PLYMOUTH RIVER

A HISTORY OF THE LAIRA AND CATTEWATER

CRISPIN GILL

PLYMOUTH RIVER
A HISTORY OF THE LAIRA AND CATTEWATER

CRISPIN GILL

DEVON BOOKS

First published in 1997 by Devon Books

British Library Cataloguing-in-Publication data

Catalogue record for this title is available from the British Library

ISBN 0 86114 911 4

DEVON BOOKS
Official Publisher to Devon County Council

Halsgrove House
Lower Moor Way
Tiverton, Devon EX16 6SS
Tel: 01884 243242
Fax: 01884 243242

The author and publisher are grateful for the financial assistance
provided in support of the publication of this book by the
Cattewater Commissioners and the Barbican Association.

Thanks are also given to the *Evening Herald* for their generosity
in permitting the use of aerial photographs used in this book.

Printed and bound in Great Britain by BPC Wheatons Ltd., Exeter

CONTENTS

*The mouth of the Plym, with Mount Batten in the foreground. Sutton Harbour and the area
of the medieval town can be seen above, with the Tamar gleaming on the far side of the city.*

INTRODUCTION

The City of Plymouth in reality has two rivers; the Tamar which makes its western boundary and the Plym, which flows through the city on the east. But until 1914, when Plymouth amalgamated with Devonport, the Tamar was firmly Devonport's river. In Devonport's early days its people took a boat regularly to Saltash market; right up until 1939 the market gardens of the Tamar Valley kept Devonport Market supplied.

In the days before the Dockyard was founded and Devonport began to grow outside its walls, there was no cause for Pymouth people to go to Devonport. Indeed the site of both town and dockyard was an empty shoreline backed by empty fields. Nor was it easy to get there; the great marsh of the Sourpool blocked the Union Street approach. Beyond that was the long arm of Stonehouse Creek, reaching up to Pennycome-quick, so that the only way to reach Tamarside from Plymouth was over Stonehouse Bridge (and that was only built in 1768-73), over the Millbridge or the long way around by Pennycomequick. Those are the only ways from Plymouth to Devonport today. Even to go to Cornwall one used the Cremyll Ferry from Devil's Point, before the Torpoint Ferry was started in 1790.

So Plymouth grew up around Sutton Harbour, and the Cattewater was for centuries just used as the deepwater anchorage. Not until industry had filled up Coxside did it begin to flow up the Cattewater shore to Cattedown and Prince Rock, and not until the railway came to the shores of the Cattewater did commercial quaysides begin to be built. Not until that time, the second half of the nineteenth century, did Plymouth houses start to spread eastwards. Not until this century did Plymouth people find homes across the river, swamping the little town of Plympton and the villages of Plymstock, Oreston and Turnchapel.

The Admiralty, having taken the Hamoaze to themselves, have dog-in-the-manger style stopped any attempt by Plymouth to make the Cattewater a major port. They did not want commercial ships getting in their way in Plymouth Sound. Even after World War I, when they were cutting down naval and dockyard employment as fast as they could, they blocked Plymouth's biggest chance of becoming a major industrial centre.

When Ford wanted a factory in England they looked at Cattedown but finally chose Dagenham. The Admiralty were frightened that if Ford came to Plymouth the high wages of the car industry would force up the wages they paid in the Dockyard, and so persuaded the Town Council that such a development would be a 'bad thing'. For the past seventy years Cattedown might have held one of the biggest car making plants in Europe. In hindsight, this must be the greatest mistake that Plymouth has ever made.

The mouth of the River Plym has always been important to Plymouth. It even gave the city its name. But how many Plymothians have sailed its waters? How many can find their way to Turnchapel and Oreston? For that matter, how many have ever been in Cattedown? It is a forgotten land, but things are happening there. It is possibly on the edge of the biggest developments in its history.

'Oreston and Cat-water, near Plymouth' from Britton and Brayley's Devonshire and Cornwall Illustrated, *1832.*

PART ONE - THE EARLY DAYS
CHAPTER ONE

CATTEWATER: NAME AND ORIGINS

Seamen have found safe harbour since the dawn of history in the mouth of the Plym. They were trading at Mount Batten twenty-eight centuries ago.

When the early inhabitants of the little town of Sutton, or Plymouth as the name became. strolled seaward towards Fisher's Nose they would look up the river. A strangely-shaped rock stood on the northern shore, just short of the turn of land, which they thought looked like a cat. So it was called the Cat Rock.

When some seamen were drowned in 1281 - maybe they were rowing back to their ship after sampling the local beers - it was said to have happened 'apud the Catte', that is, near the Cat. Support for this theory comes from that authoritative volume, *The Place-names of Devon*, in the series published by the English Place Names Society. In reference to that 1281 report it says that 'The preposition "apud" suggests that Catte was not the name of the estuary at the time but some feature on its shores ...some feature in the topography of the district suggests the use of the term ...the name came to be compounded with Down and also with Water, the name of the estuary'.

In a 1709 life of John Avery, the notorious pirate who was born in Cattedown, the Cattewater is said 'to take its name from a mountain or down which at once swells above and defends it from the insults of tempestuous weather'.

In later centuries the wind and the rain weathered the rock and people then thought it looked more like a bear. It was used as a landmark in drawing up the town's boundaries in 1439, and was called the Bear's Head from its shape. An article in Volume 4 of a Plymouth magazine, *The South Devon Monthly Magazine*, published in December 1835, describes Bear Rock and remarks that weathering is changing its

The Bear's Head, from the South Devon Monthly Museum, *December 1835.*

Half a century later, the Bear's Head drawn by Hansford Worth for his father's History of Plymouth, *1890.*

shape, and from the front it looks more like a water spaniel. According to the memoirs of Thomas Pitts, the maltster and leading member of the Council, it was destroyed when the Corporation built a 'soil quay' on the site in about 1890. ('Soil' was the street sweepings of horse manure collected for sale to the Tamarside farmers). The spelling changed from 'Catwater' and 'Catdown' to the present 'Catte' at about that time - a touch of 'ye olde' nonsense.

Another suggestion linking Bear Rock with the name Cat is contained in a map accompanying the sale by auction in 1820 of the Sutton Pill Estate. In this only the fields immediately behind Bear Rock are called 'Catdown', and the fields opposite, on the other side of Cattedown Road, are called Cattyhorne.

ORIGINS

The Cattewater's shape was first carved out in geological times, when a coral reef was laid down under a warm sea covering the whole area. As time went on and land emerged from the sea, this became a ridge of limestone running from Cremyll through Devil's Point and the Hoe to Mount Batten, Cattedown, Turnchapel, Oreston and away eastwards until it peters out around Yealmpton. The Tamar breaks through this ridge between Cremyll and Devil's Point, the Plym between Cattedown and the eastern shores of the estuary. In three places the Cattewater breaks out of its limestone confines, into Sutton Harbour, Hooe Lake and Pomphlett Creek, on geological faults. Otherwise the cliffs originally fell sharply into the water right up as far as the present Laira Bridge.

The Plym, like the Tamar and all the estuaries of the south coast of Devon and Cornwall, is a ria, a drowned valley. In the last Ice Age, when much of the sea was taken up in solid ice, the sea level was 200 feet lower than today. Eddystone stood as a headland on the then coast. So the rivers cut deeper and deeper into the valleys through which they ran. The bigger river Tamar has by the force of its flow kept a deep channel in its estuary; the smaller Plym is now badly silted up, as a result of seven centuries of tin mining and more recently china clay extraction on Dartmoor. J.M.Rendel, the engineer building the first Laira Bridge, found rock at 80 feet below high water mark, through 60 feet of granite sand. Murrie Hutton, the engineer who built the present bridge, found hard rock 90 feet below the river bed.

Before so much quarrying was done on both sides of the Cattewater the cliffs rose about a hundred feet almost sheer from the water. During the Ice Age, when the sea was so much lower, it was a canyon from Laira Bridge to the Hoe, a sort of Cheddar Gorge.

CHAPTER TWO

LAIRA: NAME AND SIDE CREEKS

Above Laira Bridge the river is clear of the limestone ridge, in shillety country. Here the estuary spreads itself, enclosed by wide meadows and rounded hills. Until man interfered with nature, the estuary was wider still, with creeks running away on either side. Even the estuary name changes above the bridge, to the Laira. There is reason to believe that this is the original name of the river.

The Devon place names volume regards the name Plym as a very early back formation from Plympton - the tun or farm of the plyme, Old English for plum tree. But Plympton only stood on a branch of the river, not on the main stream. On the main stream a Domesday manor is named Leurichestona, an area now called Leigham. Leuristone stands on the main stream of the river, it may mark some prominent stone beside the river and Leurich is not so far removed from Laira. Most of the main Devon rivers have pre-English names, and Lew is a Celtic river name.

PRINCE ROCK

Once out of the limestone, above Laira Bridge, the old spread of the estuary can still be traced clearly by walking the ground. On the northwest bank the shore that was formerly under water begins immediately. Laira Bridge Road and Hele's Terrace are the boundaries, with the bus depot, the industrial sites along Embankment Lane and the playing field once under water.

The spur of high ground at the Plymouth end of Laira Bridge, once called Great Prince Rock, marked one end of this little bay. The other end, Little Prince Rock, was a point of land roughly at the present junction of Embankment Road and Gdynia Way. Fields behind these two points were all called Prince Rock in an 1820 sales catalogue map.

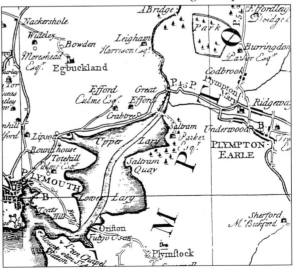

Detail from John Donn's 1765 map of Devonshire, showing the expanse of the Upper and Lower Laira. By this time the original stretches of water above Marsh Mills were more or less dry land.

TOTHILL BAY

Little Prince Rock marks the southern end of Tothill Bay, which reached right up over the playing fields and Tothill Park to the curve of Egerton Crescent. The southern edge of the bay is roughly marked by the embankment which carried the railway line to Friary Station, although at the eastern end the Lucas Terrace group of houses are on formerly drowned land, rescued by the railway. The northern edge has Lanhydrock Road following the old shoreline, just above the high water mark. Even in this century houses in Lanhydrock Road have been flooded by extra high tides.

The northern extremity of Tothill Bay was marked by Arnold's Point. Driving out of Plymouth along the Embankment one can clearly see where the railway line cuts right through the tip of the old headland, which over the centuries has been called Tothill Point, then Mount Gould Point after Colonel Gould, the Parliamentary commander of Plymouth in the Civil War, and then Arnold's Point after a more recent landowner.

At present Arnold's Point houses the Plymouth Rowing Club headquarters. With Chelston Point opposite, where the Saltram boathouse is prominent, it effectively cut the estuary into two areas which were called Lower Laira and Upper Laira.

LIPSON LAKE

The railway marshalling yard at Laira nowadays dominates the land recovered from Lipson Lake. Behind the embankment which carries the railway line curving from the main London route around to Friary station, the flat plain is occupied by two schools and a playing field, and stretches right up to where Bernice Terrace curves around to join Lipson Vale. It is probable that in very early times the creek reached right up to St Augustine's Church. The builders of the church had to penetrate a bed of sand to get down to rock.

Old Laira Road runs on the high ground above the north side of this creek, which rejoins the main stream where Old Laira Road meets the Embankment. The road from this point to Crabtree marks the original northern bank of the Laira. The link road turns off to join the Parkway at the point where another side creek starts. The twin wooded hills of Efford Warren, each now crowned by Victorian forts, and Blaxton Point across the river, mark another narrowing of the estuary.

FORDER VALLEY

The long narrow creek of Forder Valley is now filled by modern roads running up from the Marsh Mills interchange. The creek forked where the next roundabout is situated, and the Parkway follows the southern branch of the creek. This ends where the Egg Buckland-Higher Compton road crosses the Parkway. The northern branch, the longer, goes right up to the foot of Forder Hill, where traffic lights mark the junction with Novorossisk Road. The eastern side of the narrow creek curves at the end around the Leigham peninsula to meet the Plym valley proper.

TO PLYM BRIDGE

All the area around the present road junction of A38, the Parkway, the Plymouth and the Plympton roads, is very rightly called Marsh Mills. There was a mill in the middle of marshland. It was a marsh by the early seventeenth century, and on the six-inch Ordnance Survey maps in use as late as the 1930s the field between Longbridge Road and the River Plym is called May's Marsh, and the other side of the river, until recently occupied by the Royal Marines, is called Coypool Marsh. The wide water meadows which stretch on either side of the Plym right up to Plym Bridge were originally all part of a tidal creek, and Plym Bridge, first named in 1238, was built just above the highest point reached by the tide. At present the highest point reached by tidal waters is about level with the present headquarters of the Plym Valley Railway Preservation Society.

PLYMPTON MARSHES

The road from Marsh Mills to Plympton follows the northern side of the longest creek of the river, which reached right up to St Mary's Church and there forked, one arm towards Colebrook and the other to the foot of Plympton Castle. The tide certainly flowed up to Colebrook, and recent excavations have found sea sand and shells some ten feet below street level. It is claimed at the Colebrook Inn that fish were once landed just across the road. In the 1890s Robert Burnard maintained that barges reached a quay in front of St Mary's Church, and that the Black Prince had sailed from Plymouth to Plympton by boat.

The house on the western side of the Castle is still called the Barbican, which means the water gate. In 1875 and 1893 building operations in this area, where Fore Street meets Back Lane, Dark Street Lane and Underwood Road in what used to be called Woodbine Villas, oak piles of a kind used in embankments were found, oak bollard-like posts, stones that might have made a quay, and black mud with sand and sea shells mixed in.

Underwood Road and Underlane follow the high ground above the south side of the creek. Old leases of houses on the north side of this road, which originally had much longer gardens reaching down to the streams, are said to have contained rights of fishing in the waters. There

are eighteenth-century memories of boats tying up at the quay across the road from Plympton St Mary Church.

CHELSTON BAY

This south bank of the Plympton branch curves around at Marsh Mills into Saltram Park, where the river still flows close under the wooded slopes of Blaxton Point - originally called Blackstone Point. Blaxton Meadow is a small area of land recovered in 1850. In 1994 the National Trust broke the embankment holding back the tide and made a sill, so turning the meadow back into a tidal marsh - the aim being to encourage the wild life of this disappearing type of marsh.

Below Saltram Point, identified by the boathouse , the old river shore bent around to make Saltram Park a promontory. Chelston Meadow, serving as a tip, is one of the largest reclaimed areas and the old shores are clearly identified, not swallowed by modern buildings.

This street at the bottom of Plympton St Maurice's Fore Street, once called Woodbine Villas and now labelled as the start of Underwood Road, was in medieval times a quay serving coastwise shipping.

CHAPTER THREE

FORDS, BRIDGES AND EARLY ROADS

The oldest crossing of the Plym is remembered in the name Efford, the ebb ford. A prehistoric trackway ran along the southern edge of Plympton Creek, the line now followed by Underwood Road and Underlane. The present road ends at Cot Hill, opposite Cot Lodge, a thatched cottage which was a lodge to a former entry to Saltram Park. A field track continues the line of the road. On the 1784 O.S. map this is a road which runs down to Blaxton Meadow and the eastern end of the Ebb Ford. In the 1823 Embankment Act the Ebb Ford is described as 'a public highway across the sands'.

On the western side the track came up from the sands at Lower Crabtree, roughly opposite the petrol filling station beside the road. As the ford could only be crossed at low water - the 'ebb' ford, travellers would often have been delayed by the tide. So the Crabtree Inn came into being where travellers could wait on the western bank, probably very early indeed. It survived until 1974, when the dual carriageway was built.

A road formerly known as Saltash Lane led up the hill to the ridge of Efford, on to Higher Compton and by Ham Lane to Weston Mill and Saltash Passage. Its route has now been disguised by military roads to serve the nineteenth-century forts, and post-war housing estates, but is still possible to follow it.

John Leland, the earliest traveller about England to leave us a record of his journeys in the 1530s, records that 'From Plymmouth I crossid over Plym River at the Ebbe...rode about half a mile along by Torey Brooke, whose colour is always redde by the Sand that it...caryeth from the Tynne Workes with it; and so to Plymtoun Marie...'

A former president of Plymouth Athenaeum, J.J.Beckerlegge, said in a lecture in 1943 that before 1758, when the Longbridge was improved, this Ebb Ford was the most accustomed route from Plymouth to Plympton, across the sands from Crabtree to Blaxton.

WOODFORD and SHALLOWFORD

There was a higher ford across the Plympton creek, still remembered by the place name Woodford. The name itself can be found in Domesday Book, like Efford, as the name of a Saxon manor, which shows the antiquity of both fords. There was also a ford across the Forder Creek, remembered in the name Shallowford.

The Embankment Act also mentioned a ford across the sands between Arnold's Point and

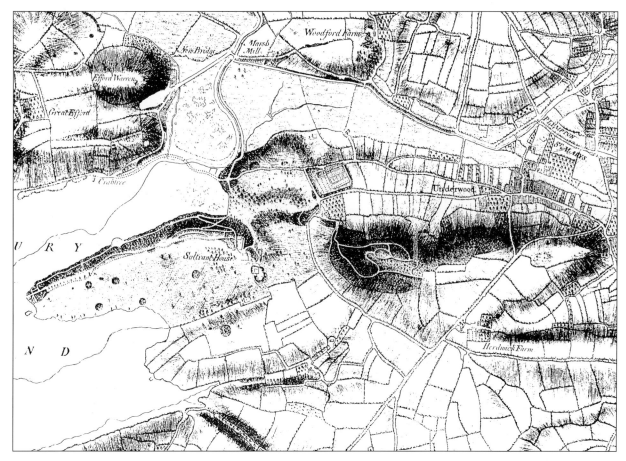

England's earliest Ordnance Survey map of this part of the world, made in 1794, marks the Ebb Ford by two dotted lines reaching from Crabtree to Blaxton Point, whence it continues to Plympton. The New Bridge (as it really was then) is shown carrying the turnpike to Marsh Mills and on to Plympton.

Saltram Point. It was approached by Tothill Lane, on the northern side of Tothill Bay and now called Lanhydrock Road. It seems a wide and hazardous crossing, and does not seem to have been much used.

LONGBRIDGE

In 1618 the old Plymouth accounts show the town giving 'by a free concent towards the buylding of the stone bridge in Plympton Marsh, 40s'. But the amount is struck out; so it appears that the money was not paid and the bridge not built. In 1642 one

of the earliest battles of the Siege of Plymouth occurred at Longbridge, where Lord Grey de Ruthven, commanding the garrison, held the narrow passage of Long Bridge for three hours against the onslaught of a force of 2,500 men under Sir Ralph Hopton, who finally retired to Plympton.

The Long Bridge precisely refers to the causeway which reached across from Crabtree to what we now call Marsh Mills. Before it was built in 1758 there was merely a beaten track across the marshes, frequently flooded. The Plym and then Tory Brook were crossed by fords. When a bridge

The 'Long Bridge' or causeway which stretched from Marsh Mills Bridge over the Plym to the Rising Sun at Crabtree, seen in this photograph at the foot of the hill surmounted by Crabtree Fort. All this road is now buried under Marsh Mills roundabout.

The New Bridge at Marsh Mills, from the South Devon Monthly Museum *of May 1835. The lodge and gateway to the new Saltram drive can be seen right.*

was again proposed in 1758, to carry the new turnpike over the river, there was a considerable dispute, one side led by Mr Parker of Saltram wanting to use the Ebb Ford route and the other side championing the Long Bridge route. Long Bridge won.

An Act of 1757 empowered the Plymouth Eastern Trust to build this road as part of the Great West Road, meeting the Ashburton Trust's road at (South) Brent Bridge. There was a 'turnpike', the Leigham gate at the end of the present Longbridge road where passengers joining the road by the Forder Valley road from Crownhill would have paid their toll. A new bridge was made over the Plym, at the end of the raised causeway, and a new road constructed along the northern side of Plympton Marsh (as it would have been by that

time). This was called New Bridge, as distinct from Plym Bridge, and was just ten feet wide. In 1835 a replacement bridge was designed by James Green, surveyor of the county bridges, 24 feet wide and built by William Dwelly of Plymouth on a contract for £1,050. In April 1835 the old bridge was almost demolished and a temporary bridge of wood served the road. The new bridge, of three arches was completed by 1838. It served until the 1930s when it was widened again to facilitate road widening. It was widened again with the dualling of the road to Plympton in 1987.

PLYM BRIDGE

Before Longbridge was built the traveller going east from Plymouth and not wishing to brave the

Ebb Ford would have had to go through Egg Buckland to Plym Bridge and so down to Plympton. He would have gone along Exeter Street (now Bretonside) to the North Street junction, up North Street to the Gascoigne Gate, just north of the public house (rechristened the Fool and Firkin in 1994), up Gascoigne Place and Lipson Hill, down the northern side to the head of Lipson Lake, and then through Lower Compton village to Egg Buckland - much of the route past the Ashford Road railway arch remained as pathfields until buried in post-1945 building. Beyond Egg Buckland he would climb Goosewell Hill and down the other side to the head of the Forder Valley to Plym Bridge Road, a route now hard to sort out on the ground. This route has to skirt around the head of both Lipson and Tothill creeks. If of course the traveller was using the Ebb Ford, once around the head of Lipson Lake he would have followed its northern bank along what is now Old Laira Road to Crabtree.

Plym Bridge is first mentioned in 1238. It served not only the Plympton-Plymouth route but also the Plympton-Tavistock road, and the early existence of monasteries at these places may have generated traffic needing the bridge. The need would have increased with the discovery in 1156 of tin on Dartmoor, and its transport by packhorse to the port of Plympton. In 1194 Plympton was made a stannary town, which meant that all tin from south-west Devon had to be weighed there.

A medieval chapel dedicated to St Mary the Virgin stood near the bridge, of which only one arch remains, on the right bank just above the bridge. In 1450 a papal letter ordered the Prior of Plympton to depute priests to hear confessions there and to absolve 'the great multitude of faithful from diverse parts of the world' who

A 1785 road map showing how the main road to Exeter had to wind around the head of the Laira creeks before the Embankment was built, and how even the turnpike to the South Hams was originally routed through Plympton.

resorted to the chapel 'on account of the many miracles which God has wrought therein'.

The present bridge replaced the original bridge in the eighteenth century, but traces of the former can still be found.

CHAPTER FOUR

THE FERRIES

The only way to cross the Cattewater was by ferries. John Beaupre was operating a ferry from Sutton (which probably means Cattedown, which was within the manor of Sutton) to Hooe as early as 1281, charging a halfpenny. A man called Dickie Pearn was operating on this route in the 1860s, charging sixpence for the single journey.

The ferry from Cattedown to Oreston, which led to Plymstock and all that eastern shore of the Plymouth Sound, is another early starter. The earliest name of this crossing, Worston Passage, appears in 1466. *The Place-names of Devon* suggests that the name Oreston probably contains the 'Har' prefix, which means a ferry. An early name for the road from the ferry over Cattedown to Plymouth was Horestone Passage. There is still a Passage House Inn at the back of the ferry beach in Cattedown. It was rebuilt in 1902 when the old Passage House Inn was pulled down. This very old building, a much-needed place of shelter and refreshment for those waiting for the ferry, would have been necessary from earliest days.

In the nineteenth century one of the more mournful jobs of the ferry was to carry the coffins of Methodists from the little waterside community of Cattedown to burial in Oreston Methodist graveyard. The ferry itself continued right up to the 1920s, with Dockyardees paying a halfpenny toll for the rowing boat crossing. The road from Cattedown Corner to the ferry was walkable until a few years ago. Quarrying on either side has left it perched on a narrow ridge. Then a side fell in at one point, and the route was finally breached by the new Macadam Road.

A rowing boat ferry service was operated between Turnchapel and Cattedown Steps from the mid-1890s until about 1949, carrying workmen between their homes and their employment. There was also a rowing boat ferry across the narrow entrance to Hooe Lake, carrying Turnchapel men to work in Oreston for the timber yard or the quarries.

In 1823 watermen could be hired at the Western Pier in Sutton Harbour who would convey a passenger to a ship in the river for a shilling (5p). It was the same fare to Oreston or Hooe, but Saltram Point was 1s6d (7p) and to go around to North Corner in the Hamoaze was 2s 6d (12p).

THE P. & O. LINERS

In 1869 two steam ferry companies began operating, the Oreston Steamboat Company with the *Little Pet* and the *Favourite*, and the Turnchapel

Passage House Inn, the old pub on the Cattedown side of the Oreston ferry, replaced by the present pub building in 1902.

Announcement of the first Oreston steam boat ferry service, 1869

Steamboat Company with the *Eclipse* and the *Greyhound* (which also served as a tug helping sailing vessels in and out of the Cattewater). Two years later the two companies joined forces to form the Oreston & Turnchapel Steamboat Company: one of the resolutions of the new company was that there should be no racing between the boats!.

The service ran from Oreston to the Mayflower Steps, calling at Turnchapel each way, the fare a penny between any two places. For a time the ferries called at Cattedown ferry beach after leaving Oreston, and later steps were built between Cattedown Wharfs and Sparrow's Wharf.

One side result of the service from Plymouth to the far side of Cattewater was that Radford Woods and duckponds, as well as Jennycliff, became a popular excursion for Plymouth people. Jennycliff and Mount Batten beach became more easily reached after the company secured landing rights at Mount Batten in 1881, and the landlord of the Castle Inn at Batten laid on all kinds of added outdoor attractions. On Bank Holiday, 1905. the

An announcement that the Oreston steamboat ferry will call at Cattedown.

Percy Elford, a grandson of the founder of the Oreston steamboat company, with the models he made of the ships of the company's fleet.

ferries carried 10,000 passengers to and from Mount Batten and Turnchapel.

There was competition, and as early as 1871 a rival steamer the *Teaser*, operated by the Greaney family, was running. The Greaneys built up their yellow funnelled fleet to three steamers. The traffic was insufficient for two firms, however, and in 1890 P&O bought them out.

In 1891 Henry Emanual Elford of Oreston, who had been one of the original directors of the company, became the effective owner. From thence forward it was a family concern. The Elfords were strict Methodists. Crews were forbidden to smoke or swear, or to sound the ship's sirens on a Sunday except in emergency.

A jetty was built at Oreston in 1884, outside the King's Arms, although at low water passengers had to use a pontoon a few yards upstream. The jetty survived until 1954. Later on a couple of hands discharged by the company began running a rival service, using the public landing place at Turnchapel as did the Elford steamers. So in 1889 a new pier, much closer to the village, was built at Turnchapel for the exclusive use of the Elford fleet. The winter before all the Elford wives and daughters had to go without new dresses, to pay for the pier.

In Plymouth the Corporation built Phoenix Wharf in 1894 to ease congestion at Mayflower Steps, and in 1895 gave the company free use and priority on the northern side. It meant that passengers had further to walk than if the ferries were using Mayflower Steps. but it remained the company's Plymouth base for the rest of its life. By 1895 the company had built new and better ships, the *Rapid*, *Lively*, *Dart* and *Swift*, which with their red funnels with black tops (like Cunard!) were to serve the company for the rest of its life. It was a firm favourite with Plymouth people, who called it the Red Funnel Line, or with mocking affection the P&O, using the name of a mighty

shipping company for the little steamers.

In 1894 an iron steamer, the *Countess of Morley*, had been added to the fleet for excursions up the Tamar - she was sailed down from Liverpool by two of Henry Elford's sons. She served until 1903 when the *May Queen*, designed by Sydney Elford, another son, took over her work. The ferry service ran continuously through World War I, although the Mount Batten call was added from 1916 onwards only to collect and return servicemen for the seaplane station.

In 1929 the motor vessel *City of Plymouth* joined the fleet for excursion work, and the *Lady Beatrice*, which had augmented the Torpoint Ferry as a passenger steamer, was bought in 1932. The P&O service had successfully competed with the train service as a means of commuting to Plymouth, but by now the bus service to Oreston was beginning to reduce the number of passengers.

In World War II the *May Queen*, *Lady Beatrice* and *City of Plymouth* were taken over by the Admiralty, just as *Lively* had been in World War I. But while *Lively* came back after extensive repairs, these three never did. A new *May Queen* was built, mainly for excursion work.

Then in 1948 the bus service was extended to Hooe and Turnchapel. The ferry began to collapse under the competition. *Lively* was sold in 1951, and *Rapid* in 1955. Harry Elford, the founder's grandson, was now managing director and his health was failing. In 1957 the ferry was taken over by C.A.Partridge of Plymouth. He tried running the service with motor boats but it still did not pay, and was finally closed down in 1965.

An attempt was made to revive the service by the motor launch *Weston Maid* which ran a service to Cawsand, in the early 1990s, but it only ran to Turnchapel for one season. Another ferry service was started from Queen Anne's Battery Marina to the Barbican end of Commercial Wharf.

CHAPTER FIVE

EMBANKMENTS

SALTRAM DRIVE

If the first change to the medieval layout of wide side arms of the Laira was made by the Long Bridge at Marsh Mills, the second came just on the Plympton side of the bridge, in the early nineteenth century. By this time the highest creeks, Forder, the Plym above Marsh Mills and the Plympton arm, had largely silted up and become marshes. In 1784 the first Lord Boringdon made a new drive to the fine house his father had made out of Saltram, linking it with the new turnpike road to London. The stretch of turnpike from Marsh Mills to Plympton was straightened at the same time. The new Saltram drive crossed the Tory Brook by a bridge and an embankment carried it to the wooded slopes of Saltram Park. This embankment considerably speeded up the drying-out process of the Plympton Creek.

PLYMOUTH EMBANKMENT

The idea of enclosing Tothill Bay, to make the marshes into dry and profitable land, had already been under discussion for some years. As early as 1749 a plan was prepared to embank Tothill Bay, with various routes onwards from Arnold's Point. Two more plans were drawn up, but nothing was done.

In 1802 a group of Plymouth business men led by the second Lord Boringdon obtained an Act of Parliament to embank the west side of the Laira, cutting off both Tothill Bay and Lipson Lake. It was to stretch from Great Prince Rock through Mount Gould Point (otherwise known as Arnold's Point) to Crabtree Village, and enclose 181 acres. The purpose of the Act was to recover this land from the sea, which the proprietors could then sell, and the only tolls proposed in the Act were for the landing of goods on any jetties on the Embankment.

A number of landowners whose interests might be affected by the proposal are named as proprietors. There is John Bastard of Kitley, Sir Lawrence Palk (who is more commonly associated with Torquay) and Paul Treby of Plympton. Then there are lesser property owners in the area, many of whom also had business interests in Plymouth; Erving Clark of Efford House and lord of the manor, George Soltau of Little Efford, Symons of Plympton and James Elliot of Leigham. The rights of Lord Boringdon as lord of the manor of Plympton are to be protected, as are the rights of the Prince of Wales (as Duke of Cornwall) and the boroughs of Plymouth and Saltash. The business men have well-known names; Collier and Hawker

An 1850 drawing by Philip Mitchell of the Embankment at Arnold's Point. The building is possibly the toll house at Lanhydrock Road. Crabtree is in the distance, the boathouses at Saltram Point are just right of the sail and Saltram House in the trees extreme right.

the wine merchants, Sir William Elford the banker and his son, Fox, Fuge, Harris, two Langmeads the brewers, Lockyers (they had many interests, including a row of cottages at Little Prince Rock), Prance, Pridham, Shepherd the wool merchant. 52 are named in all; they were empowered to raise £8,000 in £5 shares, an extra £6,000 if that was not enough, and could mortgage or sell the land recovered from the sea. They were to hold their

first meeting in the Pope's Head Inn, Plymouth (now the Arts Centre at the top of Looe Street) on the first Monday a fortnight after the Act became law, and seven were to be selected as a committee of management. If these seven were known we should know who were the movers and leaders of the scheme, but from what we know of Lord Boringdon he was probably the moving spirit.

No time was wasted. Tenders were invited for

embanking Lipson Lake, and one from Mitchell Samson of Gwennap accepted. The same firm also contracted for embanking Tothill Bay to Little Prince Rock. In his diary of 10 October 1802, Henry Woollcombe, secretary of the company, wrote, 'I had the pleasure this evening of seeing the tide kept out from Lipson Bay for the first time since the creation of the world. The Embankment across it was closed this afternoon. I hope it will endure for ages against all accidents.'

In 1808 a miner called W.Kitto agreed to embank the little bay between Great and Little Prince Rock, and the terminal of Lord Boringdon's ferry to Pomphlett Point. The completed Embankment was finally opened in 1809, with great celebrations. On the day of opening a salute of fifty guns was fired at sunrise. Crowds poured out from Plymouth to meet the Embankment directors at Crabtree. A procession was formed back into the town; prominent in the parade was 'an imposing array' of Russell's wagons, which would henceforth be spared the long climb up Lipson Road and the corkscrew descent into Lipson Vale. Each horse was decorated with the couplet:

> Sirs, for the road on Laira's banks
> Accept the wearied horses's thanks.

An ox was roasted on the Hoe, and that evening the Mayor and Corporation dined the directors at the King's Arms, not only the principal hotel in the borough at the time but also at the end of the linking road the Corporation built to meet Embankment Road.

EMBANKMENT ROAD

Plymouth East Trust, set up under the Turnpike Act of 1756, promptly began building a new road along the Embankment. It would be interesting to know how many directors of Plymouth East were also Embankment directors; certainly in later years the two companies shared the same secretary, Henry Woollcombe, and the same office in Frankfort Place. The turnpike company was working on plans for a new road in the very year the Embankment Act was obtained. In fact, on the morning of the day that Woollcombe saw the tide excluded. a meeting was held in the Mayoralty House to consider improving the route into the town by widening Higher Street. The scheme was voted down by a majority and Woollcombe lamented that 'it will now be left to a more enlightened period of society's progress'. Higher Street was a narrow lane, lined with ancient houses, on the line of the present Bretonside and Exeter Street, reaching to the corner of Sutton Road. But it was widened eventually, and by 1810 Plymouth Corporation had also built a continuation road from the corner of Sutton Road to Cattedown Corner, which they called Jubilee Road to celebrate the jubilee of King George III. This linked with Embankment Road leading to the new route across the Embankment.

The Embankment was bought by Plymouth Corporation in 1897, the year in which they also bought Laira Bridge. They paid £22,500 and tolls made an annual profit of £1,000. Not until 1924 were the tolls removed, the last toll road to be freed in the area. That year the road was raised in height and much improved. The road has been improved since, and now is a dual carriage, four lane highway carrying very heavy traffic indeed.

CHELSTON MEADOW

The first Lord Boringdon enclosed the Plympton marshes with his new drive. His son, having led the Plymouth company which built Plymouth Embankment across the water from Saltram, realised that he could add to his estate by building an embankment cutting off the Chelston creek. So in 1807 he obtained an Act of Parliament to build an embankment 972 yards long from Saltram

The toll house at the Plymouth end of the Embankment, with the collector taking the ticket from a heavily-laden lorry.

Point to Pomphlett Point, having first paid King George III the sum of £200 to buy the royal rights to the fundus. This ended the existence of Saltram as a peninsula between the Plym and the Chelston Creek, and enabled Boringdon to drain 175 acres of land, which was christened Chelston Meadow.

He had to mortgage the estate to meet the cost, £15,000, and he changed completely the eastern shore of the Laira estuary. But he was awarded the gold medal of the Society of Arts for the enterprise.

CHAPTER SIX

LAIRA BRIDGE

After launching his plan to enclose Chelston Meadow, and realising that he could build a road along his new embankment, Lord Boringdon saw the possibility of a shorter route from his home to Plymouth. So in 1807 he planned not just a road along Chelston embankment to Pomphlett Point, but a bridge across the 550 feet gap between the point and Prince Rock. It was the narrowest stretch of the river, the place at which the limestone gave way to shillet. He engaged Daniel Alexander, engineer to both the Duchy of Cornwall and Trinity House, to survey the estuary. Alexander drove piles in the river, found the great depth of mud and the strength of the current, and advised that the expense would be enormous. The idea was dropped.

As proprietor of the ferry right between Oreston and Cattedown, Lord Boringdon could also operate other ferries across the Cattewater. So he set up a flying bridge, built for him by Isaac Blackburn, a Turnchapel shipbuilder. In this device a chain was stretched across the river which passed over pulleys in the ferry, and the ferry was wound along manually by two windlasses. It was a flat-bottomed barge with openings at each end through which 'waggons, carts, carriages and other vehicles as well as horses and cattle' could embark and disembark. It

saved the people of Plymstock, Wembury and Yealmpton a great deal of travel, and Lord Boringdon used it regularly to go to Plymouth.

The flying bridge made £200 in its first year of operation, and £650 in its last year, 1827. But it was slow and cumbersome, and not easy to control in the strong currents of spring tides. Its name was anything but accurate, and Lord

Predecessor of the Laira Bridge; the 'flying bridge' approaching the Prince Rock side of the crossing. A painting by P.H. Rogers in Plymouth Art Gallery.

Laira bridge, a drawing from Doidge's Annual for 1888.

Boringdon's sisters were very scathing in their letters about the time the crossing took.

In 1822 the Earl of Morley - Lord Boringdon had now been advanced in the peerage - was approached by a young engineer. James Meadows Rendel had set up practice in Plymouth and recently projected a suspension bridge across the Tamar. Now he was proposing a similar scheme for the Laira. Within two years Lord Morley had an empowering Act through Parliament, but not for a suspension bridge.

Rendel found two problems, the depth of mud and the speed of the current at spring tides - a large area of water drained through this 500 feet gap. So widely-spaced supports were wanted, so as not to accelerate the currents, and Rendel went for iron spans. The first cast iron bridge had only been built 45 years earlier: the Shropshire town where it was built is still called Ironbridge. This Laira Bridge was also called the Iron Bridge for the rest of its life. Rendel planned five spans, the central one a hundred feet long and 22 feet above high water springs. The spans were carried on granite pillars which rested on wooden piles driven down into the mud. Rendel also formed an artificial bottom to prevent the current sluicing away the pillar foundations.

The building superintendent of the bridge, called Pethick, was also manager of the Dartmoor Granite Works, close by the Plymouth end of the bridge, and eventually became its owner. In the first year of construction work on the bridge proper the flying bridge broke away from its moorings in the violent November gale which wrecked seventeen ships in Deadman's Bay, further down the Plym. The flying bridge was finally sold in 1827, a few months after the new bridge was opened. The Iron Bridge cost £10,500, and the first person to drive across was the Duchess of Clarence, later Queen Adelaide. Rendel was 28 when the bridge was opened, the

Laira Bridge was freed from tolls in 1904 but a stretch of approach road on the Plymouth side was owned by the Embankment road company, which charged tolls at this gate for using this short piece of road until bought out in 1924.

second largest iron structure then existing, and he received the Telford Medal from the Institution of Civil Engineers for his work.

The Iron Bridge speeded up traffic not just to the immediate neighbourhood but all the South Hams. A new turnpike was constructed to Elburton - the present road follows the line - which cut out the previous route through Plymstock. Both bridge and road were subject to tolls, although the road charges disappeared in the mid-19th century. Plymouth Corporation bought the bridge, amicably, from the Earl of Morley in 1897 for £43,500. The revenue from the tolls was £2,000, and Plymouth finally abolished them in 1904, forfeiting a profit of £1,800 a year. So the tolls (a penny for foot passengers) ended on the bridge, but a short stretch of the approach on the Plymouth side was owned by the Embankment Company, who also charged a halfpenny for pedestrians to the bridge. The company was not bought out until 1924, when not only the bridge approach, but also passage along the Embankment. was freed.

The Iron Bridge, with its 24 feet roadway between railings, lasted with only widening until after the Second World War. Then, with the vastly increased traffic, widening was not only necessary but it was found that the weight of traffic was causing one pier to start sinking. A new bridge was planned in the City Engineer's department,

The new Laira Bridge under construction in 1961, with the original bridge and the railway behind.

being basically the work of Murrie Hutton.

It sprang from the same base on the Prince Rock side but crossed at a skew to the old bridge, so avoiding an awkward twist in the road on the Pomphlett side which had always been a traffic nuisance. The structure is in concrete, four spans carrying four lanes of traffic and pavements. They rest on 52 inch diameter pillars which have a steel cylinder lined with precast concrete and driven right through the mud into the solid rock. It was built by Marples Ridgway and Partners, at a cost of £565.200. In the Pomphlett abutment of the road, which reflects the original curve as it links the road into Chelston Meadow, is the original latin-inscribed commemoration stone of the building, starting with the words HUNC PONTEM which have fascinated generations of children. The latin was approved and amended by George Canning, the Prime Minister in 1827 when the original bridge was opened. His mother lived in Plymouth and Mr Canning was a frequent visitor to Saltram.

PART TWO - MAN ON THE RIVER

CHAPTER SEVEN

COMMERCIAL SHIPPING BEFORE 1850

PREHISTORY

Of the craft that entered the Cattewater in its prehistory days, or even Roman days, to trade at Mount Batten or careen in Hooe Lake, one can only speculate. The settlement appears to have had trade links with Brittany and possibly northern Spain as early as the eighth century BC. By the Early Iron Age the goods found imply 'contacts along the Atlantic seaways extending far south of the Armorican peninsula...linking ultimately to the Mediterranean'.

Whenever Mediterranean trade with prehistoric England is mentioned, the old idea that Phoenicians reached these shores crops up. It is more likely that the Phoenicians trading west through the Straits of Gibraltar coasted the few miles north to Tarshish, the port to which Jonah was fleeing, across the bay from modern Cadiz. There the goods they brought would have been traded for the goods of northern Europe, including these islands, and the Celtic seamen who had carried them south returned with the Mediterranean products.

Roman writers tell of a promontory in Britain called Ictis, where tin was to be obtained from the natives. 'If Ictis is an actual place, then Mount Batten has a claim to the name both on archaeological and topographical grounds, but the matter is beyond proof', wrote Professor Barry Cunliffe in 1988.

The timespan ranges continuously from the Late Bronze Age to the Late Iron Age, and right through to the end of the Roman occupation. Although the port continued to flourish, it seems that the main occupation during the latter Roman times was with a busy coastal trade.

MEDIEVAL TRADE

The earliest medieval ships trading into the Cattewater, of which we have any knowledge, were bound for Plympton. It was the first centre of any importance on the Plym, created by the Norman castle built by the first Redvers Earl of Devon. The little town of Plympton Earl (now St Maurice) grew up around his castle, and the first ship of which any records survives is one which took a cargo of slate - no doubt from Cann Quarry - from Plympton to Southampton in 1178.

But very soon even the shallow draught ships of the time were having problems in getting to the quay under Plympton Castle, or even to a quay by Plympton Priory. The only sizeable stream flowing into the Plympton branch of the estuary, the Tory Brook, would not have had enough power to scour the channel free of the mud brought down by the winter rains. The silting up was further speeded when tin streaming started on Dartmoor in 1156.

Soon ships could only reach Plympton at high tide, and would wait for the flood, or outward bound for favourable weather, at the mouth of the Plym, in the lee of Mount Batten and Staddon Heights. So more and more they were anchoring at Plym Mouth. No doubt the sailors went ashore for a pint and other pleasures at the little town of Sutton, and in no time at all the trade was being done through Sutton-super-Plym Mouth. This is the name on a town seal of 1368.

The first record of the name Plymouth is in the Pipe Rolls of 1211, when ships took cargoes of bacon to Portsmouth, and wine for Nottingham. Since 1154 all the western seaboard of France had been under English rule, and Plymouth men were trading to Bordeaux and the Biscay ports. After King John lost Normandy in 1204 the only English possessions left in France were these Biscay provinces. So these western seamen accustomed to sailing around Ushant became especially important and Plymouth became increasingly a base for military operations in these areas.

These little ships could use Sutton Harbour, but it all meant more shipping in the Cattewater; ships waiting for berths, or waiting for winds. In 1303 the first names of Plymouth ships are known, the *Santi Salvatoris* and the *Sancta Michaelis*, both of 'Plemua' , and then in 1308 the *Santi Andrei de Plomuth*. They were bringing wine from Bordeaux. In this century Plymouth, and its trade, grew considerably.

The Cattewater was important to this trade. Leland called it 'a goodly Rode for great shippes betwixt the haven mouth and the creek of Schileston', which must be Chelston. There was worry from very early times about the damage done by the tinners, with a commission to survey the haven set up in 1486, and the Lord High Admiral was taking a 'view' of the Cattewater in 1538. There were various lawsuits against the tinners, and Acts of Parliment to restrain the tinners sending down so much silt were passed under both Henry VII and Elizabeth. In Queen Anne's reign an Act empowered the removal of the Middle Bank, close to the entrance.

Dredging on the bank south of the main Cattewater shipping channel between Queen Anne's Battery and Mount Batten in 1973 revealed a wreck thought to be that of a sixteenth-century vessel. She may have sank at her anchorage in the lee of Mount Batten in the most exposed part of the anchorage, or else had struck the Batten Reef as she came in, and managed to sail on a distance before foundering.

MODERN TIMES

Charles I gave a charter to Plymouth in 1637 which stated that the harbour of Cattewater was decayed by earth from the tinners of the Meavy and Plym, and by the dumping of ballast. This last was a problem right up until recent years: ships would come in empty of cargo but ballasted with stone or whatever they could pick up in their port of departure, and have no compunction in dumping it over the side to make way for a real cargo. In 1709 there was an Act for preserving the Cattewater and Sutton Pool.

Another worry from early times was that the low, narrow neck of land joining Mount Batten to the mainland would be irrevocably broken in a storm,, imperilling not just the safety of the Cattewater anchorage but Sutton Harbour itself. It was breached in 1633, and ten years later the sea wall on the seaward side was being repaired. About this time every lighter and sand-barge in

A 1368 seal of Plymouth, with a drawing of a ship of the time.

Detail from the defence map of Henry VIII, c.1540, showing a ship bowling across the Sound towards Plymouth with more ships at anchor in the Cattewater. The building over a creek on the right bank of the Laira might be a tidal mill, and Plympton Priory is still on the water's edge.

the port was required each year to take a load of rubble from the Cattewater and dump it on the seaward side of the isthmus.

The Cattewater was being used more and more as an anchorage, with a Mediterranean convoy waiting for the weather there in 1672. As ships grew bigger so they anchored in Cattewater and sent their cargoes into Sutton Harbour in barges. This was the pattern right up until the last century.

In 1807 the go-ahead Lord Boringdon got a private Act of Parliament empowering him as lord of the manor of Plympton to lay a trot of buoys in the Cattewater, for the safer berthing of ships. He was empowered to charge for use of these moorings, according to the size of the vessel, which were moored fore and aft. The Act required that this chain be east of a line from Monkeydoe (the Bear's Head) on Cattedown to Ivey Cove on the Turnchapel side; actually it stretched across the river off Cattedown Wharfs.

Shipowners and merchants promptly persuaded the Mayor of Plymouth to call a meeting and lodge opposition to the Bill as soon as it was published, in 1806. They said that ships had always anchored where they would and they wanted this to go on; fixed moorings would interfere with the freedom of the harbour. Lord Boringdon got another Act in 1812 for improving the Cattewater, which gave him the power to appoint a harbourmaster. The people using the harbour opposed this as well, and when the Bill became law they petitioned to have it stopped. It was to be the pattern for the rest of the century; every time anyone wanted to develop anything at all in the river, everyone else opposed it.

In 1812 the petitioners also opposed the renewal of the East India company's charter, and wanted to be free to trade in India and China with Plymouth ships. They also opposed the creation of a private gunpowder magazine at Mount Batten. The people who wanted this magazine were worried about the danger of ships carrying large quantities of gunpowder entering Sutton Harbour, and they needed an Act of Parliament because legislation prevented any private magazine being founded within two miles of a Government magazine - in this case in the Citadel. The magazine at Mount Batten never was established.

But in spite of the screams of the protesters, when the Admiralty made Lord Boringdon lift his moorings and relay them to be clear of the channel, there was a protest signed by 48 captains and shipbuilders, the pilots and eight Plymouth

An 1830 drawing by Thomas Allom showing shipping in the Cattewater. The steamer in the centre is thought to be the Sir Francis Drake, *the first steamship built in Plymouth and launched from the Cattedown shipyard in 1824.*

merchants. By 1815 the moorings were so popular that Lord Boringdon, who that year became Earl of Morley, did not renew his permission for these buoys from the Government, and so they reverted to the Admiralty.

According to Johns's directory for 1823 a lookout was kept on Mount Batten tower, for ships in the offing, and signals hoisted on a flagstaff on the tower.

In 1824 there was a real worry for the local shipping people when the sea again broke through the narrow Mount Batten isthmus. This prompted them in 1827, after more meetings called by the Mayor in the Guildhall, to petition against any more quarrying at Mount Batten; they were afraid that the whole rocky area would be reduced to the level of the sandy link to the mainland and so remove the shelter to the Cattewater and Sutton Harbour. They were also concerned that quarry waste thrown into the sea, and washed from the shore in bad weather, was silting up the harbour. Soon after this the Admiralty halted any further quarrying at Mount Batten, because the quarry face was right up to the base of the tower and it was in danger of collapse.

In the 1820s steam vessels began to make their appearance in the Cattewater. The first steamer built in Plymouth was launched from Hill's Yard at Cattedown in 1824 and thereafter made the Cattewater the base for her coastal services to the Channel Islands, Portsmouth and so forth. About 1830 the London and Dublin Steam Marine Company began using Plymouth as a port of call, berthing in the Cattewater. In 1846 fire broke out in their steamer *Shannon*, moored in the Cattewater after coming from London. Her passengers were taken off, and she was beached at Cattedown.

But the race to make the Atlantic passage under steam was the major issue of those years. Brunel began building the *Great Western* for that purpose and another company, the British and American Steam Navigation Co, began building a rival craft. When it was clear that Brunel would win the race, the B & A hired the paddler *Sirius* from an Irish company and she just beat the *Great Western* into New York, in 1838. On her second return voyage the *Sirius* ended her crossing by dropping anchor in the Cattewater, and sending her mail and passengers by harbour craft into Sutton Harbour. The next year Thomas Gill, chairman of the company building the railway line linking Plymouth with the rest of the country, started building Millbay Pier. The new docks thus started stole the thunder, and the trade with the larger vessels, and the Sutton Harbour/Cattewater trade was soon taking second place.

CHAPTER EIGHT

WARSHIPS AND SEAPLANES

Over the years there has been considerable military use of the Cattewater. King Edward I found it useful when his admirals reformed a fleet in the harbour. It had set out from Portsmouth for Gascony in 1294 and been scattered in a storm. In each of the next three years the fleets were assembled in the Cattewater. The King himself spent a month in the port in 1297. His grandson Edward III and then his son, the Black Prince, used it continuously.

Later in this Hundred Years War the French underlined its importance in a major raid. In 1403 the Sieur de Chastel brought a force of 30 ships and 1,200 men-at-arms into the port. The entrance to Sutton Harbour was strongly defended but not the mouth of the Cattewater. Chastel sailed his ships past the defences covering the chain across the harbour mouth - where the piers and lock gates now are - and anchored in the Cattewater. His army landed on the beaches of Cattedown and attacked Plymouth from the east, burning all the houses outside Martin's Gate, the area now known as Breton Side, and were only driven back by the determined onslaught of the townsfolk.

The Cattewater was in continuous use as an anchorage by every kind of vessel, and in Tudor times batteries of guns were established along the Hoe at Fisher's Nose to defend it. They had halted a squadron of seven Spanish ship which had attempted to enter the Cattewater in 1576 These vessels came bowling up the Sound and made no effort to dip their topsails or their flags in salute. So they got one shot at the admiral's flag, which did not deter them; and a second shot which 'raked the admiral through and through'. Then they went about, anchored in the Sound, and complained to the Mayor. They got little change.

A bulwark and three guns were established on Mount Batten in 1587, enlarged in the year after the Armada. When the counter-Armada fleet was assembling in the summer of 1588, over a hundred vessels were in the port. The biggest ships anchored in the Sound and the rest in the Cattewater.

After various abortive forays to meet the Spaniards, including one when a gale wrought some damage, the ships that needed cleaning and caulking were careened on the Cattewater beaches, with men working night and day. Some ships were plague-ridden and hundreds died. Mass burials on the foreshore at Mount Batten may be accounted for by these deaths.

THE STUARTS

Charles I's equally plague-ridden fleet of 1626, which failed under Buckingham's leadership to achieve anything at all in a raid on Cadiz, anchored in the Cattewater. When Plymouth declared for Parliament in the Civil War an outlying defensive position was established above Turnchapel and called Fort Stamford. This was captured and held for a spell by the royalist besiegers, so denying the use of both the Cattewater and Sutton Harbour to the town.

Mill Bay was used for the first time as a shipping base. There were also small forts at Cattedown and Prince Rock, built as part of the outer ring of defences. These were never challenged, even though Pomphlett Creek was

One of three cast iron 9 pounder guns mounted on top of Mount Batten Tower following the completion of conservation on the gun platform there in the 1980s.

pressed into service by the royalists. They billeted soldiers in the mill and boats were brought overland from the Yealm to the creek, with the aim of launching a waterborne attack on the town.

A spell of dredging off Cattewater Wharfs in 1887 (14,000 tons of silt, rubble and rock were removed) discovered a wreck covered in sand. Of 300 tons, 80-90 feet long, she was a ship of the Civil War period. A canon found marked with a P was still loaded with a half pound ball, wadding and powder charge. She is thought to have been a Parliamentary ship run aground under cover of Parliamentary guns on Cattedown after being damaged by royalist guns on the far bank..

In the Commonwealth, Cromwell's efficient use of a revived Navy in the Dutch wars saw his agent, Captain Henry Hatsell, establishing a base in the Cattewater. To defend it a round tower was built, about 1651-52, on the tip of the peninsula, very like the 'Cromwell's Castle' of this period on Tresco, in the Isles of Scilly. It was called Mount Batten, after the Captain Batten who had commanded the Parliamentary naval forces in Plymouth during the siege. This solidly-built stone tower had two rooms above a cellar, with a top platform designed to carry ten guns. It first appears on a map of 1646. The tower still stands, and in recent years three small canon have been set up on the gun platform.

In these Commonwealth developments repair yards for the Navy were set up at Teat's Hill and Turnchapel, and in 1657 a hulk, the Spanish prize *Elias*, was moored in the stream to house shipwrights. Then in 1672 the Navy Board ordered that dockyards be established at Plymouth and the hulk offered for sale. But there were no takers, and in 1665 her workmen converted two Dutch prizes into English warships.

A map of that year marks the area between Turnchapel and the entrance to Hooe Lake as 'the

King's Land fitting for a dock'. Within two years the beaches in front were being used to careen and repair naval craft. John Lanyon, who had replaced Henry Hatsell as naval agent on the Restoration of the monarchy, urged the building of a dry dock on the Cattewater to act as a base for a western squadron, but nothing was done. Even the hulk was condemned in 1684 and taken out of service.

To strengthen the Cattewater defences in the Commonwealth wars with the Dutch, a battery of five guns was set up on Pig's (or Peake's) Point, in 1667, just after the completion of the Citadel. Later on, in a French scare, £88 was spent by the town on strengthening these defences.

In 1714 Col. Christian Lilley, an engineer inspecting the port defences, said they were all useless and had the fourteen guns of the battery removed - 'better employed in the Citadel'. As Chris Robinson points out, Queen Anne had already been dead for two years. But by 1835, when the battery was described as an irregular curve with fourteen portholes for guns, but long decayed, it was called Queen Anne's Battery and the name still sticks.

WARSHIP REPAIRS

The need for a western dockyard was growing. As early as 1671 King Charles II with his brother James rowed up the Cattewater while studying this and other sites for a yard. He came again in 1676, this time with Samuel Pepys, the secretary to the Admiralty. But not until William of Orange reached the throne was it decided to establish the dockyard in the Hamoaze. William after all had reason to like the West; he had landed with his army in Torbay, and when he marched away the fleet came around to Plymouth. The Citadel, which had only just been built, was the first fort in England to surrender to the new King, and his fleet anchored in Cattewater.

The crenellated wall of Queen Anne's Battery, a drawing from the South Devon Monthly Magazine *of December 1835. All the guns had been removed as early as 1714.*

From 1690 onwards the Navy was concentrated in the Hamoaze. Ships might anchor at the mouth of the Cattewater to take on supplies from the Victualling Yard, on Lambhay, but even this ceased after 1830 with the opening of the Royal William Yard at Stonehouse.

In the mid-nineteenth century the Government was alarmed by the sabre-rattling of Napoleon III and embarked on a considerable programme of land defences for its naval bases. As part of the ring around Plymouth, Stamford Fort was built in the 1860s, largely with stone from Mount Batten. Efford Fort and Laira Battery, built at the same time, were part of the landward defence. Within half a century they were obsolete; Laira Fort was being used as a holiday home and centre for children when it was finally sold in 1930 by the War Department. It became a builder's yard.

TURNCHAPEL WHARFS

Not until 1903 did the Navy return to the Cattewater. Then the Admiralty bought Turnchapel Wharfs, and five acres of the quarries behind, as a coaling wharf. Oil fuel was coming into use, and tanks were built in the quarries to store the fuel oil. The Bear Creek Oil Company sent in the first tanker in 1909. Later on more tanks were added to store aviation fuel for the flying boats at Mount Batten. Between 1935 and 1938 ten oil tanks were erected in the valley east of Radford dip, with a pipeline to carry the fuel to Turnchapel Wharf. This fuel depot ceased to function in 1971. Eventually, in 1995, it was proposed to demolish the tanks and sell the 29 acre site for housing development.

Turnchapel Wharfs also served as a base for new ideas in naval warfare, submarines and torpedoes.

The Admiralty had upset the mercantile users of the port in the 1890s by their high-handed rejection of development plans. In 1904 they stirred up a deal of indignation among the fishing fraternity as well. Under the control the Navy exercised over all waters in the naval port, they banned all anchoring in certain areas of the Cattewater, some of which had always been used by the fishing fleet, and required that a channel not less than fifty fathoms wide be kept clear all the way up to Breakwater Quarry. There had already been a rumpus when the skipper of a Breakwater barge had complained of a moored ship interrupting his passage. In 1906 there were further fears that the Admiralty would close the road from Hooe village to Turnchapel Station, and stop up the way into Turnchapel village. This never happened, but to this day the road from Hooe along the shores of the lake into Turnchapel is private, and gated.

After World War I Turnchapel became a base for the Royal Fleet Auxiliary cable ships, always manned by merchant seamen. On the Wharf large cylindrical tanks were built in which the cable was stored: their bases can still be seen. Until 1938 the Admiralty's only cableship. HMTS *Kilmun*, converted from a sloop in 1917, was based here. Then more cable ships came into service, the *Lasso* (1938) and during the war the *Bullfrog*, *Bullfinch*

and *St Margaret* (1944). *Bullfrog* was sold in 1947, *Lasso* survived until 1959 and *Bullfinch* went to the breakers in 1979. *St Margaret* remained in service until 1985 when, the oldest steamship in the Royal Navy, she left the port to be laid up.

Operating under Admiralty contract also were cable ships of the Commercial Cable Company, which about 1922 established a base in the river (see chapter 14).

After World War II, Turnchapel Wharfs became the base of two naval research vessels, the *Whitehead* and the *Newton*. The wharfs were required as a base for 539 Assault Squadron Royal Marines in 1993, when they had to move from the Royal William Yard. *Whitehead* and *Newton* transferred to the Dockyard. Something like £3 million was spent on setting up the Royal Marines base, and henceforward dockyard auxiliary craft, landing craft all all sizes, inflatable assault boats and even hydroplanes, became as familiar sights in the Cattewater as once seaplanes had been.

MOUNT BATTEN AIR STATION

World War I brought more naval activity. First of all Chelston Meadow became the base for small airships used for spotting purposes. In 1916 the Royal Naval Air Service set up a seaplane base at Mount Batten. The Castle Inn, rechristened Greenleaf House, was used for a time as the station commander's house, and later became the officers' mess (It was demolished in 1962 to make room for a sergeant's mess). The coastguard cottages facing the Sound housed the petty officers until replaced after World War II by a barrack block. Other ranks were billeted in Plymouth, and the Plymouth and Oreston Steamboat Company's little *Rapid* was taken over to transport them to Mount Batten. The first hangar, to house Short seaplanes, was of canvas. More solid hangars and living quarters were built,

In World War I Batten Breakwater was used as a parking area for Short seaplanes. They were lifted in and out of the water by a dockyard crane which trundled up and down on rails.

with slipways for the seaplanes and attendant launches. A railway track was laid along Batten Breakwater on which a crane operated, to hoist seaplanes out of the water and park them with tails over the top of the sea wall. The planes were employed from dawn until nightfall hunting U-boats in the Western Approaches

In these early days the guard house was at the top of the slope leading down to the station proper, at the far end of the Well Field and the football pitch. Not until 1935-6 was the guard room moved to the bottom of St John's Road, and the extra land taken into the station.

With the amalgamation of the RNAS and the Royal Flying Corps into the Royal Air Force on 1 April 1918. Mount Batten became an RAF station.

On 31 May 1919 the American seaplane NC-4 taxied to a Batten slipway and ashore, the first aircraft to complete an Atlantic crossing. She had started with two other planes but only NC-4 completed the crossing from New York, by way of Cape Cod, Newfoundland, the Azores (where the other two crashed), Lisbon and Plymouth. The actual Atlantic flying time was 35 hours 1 minute. The crew were given a civic greeting on Mayflower Pier a week later.

Soon after, Mount Batten was put into care and maintenance, and remained nearly empty until 1928. Then 204 and 209 flying boat squadrons were based there. The first job for the airmen was clearing the brambles and weeds that were choking the place. 204 Squadron were first

A rare photograph showing a typical Cattewater scene between the wars; a P&O ferry steaming past flying boats moored in the river with cable ships behind at moorings off Turnchapel.

equipped with Fairey IIIDs float planes, and then Southamptons, and 209 with Blackburn Iris flying boats. One of these crashed in the Sound in 1930, killing most of the crew.

In this time Aircraftman Shaw - T.E.Lawrence of Arabia - was stationed at Mount Batten and was one of the first to reach the wreck, diving repeatedly to try and save life. After this Lawrence spent much time working with the launches attached to the station, improving their performance and in some ways blazing the trail for the air-sea rescue craft of World War II.

When 209 Squadron took their Blackburns to Lee-on-Solent, 407 and 444 Squadrons Fleet Air Arm moved in, with their Osprey and Fairy IIIF seaplanes. Various changes took place over the years until in 1939 the first giant Sunderland flying boats arrived. Within a week they were engaged in the Battle of the Atlantic.

On 1 April 1940 No 10 Squadron of the Royal Australian Air Force arrived, to collect Sunderlands to fly back to Australia for coastal

defence there. Instead they were to stay at Mount Batten until the end of the war. In that time they flew a tremendous number of sorties over the Western Approaches and sank a number of U boats, as well as keeping a watch on the German battleships berthed in the ports of western France. A number of distinguished people flew in and out of Mount Batten, including Winston Churchill when he arrived in January 1942, back from talks with President Roosevelt.

A new officers' mess had just been finished at the start of the war, in a splendid position at the back of Batten Bay and looking right across the Sound. It was a casualty in one of the very first air raids, but was quickly restored. On 26 November 1940 a solitary German plane dropped a stick of bombs on Hooe Lake. Two bombs fell in the lake, one hit the railway bridge across the entrance to the lake, and the fourth hit one of the fuel tanks in Turnchapel Quarry. The fire enlarged later when another tank exploded in the heat. The burning oil flowed over Turnchapel Station, utterly

A Sunderland flying boat taxis towards the Cattewater; the Australians flew these craft from Mount Batten right through World War II.

destroying it, ran over into the lake and spread across the water to the timber yard opposite, setting it on fire. Fortunately the timber fire was soon extinguished, but the oil burnt for days. Three Auxiliary Fire Service men were killed. The pillar of smoke by day, and the flames by night, could be seen from twenty miles away.

Mount Batten itself suffered various air attacks but came through the war fully operational. The Australians finally took off for home and in November 1945 the base reverted to Maintenance Command once more.

POST WAR

Since then Mount Batten has been home to various boat units, the main meteorological office in the South-West, and a survival school. It was the base for many years of the Air Officer Commanding Coastal Command, No 19 Group RAF and headquarters, Southern Command Maritime Air Region, responsible for the surveillance of the eastern Atlantic from Greenland to the Canaries.

The old tower above the quarry, dating from Commonwealth days, became unsafe in 1962 and the Air Ministry threatened to demolish it. A huge public outcry prevented this happening, and the cliff face below was shored up to make the tower safe.

The last RAF personnel departed in November 1993 and the base was finally handed over to Plymouth Development Corporation in 1994, almost fifty years after the last serious flying boats operations had taken place.

THE AMERICANS

When the Americans came into World War I they took over Victoria Wharfs in June 1917, with headquarters in Elliot Terrace. Within weeks they had two destroyers and over sixty submarine chasers based in the Cattewater. 3,000 American naval personnel were working out of Plymouth, a thousand manning the sub chasers. Eight or nine U boats in the Plymouth area were credited to them. The base stood down in February 1919.

In World War II Victoria Wharfs again came under American Navy control, as did the old shipyards at Queen Anne's Battery. Martin's Wharf served as a 'parking lot' for the Landing Craft Mechanical used for moving equipment about the area, with the crews living and feeding in huts on the quay. Cattedown Wharf was used in 1941-2 by the Royal Navy for degaussing destroyers and large merchants vessels, and later was used by the Americans for assembling large steel pontoons.

The Cattewater became a key centre for preparing landing ships and tanks for the Normandy landings. Fleets of lorries were camouflaged under the trees in Saltram Park. When finally the V and VII Corps of the American Army left for D.Day, embarkation points were set up at both Queen Anne's Battery and at Sycamore Bay, Turnchapel, where a special approach road was laid down and concrete hards built across the beach. The road and hards remain as the only monument to the American occupation.

In World War II Queen Anne's Battery was the centre of operations for the American amphibious craft based in the Cattewater, preparing for the Normany landings.

CHAPTER NINE

SHIPBUILDING AND SHIP-BREAKING

Ships have been built in the Cattewater since the dawn of history, although the first written record is of the Black Prince ordering a warship in 1358. When the men struck for more money he sacked them and brought in replacements from Cornwall. In those early days, and indeed well into the nineteenth century, ships were built on beaches with no benefit of slipways or graving docks. Ships were sometimes built as one-off jobs by the village carpenter, and with no formal yard. Names of shipbuilders come and go. R.N.Worth lists 7 in 1783, 10 in 1814, 13 in 1830, 8 in 1870 and 11 in 1890. Another list gives 6 in the Cattewater in 1815.

BLACKBURN

The first purpose-built facility in the Cattewater was ordered by Lord Boringdon in 1797 at Turnchapel. The site is now occupied by the Royal Marines boat section. It was leased by John Cater, and then Isaac Blackburn. He built the flying bridge in 1817 which was Boringdon's first attempt to speed the Laira crossing. In that year Blackburn also had his first commission from the Royal Navy, the *Derwent*, a brig-sloop of 18 guns. Her first commission was suppressing the slave trade off the African coast. She saw more action back in the Channel when she captured a French privateer in 1810 and another in 1813. But with the war over, she was sold in 1817.

In 1810 Blackburn built the *Armada*, a third rate of 74 guns and the biggest warship built locally outside the Dockyard. She had a figurehead of an Armada hero, and the Plymouth coat of arms on her stern. *Armada* was launched by Mrs Pridham, wife of the Mayor of Plymouth, and 300 ladies and gentlemen sat down to dinner afterwards in his loft. Blackburn proposed two toasts, to the 'Pious memory of Sir Francis Drake', and 'Success to HMS *Armada*'. The ship saw a deal of action in the Napoleonic wars, and was not sold out of the service until 1863.

Another third rate of 74 guns, the *Clarence*, was built in 1812 and her launch is recorded in an oil painting by John Rogers in Plymouth Art Gallery. This too was obviously a fashionable occasion. She spent a couple years blockading French ports, but was paid off before the end of the war. In 1827 she was cut down to 50 guns and renamed the *Centurion*, but was not apparently a success because she was broken up in 1818.

Two other warships are by some authorities said to have been built at Turnchapel, but others credit

The Turnchapel shipbuilding yard, long after the glory days of launching 74-gun warships in the Napoleonic wars and before conversion into Turnchapel Wharf. On the left, behind the masts of the barque at anchor, there are ships drawn up on the Cattedown foreshore by Hill's shipbuilding yard.

them to Devonport Dockyard. They are the *Circe* (which eventually became one of the ships in the *Impregnable* group of training ships at Devonport and survived until 1922, and the *Nile*, which was eventually converted to steam and renamed the *Conway* in 1876 to become the third training ship of that name. She survived until stranded in the Menai Straits in 1953.

It may have been the influence of the naval dockyard that made Plymouth shipowners proud to boast that 'only the very best vessels are built in our home port'. The standard of work required at Devonport was very high, and men apprenticed outside the dockyard were always anxious to seek employment in the yard, which carried with it a pension. Plymouth shipyards might be more expensive, but their vessels lasted longer.

POPE

In 1825 (or 1830, sources do not agree) the Turnchapel Yard was sold to John Pope. The

family had been in the business for some time, for when in 1817 two Pope brothers were established in Prince Edward Island, one of the Atlantic provinces of Canada, they were described as of a family of Plymouth shipbuilders and timber merchants. An 1856 chart of Cattewater which names the Turnchapel site as 'Pope's Yard and Dry Dock' also marks a dock at Mount Batten as 'Pope's old Dock'. One of John Pope's early jobs at Turnchapel was to build in 1832 the first chain ferry for Saltash to the designs of James Rendel - who had earlier designed the flying bridge for Lord Boringdon. Timber was plentiful in Prince Edward Island and a good business was made of building ships in the island, sailing them to England (with a cargo of timber) and there selling them. The Popes flourished in Canada, and became important members of the community. One report says that the family sold the Turnchapel yard in 1859 to N Were: maybe Canada beckoned. Another version says that the Popes went bankrupt towards the end of the century and the yard was taken over by the Plymouth Naval Bank. Orlando Davies, a shipping agent writing in 1910, suggests that they had been there within his memory.

ROUTLEFF and KELLY

There were more yards a little further down the river, at Turnchapel and Mount Batten. William Routleff was at Mount Batten by 1850, and built the second Saltash chain ferry in 1852. He died that year and his son, also William, carried on the business. Typical of the Routleff craft was the *Batten Castle*, built in 1851, square-sterned, sloop rigged, 57 feet long, 61 tons. Various members of the Routleff family owned a quarter of the shares, but half were in the hands of Charles Couch, a shipowner of Plymouth. Couch's son, Theophilus, was master throughout the *Batten Castle's* career. Her home port seems to have been Mevagissey. Most of her voyages were between Plymouth, Pentewan and the Clyde, carrying china clay for Shanks of Barrhead, makers of sanitary ware. She brought back a variety of goods, mainly iron, to the Cattewater, and then sailed to Pentewan in ballast. In her fourteen years life the ship rounded Land's End 145 times, and made 255 calls at 44 different ports to load or discharge cargo. She was finally lost in September 1866 on Breaksea Point, in the Bristol Channel.

The Routleff yard was taken over in 1882 by W.S. Kelly, who moved down from the Sand Quay at Dartmouth. He continued to build hookers and other fishing boats, coastal craft and yachts, of which the most celebrated in racing circles were the *Mabel* and the *Florence*. Kelly's last ship, built in 1878, was the *Alfred Rooker*, named after the distinguished Plymouth Liberal leader who was instrumental in building Plymouth Guildhall. She was commissioned by the Plymouth & Oreston Timber Company, and later converted by William

Lucas at Oreston for Arctic work. Only in 1930 did she stop work, due to trade being slack.

DARTON, BURLACE and LUCAS

Alongside Kelly's yard at Mount Batten was the yard of John and Isaac Darton. Dartons built ships for the Oreston and Turnchapel Steamship Company, and possibly their rivals, the Greaneys. They also built the *Kitley Belle* in 1900, specially for the Yealm service between Steer Point and Newton Ferrers. She was still in service in 1929 when the railway to Steer Point and Yealmpton closed down. Dartons built the yacht *Mayfly* for 'Squire' Bewes of Beaumont House. Other names crop up at Mount Batten, among them England, Hines and Frost.

In the mid-1860s Alfred Burlace was building ships and boats at Turnchapel; possibly some for the steamship company as well as hookers and other fishing craft. Further up the river, at Oreston, William Lucas, William Lapthorn and George Underhill were active in the second half of the nineteenth century. Even the landlord of the King's Arms, Edward Pile, built boats for a spell. In the 1920s Stanley Lucas ran the family yard, which was at the western end of the village, its slipway now used for yacht storage. He could haul up for repair the fishing boats, coal hulks,

A 1905 postcard of Mount Batten, showing the Castle Inn on the foreshore, with Darton's boatyard to the right.

Bayly's lighters, and other local craft. He died in the 1930s. His sons eventually gave up the yard, before World War II, when it was taken over by the Admiralty to repair motor torpedo boats. Between Lucas's yard and Bayly's yard was a smaller yard run by Sydney Harper, who had been an apprentice with Lucas.

RICHARD HILL

On the Cattedown side the trade was much more formalised, with two yards equipped with slipways and graving docks. Under the modern Cattedown Wharfs is the yard of Richard Hill & Sons. They were there for three generations, probably established by the 1820s, and when they went out of business in 1885 they had a wet dock, building slip and a patent or railway slip that could take ships up to 1000 tons.

The yard was originally that of Alexander Brown, and in 1823 the first steamer built in Plymouth, the *Sir Francis Drake*, was reported in two local newspapers as having been launched from 'Brown's Yard'. In that year Brown went bankrupt, and Hill took over the yard, which explains why an old man of 96, telling in 1906 the story of her launch, said it happened in Hill's Yard. In his story, when the *Sir Francis Drake* was launched her stern went under water, and an East Street druggist, John Prideaux, standing aft, came up drenched. The *Drake* continued her coasting service, mainly to the Channel Islands, until 1873.

To start with, Richard Hill was building ships at Oreston for some years,and continued building ships there after taking over the Cattedown yard. In Oreston they built in 1829 the topsail schooner *Richard Hill*, 62ft, 79 tons, and, as was often done, she was kept in family ownership. She traded to Brazil, Norway, America and the Mediterranean until in 1841 she was sold to an Exeter coal merchant and went coasting. In 1857 she was

auctioned at Ilfracombe and transferred to Barnstaple. She was sold again in 1860 to Beava brothers of Appledore, and continued trading until 1877, when she was injured in a gale. The *Richard Hill* was repaired but never sailed again, and was broken up in 1884, a working life of forty-six years.

The second Richard Hill died in 1876 and in his will left his lease of Marine Villas, which were two houses at Oreston, as well as shipbuilding yards and sheds held under lease from the Great Western Dock Co, who owned Millbay Docks. By this time, when iron and then steel ships were coming in, it became more and more difficult for the wooden shipbuilders to make a living. They tried building bigger and bigger ships 'on spec', hoping to find a buyer, and often were left with these craft on their hands. This was a common, and expensive, practice throughout the West Country as builders tried to stay in business. The third Hill had to mortgage the yard in 1881 but still went bankrupt and sold out to Burnard & Alger in 1885. They built Cattedown Wharfs on the site.

BANKS

The other big yard was at Queen Anne's Battery, and the slipways and docks can still be seen on the north-west side of the marina, used by the University of Plymouth's marine facility. It was developed by Joseph Banks, who had started at Mutton Cove and in 1830 moved to the Cremyll yard now occupied by Mashfords. In 1852 he bought the Queen Anne's Battery site from a man called Rowland, and built a dock capable of taking two ships,one lying astern of the other, as well as a dry dock. Family legend is that the dry dock was unsatisfactory because of a spring uncovered when it was being dug out.

But iron ships were beginning to take over from

the little wooden ships. In 1865 the Plymouth Ship-Building, Dock and Iron Works Company was formed with the intention to taking over the yard. It planned to build and repair iron ships and make considerable extensions to the dock. It was going to be managed by Joseph Banks, and would have been the first iron shipbuilding works in Plymouth. But nothing came of it.

Joseph Banks tried another tack, trying to compete in the changing market with a bigger and better wooden sailing vessel. In 1870 he was launching 'the largest ship that has ever been built in Plymouth', according to the *Western Morning News* of August 12 that year. 'The vessel, the *Nimrod*, was commenced about four years since, and has been ready for launching for some considerable time past, but this, for some reason, has been delayed. She is 1,127 tons burthen, 188 feet long, 36 feet 6ins broad and 21 feet 8 ins deep, and will not be completed until purchased.'

Things took a better turn when Joseph's daughter Bessie married John Westcott, the shipowner and coal merchant who had his coalyard quite close in Coxside Creek. Bessie's brother David, who had taken over from his father, built eleven ships between 1873 and 1894 for his brother-in-law; three schooners, six barges and two tugs, the *Stormcock* and the *Herbert*. He owned several of the vessels that he built and after his father's death his widow, David's mother, Jane Tonkin Banks owned shares in his vessels. Banks was still busy in 1882, but work was falling away for him as for everybody else.

In 1910 Orlando Davies, writing about the industries of Plymouth, said that 'shipbuilding, which was at one time a thriving and important industry in the port, has practically ceased to exist. The Queen Anne's building slips and dry dock, Hill and Sons' building slip and yards, Pope's dry dock and building slips at Turnchapel, Moore's, Shilston's, Gent's (all in Sutton Harbour), Kelly's

building yards and railway slips, all have disappeared, and with them the allied trades, and the sound of the chisel and mallet has ceased'.

SHIP-BREAKING

The closeness of Devonport Naval Base, where a great many ships were laid up at the end of their working life and eventually sold for breaking up, was a considerable source of income to the Plymouth breakers.

EDRED MARSHALL

Edred Marshall established a considerable establishment in Deadman's Bay with docks and slips for ship-breaking. Examples of the vessels he handled in this way are:

Pilot, a 16-gun brig launched in 1838 which had seen service in the East and West Indies before Marshall bought her for £802 in 1862 to break up:

Armada, built at Turnchapel in 1810, was bought for £2,600 in 1863 for breaking up:

Lancaster, a fourth rate of 50 guns built in 1823, spent nearly all her life laid up at Devonport until she was sold in 1864 to Marshall for £3,025:

Cerberus, a third rate of 42 guns launched in 1827, also spent her life laid up at Devonport until sold in 1866:

Pantaloon, a screw steam sloop of 11 guns, launched in 1860, sailed for the Cape of Good Hope station. She was wrecked on a coral reef, refloated, recommissioned in Bombay and sailed home in 1866 to be sold for breaking up for £1,610.

The biggest ship broken up in Marshall's yard was the 84-gun *Sans Pareil*, launched as a sailing ship in 1845 and converted three years later to a 70-gun steam screw battleship. First commissioned in 1852, she played a prominent part in the Crimean War, taking part in the bombardments of Odessa and Sebastapol. She

The old Defiance *which was broken up by Castles in 1931. It is possible that she was broken up in Millbay Dock.*

subsequently sailed to China and was in the assault of Canton, returning to India to subdue Calcutta in the Indian Mutiny, and completed her service life in comparative quiet. She was sold to Marshall in 1867.

But the Navy had stopped building the wooden walls many years earlier, the number coming for breaking up was dwindling and the supply of smaller commercial vessels was little compensation. So in 1892 Edred Marshall sold the yard to Cornelius Duke and moved to the other side of Sutton Road where he set up a box-making business - 'the mechanical marvel of the town', wrote Whitfeld. This was operating until World War II.

CASTLES

In 1920 Sidney Castle moved to Plymouth, a member of a family renowned in the ship-breaking business at Rotherhithe since the seventeenth century. They had bought many vessels from Devonport and taken them to their yards on the Thames in that time. He established a breaker's yard between Cattedown Wharfs and the Corporation Wharf, but also broke up ships in Millbay Dock and Ocean Quay, Devonport. He was mainly handling steel ships, unlike the wooden vessels broken up by Marshall.

Among ships he broke up at Cattedown are:

1920: *St George*, 1st class cruiser, 7,700 tons. 2 nine-inch, 10 six-inch guns, built 1892.

1921: The training ship *Mount Edgcumbe*, which had been moored off Cremyll since 1874 and used by the Devon and Cornwall Industrial Training Ship Association. She took orphans and boys from poor homes and trained them for employment afloat, although the hard training they received resulted in most graduates finding other employment! She had been built in 1822 as the *Winchester* and had a brief spell as the *Conway*

training ship before coming to Plymouth. A hundred years old, it is no wonder that she was in a poor shape at the end.

1931: *Defiance*; for long a familiar sight in the Plymouth waterways as the torpedo training establishment off Wearde Quay, at the entrance to the Lynher. Built of wood in 1861 as a 2nd rate with 34 eight-inch guns, she was in the Lynher from 1884 until 1931.

1932: *Tintagel*, S class destroyer, built 1918.

1952: *Research*, an unusual ship built at Dartmouth entirely of non-ferrous metal as a survey and research vessel. Laid down in 1939, she was never completed and was sold to Hocking Brothers, who had been taken over by Castles.

With ship-breaking business falling off between the wars Castles had started a sideline in building furniture. Early in World War II they began making ammunition boxes for the forces, and after the war the making of kitchen units gradually became their dominant occupation. They had completed the changeover by 1982, when they moved their establishment to Estover and changed their name to Castles Kitchens.

DAVIES & CANN

For many postwar years cars driving to Plymouth over Laira Bridge had the spectacle of warships and submarines being broken up alongside the quay close on their left hand.

Davies & Cann had been established at Cremyll Street, Stonehouse as iron, steel and non-ferrous scrap metal merchants for some years when they were taken over by Eddie Smith in 1951. He bought Martin's Wharf, between Laira Bridge and the power station in 1955 from English China Clays, and soon after bought from Coles, the timber merchants, their wharf on the other side of the river, between Laira Bridge and Pomphlett Creek.

In 1966 he turned to ship-breaking, and the first job was the wartime frigate, HMS *Loch Ruthven* of 1,435 tons. Three years later the company was breaking up an ocean salvage tug, the *Prince Salvor*, and in 1977 they began breaking up two famous submarines. HMS *Andrew* was the first submarine to have crossed the Atlantic submerged for the whole voyage, and the last submarine to carry a deck gun. HMS *Rorqual* had been used in the film *On the Beach* with Gregory Peck in the lead, and preservation societies tried very hard to keep these vessels.

Other interesting ships broken up by the Smiths included the sonar trials vessel *Broadway* (1980),

which had featured in the Portland spy trial, and the elegant 1900 luxury steam yacht *Norian* (1976). For fifteen years four of the disbanded Reynolds fleet of steam tugs from *Torpoint*, *Trevol*, *Tactful*, *Carbeill* and *Antony*, lay off the yards. They were the last steam tugs on the South Coast, and there were hopes of their preservation. Scrap metal was sometimes loaded into 500 ton ships for delivery in South Wales.

Eddie Smith's sons, Michael and Tony, had taken over from their father some years before they ceased trading in August 1992 and sold their yards in 1993.

A submarine can be seen awaiting break-up at Davies & Cann's yard at Laira Wharf, and across the river the Reynold's tugs await the same fate at the company's other yard.

CHAPTER TEN

CATTEWATER COMMISSIONERS AND BATTEN BREAKWATER

A sore point for centuries in Plymouth was the right of the manor of Trematon over the Cattewater and Sutton Pool. For years the borough of Saltash, as lords of the manor, collected dues from ships anchored in the Cattewater, but in 1637 a wreck was considerably hampering navigation and Saltash refused to do anything about its removal - estimated to cost over £2,000. So Plymouth appealed to the authorities, who ruled that Plymouth Corporation should receive various shipping dues and that Saltash should remove the wreck. Saltash then came to terms with Plymouth and agreed in future to joint control of the Cattewater.

Lord Boringdon's Acts of 1807 and 1812 gave him the rights to improve the harbour within his manor of Plympton, and to appoint a harbourmaster, and Saltash seems to have abandoned its claims.

There were earlier Acts of Parliament concerned with the Cattewater, mostly for its 'preservacion', for control of silting up by waste from the tin mines and from dumping of ballast, and for its general improvement. In Queen Anne's reign an Act empowered the removal of the Middle Bank, close to the entrance.

The building of Plymouth Breakwater 1812-1844 much improved the safety of the Cattewater as a harbour, but the reef of rocks that ran out from Mount Batten was a danger to vessels seeking the Cattewater's shelter. Recorded wrecks start as early as 1627, when fifteen ships were ashore in the Hamoaze and five in the Cattewater. The *Dutton* troopship struck these rocks when running for the Cattewater in a January gale in 1787, finishing up on the rocks under the Citadel where some 600 people were rescued.

In 1811 HMS *Amethyst* was lost on these rocks with the loss of 600 lives. Six years later HMS *Jasper*, a brig, went ashore there with the loss of 72 of its crew of 76. Five ships were driven ashore on Batten Reef in January 1828, and during a storm in 1872 four ships were lost there.

Ships at anchor within the Cattewater had also been cast away. A storm in 1787 sank five merchantmen. More ships were lost there in 1803 and 1804. In November 1824 a great storm created havoc in the Cattewater. In the area between the eastern pier of Sutton Harbour and the Bear Rock, exposed to the full blast of a south-westerly gale, forty-eight ships were wrecked and 144 seamen drowned. Ever since that stretch of shore has had the dread name of Deadman's Bay. Four vessels were wrecked there in October 1877 when two

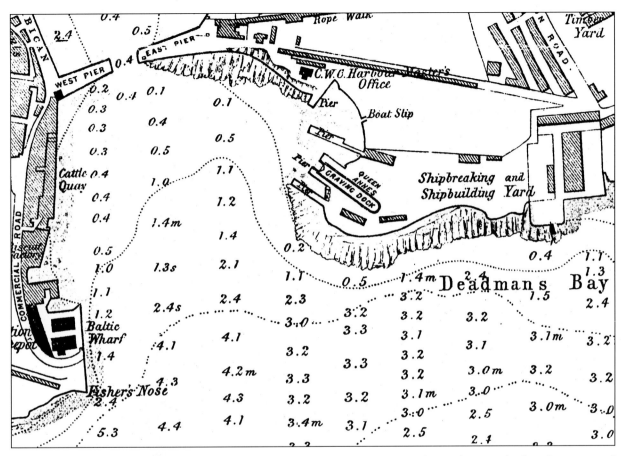

Detail from an 1877 harbour plan showing the Cattewater outside the entrance to Sutton Harbour. Top centre, the letters 'C.W.C.' mark the Cattewater Commissioners' harbourmaster's office, on Teat's Hill.

more went ashore as far up the Cattewater as the Bear Rock.

An inner breakwater built out across the Batten Reef, and sheltering Deadman's Bay, was the obvious answer. But not until November 1873 was any action taken. Then a meeting was called of shipowners and business men concerned with the Cattewater. It was presided over by one of the principal landowners in Cattedown, Lord Graves.

As a result of that meeting, and many more, on 7 August 1874 the Cattewater Harbour Order completed its passage through Parliament. It set up the Cattewater Commissioners, whose principal business was to be the construction, maintenance and regulation of a breakwater and pier on the Batten reef of rocks. They were also empowered to dredge, deepen, scour and otherwise improve the harbour, and to lay down buoys and moorings. They were empowered to buy land, to maintain the Cobbler Buoy at the entrance to the Cattewater and to take over from the Admiralty all other buoys within its boundaries (which were laid down as all the tidal waters within a line from the Cobbler Rock to Fisher's Nose, except Sutton Harbour within the piers, and not extending beyond the Laira Bridge. To do all this it was empowered to borrow up to £30,000.

This meant that Plymouth had yet another port authority. The captain of the Dockyard and the Queen's Harbourmaster had authority over the whole port. Sutton Harbour controlled its own waters. Millbay Docks had a harbour master and control of its own waters. The Cattewater order set up a third civilian harbour authority and a little later on the Stonehouse Creek Improvement Company created another authority. As long ago as 1928 the Labour Party on the Council wanted one port authority, and Jimmy Moses, the Labour leader, moved that the city should buy out both the Cattewater Commissioners and the Sutton Harbour Improvement Company. A general conference of the corporation and all the harbour authorities came out strongly against unified control. Nothing came of it, and the Port of Plymouth staggered on with four civilian authorities all under the thumb of the Royal Navy.

In 1995, with the Admiralty saving money as hard as it could go and cutting down in all directions, it set up a scheme whereby the Cattewater Commissioner would take over the general responsibility from the Queen's Harbourmaster. Sutton and Millbay were to retain their limited control.

There have been various Cattewater Harbour Orders made since 1874, mainly to increase the borrowing rate. The original order laid down that the seventeen commissioners should consist of one each appointed by the Admiralty, the War Department, Trinity House, the Duke of Bedford, the Earl of Morley, Lord Graves, Lord Blachford, the local marine board and two town councillors. A 1915 Revision Order added that six 'frontagers' were to be elected to represent the owners and lessees of property fronting on the harbour, two of whom were to be re-elected each year. The 1915 Order also gave new powers for buying land, building wharfs, laying moorings and controlling vessels using the Cattewater. This order laid

The present Commiss-ioners office at 2 the Barbican.

down that the Commissioners were bound to act in consultation and agreement with the Admiralty, which in practice means the approval of the Queen's Harbour Master, and Trinity House.

The Commissioners have never owned the foreshore or fundus of the harbour, but hold these right on licence from the Duchy of Cornwall. A series of 30-year leases gave way in 1994 to a long lease of 125 years, to enable all concerned authorities to enter into long-term plans.

Various Revision Orders have also made allowances for the changes of ownership of the foreshore. revision of rates and greater powers of wreck removal. For many years the Commissioners had their office at Teat's Hill. Between the wars the offices were in the Exchange in Woolster Street but this was destroyed in 1941. Since then they have been installed in the old Seamen's Mission building on the Barbican, opposite the end of the Mayflower Pier and looking up the Cattewater. The local Coastguards were on the ground floor, the pilots on the first floor, and the Commissioners occupy the top two floors.

In 1987 the Pilotage Act transferred the responsibility of providing pilots from Trinity House to local harbour authorities. Plymouth has three such authorities, but the Cattewater Commissioners were elected as the pilotage authority.

The modern powers of the Commissioners cover the provision of lights and buoys and beacons, regular hydrographic surveying, the preparation of charts, and dredging to maintain the navigational channels. In the early days dredgers were hired, but after World War II the *Sandswallow*, a single-crane dredger, was bought. Captain Stan Daymond, formerly of Reynold's tugs, was the master, and when not at work in the Cattewater, *Seaswallow* was hired for outside jobs, as far away as Exmouth and Brixham.

In 1954 she was joined by an ex-Dockyard steam dredger, which was renamed the *Plym*. She had to be fetched from Leigh and Captain Daymond, who took a crew up to fetch her, had a rough passage of the North Sea in which most of the extra coal for the passage, carried as deck cargo, was washed overboard. *Plym* found outside work at Newport and Swansea. Once she had proved herself, *Seaswallow* went. A motor-hopper which had been laid up for some years in the dock at Breakwater Quarry, was bought in the late 1950s and refitted to work with a crane barge. In 1969 *Plym* was replaced by a diesel electric dredger from Liverpool, renamed *Plymsand*. She was sold in 1984 and contract dredgers employed. An 80-ton tug, the *Plym Echo*, was purchased in 1996: she could also serve as a dredger and act as an auxiliary pilot boat.

The Cobbler Channel from the Mallard Shoal, off Batten Breakwater, has a leading light in the clock tower of the Royal Western Yacht Club. Off Queen Anne's Battery Breakwater the channel swings just south of east. with a leading light and beacons on Cattedown. Off Victoria Wharfs it turns a little more to starboard, with leading light and beacons on the high ground behind Turnchapel. At a point off Turnchapel the channel swings to port between the two wharfs. All this is dredged to five fathoms, with deeper water maintained off the quays. The channel on to the Stone Jetty, swinging over to the Oreston shore to circle the Cockle Bank, is only maintained to two metres. A few buoys mark these passages.

A triumph of navigation in the Plym is regularly performed by the 300-ton sludge vessel *Douglas McWilliam*. Specially designed by Mark Gatehouse, owned by Dean & Dyball and chartered to South West Water, she regularly passes under Laira Bridge and finds her way up an almost unbuoyed channel to the sewage works at Marsh Mills. There she loads from a pipeline in the river where it narrows above Blaxton. She has also lifted sludge from Radford and Camel's Head, all of which she dumps in the approved ground west of Rame Head.

Batten Breakwater in 1994, showing the stones dumped in the sea on either side to protect it from storm damage.

Harbourmasters since World War I have been W.S.Watt, Captain J. Snowden, Captain Hunt, Captain Davis and Captain T.Hornsby. Lieut Cdr A.G.Dyer, was appointed in 1983 and resigned in 1996.

In 1994 the Commissioners were: Admiralty, the Queen's Harbour Master; Minister of the Army, CO Amphibious Squadron, Royal Marines; Minister for Air, vacant; Trinity House, Capt. R.Golding; heirs and assigns of Duke of Bedford, Mr V.Stimson; Lord Graves and Lord Morley, both vacant; heirs and assigns of Lord Blachford, Mr M.N.Booth (ECC Quarries); City Council,, Mrs J. Nelder and Mr J. Finnigan; Chamber of Commerce, Messrs L.P.Stribley (chairman) and R.Love; frontagers, Messrs P.G.Adams, M.G.East (deputy chairman), D.B.Godefroy, M.A.Gatehouse, J.S.Gill and M.Smith.

BATTEN BREAKWATER

Once created, the Cattewater Commissioners wasted no time in starting work on Batten Breakwater. By May 1878 an engineer had been appointed, James C. Inglis. He was engineer to the Great Western Railway, who were competing fiercely with the London and South Western for Plymouth's harbour business. Inglis was later to design the old Fish Market in Sutton Harbour, which has always looked like a GWR station. In 1902 he became general manager of the GWR and was knighted.

In October 1878 the work already started was damaged in two successive storms, but by October 1879 the breakwater was finished, 855 feet long and 40 feet wide. It took longer to build than estimated, and cost more, so that an extra borrowing power covering £10,000 had to be taken. Later there were plans to extend the breakwater to include the Mallard Shoal, but this was abandoned in 1898 because it was found that the Cobbler Channel, between the end of the breakwater and the Mallard was too deep, and the bottom not suitable for building.

Batten Breakwater was maintained through the dues the Commissioners were empowered to levy on vessels using the harbour. Then in 1926 the Air Ministry took over the breakwater, buying out the Commissioners' rights for £14,000. This was less than it had cost to build, but relieved the Commissioners of the costs of maintenance. In 1984, for example, the Ministry of Defence spend £2,000,000 on repairing the breakwater and strengthening it by dumping large blocks of stone around the pier. Unfortunately they did not carry this through to the root of the pier, where the outer skin was badly damaged in 1989. Only first aid repair work was carried out, and in 1993 ownership of the pier, along with the whole air station, passed into the hands of Plymouth Development Corporation. They promptly set about completing the work on Batten Breakwater that the M.o.D. had skimped, and restored it to first class condition at a cost of £800,000.

The breakwater has been repaired at about thirty-year intervals, and the current work is expected to last as long. The need for the breakwater is now rather different; when it was built vessels using the Cattewater anchored and were serviced by lighters; now they berth alongside quays.

The breakwater today benefits recreational as much as commercial users, such as the dinghies based around Phoenix Wharf and the yachts using marinas at Queen Anne Battery. The marina would have had to been built much more robustly had there been no Batten Breakwater. It is considered that in future the cost of maintaining the breakwater will need to cover both groups of users.

CHAPTER ELEVEN

THE FIRST WHARFS, LAIRA AND CATTEDOWN

LAIRA WHARF

The oldest quay on the Cattewater was planned as the terminus to a spur of the Plymouth & Dartmoor Railway, which actually finished alongside Coxside Creek in Sutton Harbour. It was completed in 1825; the wall of the quay naturally being in granite as the purpose of the horsedrawn railway was to bring granite from the Moor. The railway's customer was the granite company, Johnson & Bryce, who had the contract both for surfacing Plymouth Breakwater, under construction at the time, and for the piers of Laira Bridge, which was just above the quay. Granite was probably transferred from truck to barge at the quay for Laira Bridge, which was alongside, and the Breakwater.

Laira Wharf took a new lease of life in 1853 when the Lee Moor Railway was built to bring china clay there for onward shipment. The wharf was soon known as the China Clay Wharf, or Martin's Wharf after the principal owner of the clay pits. Much was brought down from Lee Moor packed in casks, which could easily be loaded on the ships alongside the quay. On the quay was built a storage shed, a house and stabling for the fourteen horses which hauled the train of wagons. Traffic fell off after 1927 with the opening of new drying works at Marsh Mills, and virtually ceased during World War II. After 1945 the line ended at Maddock's (now Heywood's) concrete works on the Embankment, and Martin's Wharf was left idle.

English China Clays had taken over all the Lee Moor operations in 1919, and they sold the wharf

Martin's or Laira Wharf in 1830, a drawing by T. Allom. Notice the sailing ship lowering its mast, without dropping the sail, to pass under the bridge.

to Davies & Cann in 1955. They set up a scrap metal operation (see chapter nine), but when they ceased trading in 1982 the wharf was leased by two brothers, Andrew and Ian Sleep, for development as a yacht storage facility.

CATTEDOWN WHARFS

In the early 1880s the control of Burnard & Alger, the chemical works at Cattedown, had fallen to the hands of a new generation. W.H.Alger, in his forties, and Robert Burnard. in his mid-thirties, were in control. Shipping in the river was showing a dramatic increase as a result of the London & South Western Railway arriving in 1874; in their first year of operation the Cattewater trade figures jumped ahead of the Sutton Harbour returns. But the old Cattedown Quay, built to cope with the small sailing vessels carrying limestone about the local coasts, was a tumbledown affair. Ships had to anchor in the river and send their goods ashore by lighter. On the waterfront across the road from Burnard & Alger's factory the old shipyard of Richard Hill was struggling to stay in business. So it was decided to buy the shipyard and build a quay where ships could berth, cutting out the lighters.

The landowner, Lord Graves, made the first application to the Admiralty for a quay, but was refused. So he made a second, modified application, which succeeded. Then his tenants took over. In 1884 Burnard & Alger bought part of the foreshore from the Duchy of Cornwall, and Hill's yard as well. Across the road from their factory they began to build Cattedown Wharf. It was the first deep water berth at Cattedown. In 1888 a steamer brought in 3,000 tons of wheat from India and an iron sailing ship from Hamburg landed 1,700 tons of guano.

The original jetty, built out over the shipyard slipways, was of wood, 521 feet by 30 feet. The Hills had their private house in the yard which was retained until 1912, but various shipyard stores and stables remained even longer. Eight stone warehouses were built at the back of the wharf, which was equipped with three fixed-jib hydraulic cranes. In July 1890 the *Western Morning News* declared that by building the wharfs, Messrs Burnard and Alger had conferred a great benefit on the eastern end of Plymouth. Magnificent vessels had entered the harbour in the two years they were open, and in the last week the largest sailing ship ever seen in the Cattewater came in, the *Boedicea*, 264 feet by 39 feet beam and 23.6 feet draught, carrying 3,000 tons.

As soon as Prince Rock power station was in business, the wharf installed electric light in 1899, at a cost of £356. In the early days it was almost solely engaged in loading and unloading fertilisers for Burnard & Alger and the neighbouring factories. A table of wharf rates for August 1901 shows the kind of cargoes being handled. They included guano, grain, nitrate, petroleum per barrel, phosphates, coals and general cargo. There were different rates for steam ships and sailing ships. But from the start imports were always in excess of exports. In 1906, for instance, 58,135 tons came in over over the wharfs, but only 20,746 went out. These figures stayed fairly constant until the war years.

Then in 1914-15 there was a great increase in imports due to prize ships brought in, and munitions arriving, but a sharp decrease in china clay and fertilisers exported. Exports fell to just over 4,000 tons in 1915 but imports were up at 82,000 tons. In these years the Admiralty did much dredging off the wharfs, which had been extended to 500 feet in length, and by 1917 there was 24 feet of water at low water springs for the full length.

A major change came in 1920. The fertiliser factory was sold to Anglo-Continental and

A mixture of sail and steam in the river, with Cattedown Wharfs behind the masts. The houses of the old waterside settlement can be seen left with Burnard & Alger's works behind.

Cattedown Wharfs Co.Ltd formed, with the second generation in control. Harold Alger, who had joined the company in 1891, was managing director. Lawrence Burnard, who had joined the firm in 1896, and Col. A.H. Bagnold, were fellow directors. The new company promptly began extending the jetty, lengthening it eastwards to 651 ft. Then they improved the road outside the wharf, increasing the width to 40 feet and planning to extend it to meet the new road being built from Prince Rock. Exports were recovering after the war, matching the prewar figures with 24,000 tons by 1920-21. Imports in these years included fertilisers, pyrites, superphosphates, gas and fuel oil, motorspirit, timber, and general cargo. Guano was still arriving in 1939 but only a few hundred tons.

But the petrol companies were building new installations, and in the 1920s agreement was reached with them that the wharf would become the major oil terminal for the port. Hydraulic pumping machinery was modernised. By 1931 imports had risen to nearly 128,000 tons, with petroleum products over 100,000 tons of that total. Exports were down that year, to 8,000 tons, but apart from china clay and stone Plymouth has always had very little to export. In 1936 the wooden jetty was demolished, replaced by a reinforced concrete quay, and extended even further east by 114ft. The berth was now 952 feet long, and could accommodate 500 feet ships of over 20,000 tons. An embankment was added at the east end which meant that railway trucks could come in at each end. A double track was laid the length of the quay.

By 1939 the total tonnage handled was 195,000 tons, with exports of 33,000 but imports over 161,000 tons. Of this 135,000 tons was in petroleum products and other business was in decline. The directors were worried that so many eggs were in one basket, but at least could be gratified that as some trades fell off, another was more than taking its place.

In the bombing of World War II the worst damage to the wharfs occurred in 1940, when a 1,000lb bomb scored a direct hit, demolishing one warehouse, damaging others and causing extensive damage to the wharf itself. In January 1941 there were firebombs to contend with, and in the Blitz of March 1941 a high explosive bomb went through a warehouse, with more high explosive and fire bombs in the April blitz. In spite of this the Army was making full use of the facilities, with vessels loading motor transport for forces overseas. Later the Admiralty were berthing destroyers and merchant vessels alongside the wharfs to degauss them, 191 were handled in 1941-2, with 285 degaussed the next

A post World War II photograph of Cattedown Wharfs, with an oil tanker alongside and Fisons Fertiliser works to the left.

year. After the Americans entered the war their store ships were using the wharfs.

After the end of the war fertilisers still formed a substantial part of the traffic. Clinker was going out to Northern Ireland, gypsum and coal coming in to be loaded directly into lorries for local work. Bagged cement was being handled. By 1950-51, of the total of 284,000 tons handled, 17,000 were exports and 267,000 tons imports. Oil exports made up 169,000 tons, which showed a healthy recovery of other imports to nearly 100,000 tons, better than the early days before bulk cargoes of oil.

In 1957, although there were still Algers on the Board, only Jack Burnard, who had joined the company in 1926, and Albert Soper were active directors. (Bert's son Tony became the distinguished broadcaster and naturalist). Jack Burnard was effectively the owner of the company and he wanted to retire. So Cattedown Wharfs were sold to F.T. Everard and Sons Ltd, a group of shipowners which had grown out of an original fleet of Thames spritsail barges. It is still based at Greenhithe in Kent. Albert Soper became managing director of Cattedown Wharfs with Lionel Stribley as company secretary and Robin Love as Chief Clerk. Mr Soper retired in 1969 and Stribley and Love each moved up one; when Lionel Stribley retired in 1993 then Robin Love became managing director.

Over the years 1967-71 more modern machinery was installed, giving faster service to ships. By 1972 a berth had been established at the west end of the wharf for oil tankers, with a complex of five marina discharge arms used by all the companies. These were linked by a pipe system to the various oil storages of the different companies. Most of the warehouses were rented out.

In 1979 dry cargo imports included 60,000 tonnes of bulk fertilisers, 58,000 tonnes of coal and gypsum. Among the exports were 85,000 tonnes of clinker. 220 dry cargo vessels were handled and 217 tankers discharged 647,360 tonnes of oil products, a four-fold increase in thirty years. New traffic included pumice from the Mediterranean for the building industry, salt from East Germany, and fish unloaded from trawlers, packed in the wharf stores and sent to Scotland in refrigerated vehicles.

Oil products built up to the million tonnes early in the 1980s but with the recession fell away again, only breaking the magic figure again with 1,017,608 tonnes in 1993. Other imports included fertilisers, fish, coal, grit, salt, animal feeds, petroleum, coke and bauxite. Total imports amounted to 1,100,176 tonnes but of this dry goods only amounted to less than a twelfth. This type of cargo was disappearing. Timber and coal, for instance, once large imports, were now coming to Plymouth by road. From time to time a shipload of coal came in from Pascoe Fields of Swansea, who rent a stretch of quay east from Cattedown Wharfs. From there it was sold by the Swansea firm to local merchants. Increasingly labour was only required to moor and unmoor ships, not for cargo handling. Goods out included lime, clay and fish, only amounted to 7,004 tonnes. The figures underline the old problem of Plymouth, it does not have a goods-producing hinterland. In 1993 804 vessels were handled, 287 tankers and 48 discharging dry cargo. 437 trawlers landed fish, mainly for the Interfish factory across the road. Only seven ships loaded cargoes.

ARCHAEOLOGICAL FINDS

One odd side result of the building of Cattedown Wharfs was that in its construction the old quarries at the back of Burnard & Alger were opened up for stone, and caves were exposed. One cavern of 54 feet in length was opened, with a chamber at each end. Here the bones of at least fifteen people were found, as well as animals, all dating from the Stone Age. The find was on a par with the findings in Kent's Cavern, Torquay, and led Robert Burnard to become interested in archaeology. His father's house at Hexworthy led him to an interest in Dartmoor. In 1893 he and the Rev Sabine Baring Gould founded the Dartmoor Exploration Committee of the Devonshire Association, of which Burnard was president in 1911.

The dredging in the Cattewater to make the deep water berths for the wharfs also led to the finding of a wreck of the believed seventeenth-century ship (see Chapter Three).

SPARROW'S WHARF

After the success of Burnard & Alger in getting permission for their wharf, Sparrow built a wharf (the 1885 application to the Queen's Harbourmaster was made by Messrs Sparrow and Bayly; the Bayly link not explained). It is immediately west of Cattedown Wharf and is still known as Sparrow's Wharf, where stone was once loaded from the quarry. Then there are no deep-water quays before Victoria Wharfs, only retaining walls creating the platforms upon which the Conoco tanks now stand. In tar distillery days the occasional small ship laid alongside, just as in recent times the Conoco bunkering craft will sometimes tie up there.

CHAPTER TWELVE

VICTORIA AND CORPORATION WHARFS

VICTORIA WHARFS

Cornelius Laskey Duke built Victoria Wharfs over the years 1893-1900. His father was clerk at the granite quarries at Merrivale, near Princetown, and Cornelius probably had no more education than his brother Henry, who started with the *Western Morning News*, became a barrister, an MP for Plymouth and finished up as a cabinet minister, high court judge and Lord Merrivale.

A great-nephew of Cornelius, A.J.Bolt of the Princetown family, lodged with the old man in Portland Villas. Mr Bolt remembers Duke as a very clever man and 'a bit of an engineer'. No doubt he had some of his brother's brilliance, and was proud of the fact that he had supplied stone for Plymouth Breakwater. This must have been for its reinforcement, which goes on every year, and possibly his interest in Merrivale quarries led him to the quarries on the Cattewater (oddly enough, after the Government had given up Breakwater Quarry, Victoria Wharfs in 1994 became the base from which stone was taken to the Breakwater for reinforcement, and the floating crane concerned in the work regularly came in and tied up at the wharf).

On the foundation stone by the north steps of Victoria Wharfs, Duke described himself as 'burgess of this borough and Cattewater Commissioner'. He would have been in his thirties, married and living in King Gardens where the street directory described him as a contractor. His wharfs were named in honour of the good Queen, whose jubilee was celebrated in the year before the chairman of the Commissioners, Thomas Bulteel of Radford (and chairman of the Naval Bank), opened the first part. The wharfs were, however, known for many years simply as Duke's Wharf.

The first part of the complex built was the wharf to the east, on Deadman's Bay Field, stretching up to Caldwell & Almond's site. While this was building Duke bought out Edred Marshall' ship-breaking yard, the Marine Hotel, a field between the hotel and the new dock. and a row of cottages. Here he created a dock of 250 feet in length to be dredged to 25 feet at mean low water springs, and a pier on the western side stretching 100 feet into the river.

It was originally planned to extend 300 feet but the Commissioners, fearing it would interfere with traffic using the deep water channel, reduced the length. The LSWR line was extended through the

Victoria Wharfs, a photograph taken from the brochure for the 1994 sale by Inchcape.

yards of Harvey's tar distillery and Caldwell & Almond's cement works.

Part of the eastern wharf was planned from the start to be leased by Chatterley & Whinfield Colliery Ltd, a Stoke-on-Trent company who built a depot on the site and shipped their coal through Garston in their own colliers. They installed the first mechanisation to handle coal seen in Plymouth. The coal was shovelled by hand into four-wheeled colliery tubs of about 15cwt capacity. These were lifted by steam crane to an overhead gantry, pushed along rails and tipped on

to dumps. These shippers moved to Millbay in 1912 but Victoria Wharfs continued to operate their coal wharf.

At the opening lunch in the Marine Hotel Mr Duke said that the land has been offered to the Corporation in 1893 but they were not interested then in the Cattewater. He also condemned the Corporation for not developing a level road from the end of Commercial Road to Cattedown. In 1900 when the whole scheme was nearing completion, the new Dock was opened by the Mayor, John Pethick, and an even bigger celebration was a dinner given in the Corn Exchange. A speaker at that dinner was Cornelius's brother, Henry Duke, who later in the year became a Unionist MP for Plymouth. In the same year Cornelius Duke was a Liberal councillor for Sutton Ward.

At the end of that year the *Morning News* reported that Duke was not only handling large cargoes of timber and coal, but also was cutting granite (no doubt from Merrivale) on the quay for export. The biggest ship ever seen in the Cattewater. the *Chesapeake*, 375ft, docked at Victoria Wharfs to discharge 6,000 tons of petroleum. A couple months later fourteen ships, big and small, were reported alongside the wharfs at the same time, even though the dock was still not completed. In 1901 the London & South Western Railway, trying to steal the GWR's liner trade, thought of using Victoria Wharfs to land passengers there - eventually they went to Ocean Quay at the entrance to Stonehouse Creek. Victoria Wharfs were extended in 1904, and in that year handled frozen meat from South America, and strawberries from Brest. 4,500 rail trucks were dealt with.

Duke was riding high in Plymouth. After a short five years on the Town Council he was chairman of the Finance Committee, the most important of all Council committees, and making headlines with his strong attacks on the Tories in the full Council meetings. In 1906-7 Duke put up a scheme for converting the whole of the Queen Anne's Battery site into an extension of Victoria Wharfs, fit to berth ocean liners. It was the second such scheme submitted in a decade but was again rejected by the Admiralty.

But he seems to have overreached himself. He is not listed as a councillor in 1906, and in October 1907 he filed his petition in bankruptcy. Victoria Wharfs were in the hands of a receiver. Duke continued as just manager of the wharf, and

business went on. In 1914 a new company was formed, Victoria Wharfs Ltd, which was owned by a group of Liverpool companies running coastal shipping. In 1917 the parent group changed its name to Coast Lines Ltd, who were to be the owners of the wharfs for the next fifty years. In later years Coast Lines always claimed that they had started their links with Plymouth in sailing ship days, and this was probably true of one of its constituent companies.

In his latter years Duke lived at 19 Portland Villas, a double-fronted detached Victorian house now on the edge of the campus of the University of Plymouth and next to the office of the vice-chancellor. When his wife died he was looked after by his daughter Lizzie until his own death in about 1940-41.

In the summer of 1917 the United States came into World War I and the wharf was taken over almost at once by the American Navy. They did not move out until February 1919. But as peace facilitated the flow of trade, so Coast Lines and Victoria Wharfs blossomed. One of their first acts had been to put up a scheme to enlarge the wharfs after the war, but it was turned down again by the Cattewater Commissioners who would not tolerate an extension of the pier into the deep channel. In 1922 they revived the scheme to turn Queen Anne's Battery into a liner dock, but it again came to nothing. In 1924 Coast Lines were content to improve what they had, spending three months dredging out the docks and removing some rocks which were in front. Trade was increasing, with cargoes of timber, phosphates and nitrates coming from Norway, Sweden, Germany and the United States.

Roy Eddison joined in 1926 as a boy (he retired in 1975 after 13 years as manager). He remembers the storehouses there like huge grocery stores filled with dry goods brought in by sea and distributed thence to all parts of South Devon and

A Coast Lines advertisement for Victoria Wharfs.

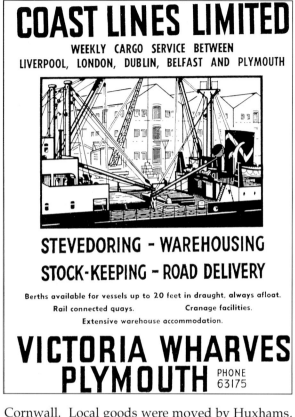

COAST LINES LIMITED
WEEKLY CARGO SERVICE BETWEEN
LIVERPOOL, LONDON, DUBLIN, BELFAST AND PLYMOUTH

STEVEDORING - WAREHOUSING
STOCK-KEEPING - ROAD DELIVERY

Berths available for vessels up to 20 feet in draught, always afloat.
Rail connected quays.   Cranage facilities.
Extensive warehouse accommodation.

VICTORIA WHARVES
PLYMOUTH PHONE 63175

Cornwall. Local goods were moved by Huxhams, a local haulier part owned by Coast Lines. They moved goods locally by horse and cart and further afield by steam waggon. More distant consignments were all loaded into railway trucks on the wharfs' own sidings. In 1955 Coast Lines would claim that they had three railway locomotives of their own operating on Victoria Wharfs. A couple horse-drawn carts were busy all day taking loads down to the GWR goods station in Coxside, at the head of the creek.

Three Coast Line ships arrived on Mondays, one from Liverpool with fruit and other goods transhipped there, and all the Unilever soaps for the West Country. Unilever even leased their own warehouses on Victoria Wharfs. Another ship

from London brought more transhipped goods, and all Procter & Gamble soaps. A third ship from Dublin came in with Guinness stout, and the half dozen Plymouth breweries of those times were all day collecting their supplies.

On Tuesdays and Wednesdays coal came in (the Wednesday ship from the East Coast). By this time Westcotts (also taken over by Coast Lines) had the coal yard; the colliers would lie beside the smaller eastern pier and the coal would be lifted across the gap by gantry. There was also a high-level gantry on the western side of the big pier which moved the dry goods straight from the ships into the warehouses.

On other days there was flour from the Co-operative Wholesale Society at Bristol, and sugar from Tate & Lyle on the Thames. They moved their cargoes in their own vehicles. Shipments of fertiliser and oil cakes (slabs 2 feet by 10ins by 2ins) for cattle feed came in, mainly moved by rail for the merchants. Fertiliser cargoes meant a great gallop all day to shift the cargo, working far into the night. In the spring there were shiploads of new potatoes from Brittany. These little ships would run up on the beach at Treguer and load from carts driven down alongside at low tide. So their time of sailing was unpredictable, and the French shipping company could ring up at all hours of the night to say that a ship had just sailed. Sometimes the top layer of these cargoes were strawberries.

If Victoria Wharfs could not take some ships, then Cattedown Wharfs would take them, just as Victoria Wharfs would help out Cattedown in emergency. When Millbay Docks were full they would send Holland Steamship Company vessels to Victoria Wharfs.

But coastwise trade began to suffer even before World War II from the competition of road transport. In a 1955 brochure devoted to their Plymouth facilities, Coast Lines had only one ship calling a week. Either the *Hibernian Coast* or the *Caledonian Coast*, both very modern motor vessels, would leave Liverpool on the Sunday and be in Plymouth 24 hours later, going on to London and so back to Liverpool by way of Dublin. They claimed to bring to Plymouth the vast majority of all margarine, cooking fats, soaps, detergents and cattle feeds consumed in Devon and East Cornwall (they now had a wharf at Falmouth). Other cargoes included linoleum, paint, disinfectants, rope, wool, groceries and fruit, fresh and canned. In 1954 the wharfs handled 150,000 tons of all types of cargo.

The building of motorways hastened the decay and even though the A38 between Exeter and Plymouth did not become a dual carriageway until 1977, the last Coast Lines ship called in 1967. Eventually they sold Victoria Wharfs to Bethel Gwyn, shipping agents who were a part of the monster Peninsular and Oriental Line. The dock under P & O had various financial controllers, last of all the Escombe Group.

Victoria Wharfs had started handling clay in 1948, 9.000 tons in all for English China Clays and Watts, Blake, Bearne and Co. The business grew as the Coast Lines traffic declined. In the month of July 1961, for instance, five Coast Line ships came in with general cargo, two with coal. Sixteen loaded clay, and one limestone. A year later there were still five Coast Line ships, but 24 clay ships. In 1966 286,000 tons of clay was handled, a thirty-fold increase in eighteen years. In August 1967, when the last Coast Line ship called, 30 other ships loaded clay.

Conveyors were set up to shift cargoes straight from the lorries from Lee Moor into the holds of ships. During the 1970s total annual cargoes fluctuated between 225,000 tonnes loaded into 315 ships, and 388,000 tonnes in 482 ships - on average one every 16 hours!. Few ships called other than for clay, three in 1972 for instance (two taking out

fertilisers), 15 ships in 1977. There were some odd cargoes, one of oyster shell in 1973, one of resin in 1977. On 24 April 1994, a random day, two ships of 2,500 tons apiece lay alongside, one loading ball clay, the other unloading palm nut kernels from Nigeria. The clay traffic peaked in 1979, and while it has declined as ECC use the rail links to Par more and more, the wharfs still handled 140,000 tonnes a year. In the last few years two 1,000 tonne grain siloes have been built beside the cliffs.

The last coal came into Plymouth by sea at the end of the 1980s, and the coal wharf, after various owners since Westcotts, was leased until 1995 by British Fuels, a subsidiary of the nationalised industry.

Victoria Wharfs were sold to Inchcape in 1992, who put it on the market in 1994 with an asking price of £1.9 million. It was bought by Mark Gatehouse and his partners, Marine Development Southampton, owned by Robert Iliffe, a scion of the newspaper-owning family. This partnership was already owner of the adjacent Queen Anne's Battery Marina. It had been anxious to take over the wharfs ever since Mark had moved into QAB, but it took ten years to realise their ambition. Planning applications for the wharf showed it and the adjacent QAB as one property, a throwback to the development ambitions of 1922. The planning permission enabled them to build an office block for renting on the frontage between the wharfs and Queen Anne's Battery, and to build new transit warehouses reaching out over the coal wharf and the old Caldwell & Almond cement works. In time they plan to extend the eastern jetty and fill in back to the old sea wall, and to increase their deep water berths.

The new owners found plenty of work for the wharfs. China clay was half their export business, and expanding. Imports included animal feeds, newsprint, fertilisers, and grain. There is much development in hand in the docks, and some ambitious plans. In 1996 Mark Gatehouse and Marina Development exchanged shares which left Marina Developments in control of the marina, and Gatehouse the sole owner of Victoria Wharfs.

CORPORATION WHARF

Cornelius Duke's attack on the Corporation's lack of interest in Cattedown in 1893 may have meant that they were only concerned with Prince Rock, at the other end of the Cattewater. He cannot have been unaware that they were pursuing land purchases there. By 1895 Plymouth had acquired all the waterfront from Laira Bridge Road to Cattedown Road, and quite a lot of land behind. Part was used for the first 'housing of the working classes', part for the power station to drive the new electric trams.

But as soon as the Corporation announced its plans to build a wharf on the waterfront - and

Corporation Wharf in front of the power station it was built to serve.

their choice of a site for the power station close to the water suggests they intended to bring their coal in by sea from the start - all the other people trying to make money from the waterfront rose up in protest. They were not going to tolerate municipal trading, having the Corporation in competition.

There was solid opposition, and not until 1904 did the town finally build a 900 feet wharf. But it was severely tied down; it was not to engage in any business as general wharfingers, and the only cargoes it was allowed to handle over the wharf was coal for its own station.

The Act permitted the building of what became known as the Corporation Wharf south of Laira Wharf, with an embankment to the south again as far as the Passage House Inn. The embankment is alongside the shallow water known as the Cockle Bank, but the channel was dredged east of the bank to enable small colliers to reach the long wharf. It is constructed on concrete piles, and is still in position.

All the coal needed by the power stations came in over the wharfs, which were fully organised with hoists, screening plants and so forth needed to handle these cargoes. 114,960 tons came in during 1950 but the next year, when Plymouth B came on stream, the figure jumped to 141,343 tons and the following year to 317,343 tons. It remains close to the 300,000 ton mark until 1958, when these imports represented nearly a third of the Cattewater's total revenue for the year.

When oil replaced coal as the power station's fuel, then the tankers were too big to reach Corporation Wharf. They berthed at Cattedown, using the general pumping facilities, with special pipes laid to the power station. At its peak the pipes were moving 350,000 tons of oil in this way. Once the power stations were decommissioned the wharf saw no more ships; a considerable diminution of the harbour's trade.

CHAPTER THIRTEEN

TURNCHAPEL WHARF AND POMPHLETT JETTY

Just as, with the collapse of the wooden shipbuilding industry, Hill's yard had given way to Cattedown Wharfs and Marshall's ship-breaking business had been replaced by Victoria Wharfs, so on the other side of the river the Turnchapel shipbuilding yard was replaced by Turnchapel Wharfs in 1898, the year after the railway line was opened.

Pope, the last shipbuilder there, had gone bankrupt. His yard was taken over by the Naval Bank of Harris, Bulteel, no doubt the principal creditor. The actual owners of the bank were the Bulteel family of Radford. Thomas Bulteel and his son Fred were already trading at a loss, but the London & South Western Railway had reached Turnchapel in 1897, and everyone had high hopes of new developments on the south side of the Cattewater. Thomas Bulteel's second son Hillersden was a civil engineer interested in railways; a few years later he was planning a railway to Wembury to serve a projected dock scheme. So, in the year the railway arrived, they secured the Turnchapel Wharfs Act of 1897. This enabled Pope's shipyard to be turned into the wharf. It was connected to the new railway line by means of a steep incline and a tunnel under Boringdon Terrace.

The next year the Bulteels sold the whole concern to Pitts, Son & King, the Plymouth maltsters. Pitts built more warehouses, and had plans for extensive development on the south side of the river, but in 1903 the Admiralty took over Turnchapel Wharfs.

It is not clear whether the Admiralty brought pressure to bear on Pitts, or whether it was an

Turnchapel Wharf with the naval trials ship Whitehead *alongside. Note the old ferry steamer pier in front of the village.*

astute move by Pitts; he was in financial difficulties at the time.

It is an odd story; A shipyard goes bankrupt. It is taken over and converted into wharfs by a banker on the verge of bankruptcy (see Chapter 31). It was bought by a grain merchant who was soon in financial trouble, and after only five years of commercial life the wharf passed into the hands of the Navy. Its subsequent story is told in Chapter Three.

POMPHLETT STONE QUAY and JETTY

All through the nineteenth century, and perhaps earlier, stone had been shipped out over Pomphlett Quay, half way up the northern side of Pomphlett Creek. It has been used for a very long time, initially with limestone for the farmers and then for building material. There was not a lot of water, but with dredging quite sizable ships were brought alongside.

The biggest vessel ever handled there by Jack Skelly, who started work there in 1942 and finally retired as wharfinger, was of 1,800 tons with 16

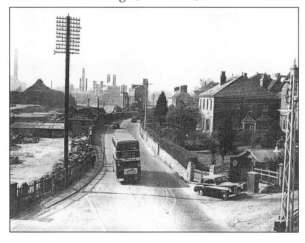

The old road alongside Pomphlett Creek, with the stone-crushing plant alongside the stone wharf (behind the telegraph pole right). This is now a four-lane highway with a roundabout in the foreground.

feet draught - and that needed a big spring tide.

In 1934 a crushing plant was built on the quay, handling stone from all the Moore quarries. It was across the Billacome road from Saltram Quarry, where the Sugar Mill complex is now. There were two conveyors, one of which could carry material direct from the lorries, and both could be used on a ship at the same time. Eventually the crushing was done in the remaining quarries and the stone quay simply had a screening plant where the stone could be graded.

The creek was used by sailing ships to load stone, and then motor vessels. But with the need for bigger ships, the new owners, ECC Quarries (who had bought out F.J.Moore in 1958) built the Stone Jetty on the south side of the mouth of the creek in 1969. Ships tie up to dolphins on the edge of the deep channel and conveyors do the loading. The stone bins from the old wharf were taken to Stoneycombe Quarry near Newton Abbot, and were still in use in 1995.

Lorries from all the ECC quarries for miles around now bring stone for shipment. They drive up a ramp and tip their loads straight into one of 16 bins, each holding 220 tonnes, according to grade. These bins discharge directly to a conveyor, which is constructed in three parts so that three different grades of stone can be loaded at the same time into a vessel alongside. The conveyor can move 900 tonnes an hour. Ships of up to 4,00 tons drawing 30 feet of water can lie alongside, but the maximum length that can be handled in the river at this point is about 325ft. On average, according to Brian Skelton who succeeded Jack Skelly, about two ships a week call, mainly taking graded aggregates to the Thames for use in making tarmac. About 200,000 tonnes of limestone a year are shipped out.

CHAPTER FOURTEEN

OYSTERS, CABLE SHIPS AND COAL HULKS

Nowadays the Cattewater, with its waterborne traffic and highly-industrialised shores, hardly seems a suitable place to go fishing for oysters. But for nearly two hundred years, from 1719 until 1887, people were willing to pay money for the right to drag or dredge these shellfish. All we know about the business comes from the surviving leases granted by the Parkers of Saltram; the business quite possibly started earlier, and may have gone on later, but the latter seems unlikely.

The 'royalty of the oysterage in Cattewater' was controlled by the ownership of the manor of Plympton, which was carved into eight shares. In 1719 John Bullock of Oreston, victualler, paid £3 a year for three-eighth of the royalty, for seven years. In 1726 Thomas Oxland of Turnchapel, mariner, paid £4 a year. John Curtis of Turnchapel had the fishery from 1747 until 1757.

And so it goes on. Joseph Knight had the oysters in 1764 but the lease was taken four years later by Mrs Grace Knight; one imagines that Joseph had died and his widow carried on. The leases seem to vary between Oreston and Turnchapel men. Rents vary over the years, getting up to £60 in 1807 and 1811 but this may reflect the scarcity of food in the war years, rather

than any quantity of shellfish. After that rents fall back again. After 1841 the series of leases ends for forty years until 1887, when Frederick Rowe of Turnchapel took the fishery for £20 a year. Whether the leases have disappeared; whether the shellfish were not worth taking once the fertiliser and chemical works started up in Coxside, whether Fred Rowe had an idea it might pay again, is all conjecture. The only reminder nowadays is the name of Oyster Cottage, in

Oreston in 1850, from a drawing by Philip Mitchell. The cottage behind the garden wall right is called Oyster Cottage and villagers still claim the right to take oysters from the foreshore.

Marine Villas, Oreston, and the belief in the village that they have the right to pick up oysters on the foreshore.

CABLE SHIPS

In October 1922 the Admiralty set up a cable depot at Turnchapel on what had been built as Turnchapel Wharf. It was a direct result of the 1921 treaty which made Eire a self-governing dominion. This necessitated the removal of the cable depot from Queenstown, the southern Ireland naval base near Cork. It was transferred to Turnchapel.

So for nearly sixty years, until well into the 1970s, the Cattewater off Turnchapel was dominated by ships of an American cable company. The Commercial Cable Company (Marine) Ltd was formed from two family concerns, the Mackays and the Bennetts - hence the ship names. Their basic contract with the Admiralty was to maintain the cables across the Atlantic. They established no shore base here but from the early 1920s had a hulk, the ex-Admiralty vessel *Mackay Bennett*, moored fore and aft just downstream from Turnchapel Wharf. The *Mackay Bennett* (1,700 tons), coal-fired and square-rigged, was launched in 1884. The most notable event in her active career came when, based at St John Newfoundland, she was called out to the *Titanic* disaster in 1912. After the war, with her engine and boilers replaced by cable storage tanks, she served as a base for the two active vessels in the company, the *Marie Louise Mackay* (1,378 tons), launched in 1921, and the *John W. Mackay* (4,064 tons), launched the following year. Both were London registered and sailed under the red ensign. When they were not at sea they would berth alongside the *Mackay Bennett*, which carried all their stores, and from her would draw cables, buoys and whatever was needed for their next job.

The Admiralty cable ship St. Margaret *steaming down the Cattewater in 1968. When she was scrapped in the 1980s she was the oldest coal-burning ship in the Royal Navy.*

From 1921 a converted steam yacht, the *George Ward*, was also based on the *Mackay Bennett*, servicing the company's European cables. At times a Western Union cable ship would also tie up alongside for a few days.

Between the wars the Admiralty cable ships, *St Margaret*, *Lasso*, *Bullfrog* and *Bullfinch* were also based at Turnchapel Wharf. On the quay there can still be seen the base of the large circular containers in which cables were stored. These vessels, serving under the blue ensign of the Royal Fleet Auxiliary, were all manned by merchant seamen. They remained at Turnchapel until the 1950s, when they were transferred to Millbay; later they were moored off Torpoint.

During World War II the *Mackay Bennett* was sunk at her Turnchapel moorings by German bombs. Another cable ship, the *Faraday*, was sunk by enemy aircraft off Milford Haven. Cables were a vital wartime need; so the cable was salvaged from these two ships by the *Marie Louise Mackay* and then, for safe storage, laid up and down the Irish Sea. Hundreds of square miles of the seabed were so covered, but the cable was safe and could be recovered in whatever length required when needed.

The *Marie Louise Mackay*, subsequently operating in the Mediterranean, cut an Italian cable running from Sardinia to Algiers, connected the Algiers section to a spare cable from Gibraltar, and so in thirty-six hours gave General Eisenhower a cable link, safe from tapping, between his African headquarters and Gibraltar, and so to London and Washington. At this time the *John W.Mackay* cut another Italian cable in the Atlantic and over a period of three weeks recovered 400 miles of enemy cable for use by the Allies.

The *Mackay Bennett* in the Cattewater was raised and restored to service as a depot ship. The *Marie Louise Mackay* was scrapped in 1961. This left her sister ship, the *John W. Mackay*, to claim the title of the oldest cable ship in the world when in 1972 she celebrated her fiftieth anniversary. Her interior was furnished with oak, mahogany and teak, and she bristled with sophisticated navigational equipment. Her first jobs had been repairing North Atlantic cables disrupted in World War I. In the 1939-45 war she was based in Halifax, Nova Scotia, repairing Atlantic cables.

The *John W.Mackay* was also threatened with the scrapyard at the time her sister ship went, but eventually was re-equipped with the latest equipment for cable laying, and navigation by satellite. One of her biggest jobs, and her last, was to act as pilot vessel to other cable layers on the 6,000 mile cable between Capetown and Lisbon.

The increasing use of radio for inter-continental communication meant a decreasing demand for cable. The *Mackay Bennett* went first, leaving the *John W. Mackay* idle in the river for some years, but she too went in 1978. Her last master was Captain W.D.Harper, born in the year that the ship was launched and in the same area. He was navigator on the *Marie Louise Mackay* during the war, and retired from the sea when his command, the *John W. Mackay*, was taken to Turkey for scrap. A long campaign was waged to keep her as a museum ship, and a trust was set up for that purpose, to no avail.

Captain Harper believes however, that her foremast, capstan, mahogany staircase and much

furniture was acquired by the KOC International Maritime Museum in Istanbul.

Frank Attwood, now of Lanhydrock Terrace, lived aboard the *Mackay Bennett* as a child with the rest of his family. Father was a ship's husband, a marine caretaker and storeman. Later they moved to Turnchapel, and young Frank served at sea in the *Marie Louise Mackay*. After a few years he transferred to the Admiralty cable ship *Lasso*.

COAL BUNKERS

Also kept at mooring in the Cattewater were hulks - one-time seagoing sailing ships no longer fit for such service, or forced into retirement by the competition of steam. They were stripped down and their holds stocked with coal which was used to supply ships calling to replenish bunkers. There were about a dozen of them, lying like a black line of ancient vessels in the river. Most had been topsail schooners; the oldest was the 80-ton *Argo* built in Prince Edward Island in 1845 and the biggest the 157-ton barquentine *James Simpson*, built at Leith in 1857.

Most coal hulks were locally owned. The hulks of Fox Sons & Co lay off Turnchapel and Bellamy's (later taken over by Cory & Strick) off the entrance to Hooe Lake. Watts's stevedores tended the Fox hulks, handling the coal entirely by hand, but Haskell's stevedores working Bellamy's had mechanical help. A steam-driven bucket hoist worked in their base hulk, the ex-naval gunboat *Elk*. Even so the buckets had to be filled by shovel: only the lift was aided.

Steamers coming into the Cattewater for bunkers would berth alongside the company's base hulk. When ships were too big to come in, one of the other hulks would be towed out into the Sound, at first by Sutton Harbour tugs and after 1925 by Reynolds's tugs from Torpoint. The stevedores worked in gangs of eight to coal a ship.

The cable ship John W. Mackay *moored in the river off Turnchapel in her last days. This photograph from Cattedown shows how the ships seem to fill the river.*

Dockers unloading coal by basket from a collier.

merchantmen alone. The hulks were a familiar sight up to 1939 but some of them had ceased to be used before then, and the trade was virtually dead with the end of World War II. As coal gave way to oil (See Chapter Eight) as a fuel supply, so these hulks were disused and finally disappeared from the river.

COAL IMPORTS

Coal was one of the largest imports into Plymouth, which ranked in the first five ports receiving coastwise imports from 1870 to 1913. The total rose from 282,000 tons in 1870 to 653,000 at the end. Not all came in through the Cattewater, but it did handle a large quantity. It was required to fuel not only the Three Towns and a large hinterland, but all the mines of the Tamar Valley.

The coal yard at the eastern end of Victoria Wharf, originally rented by Chatterley & Whinfield Colliery from the wharf company, was operated in the 1920s by John Westcott, whose coal business by this time had been taken over by Coast Lines, the owners of Victoria Wharf. It was later operated by British Fuels, the national company which has taken over various local coal merchants. They had to move from Bayly's Wharf in Coxside Creek when the area was needed for the new fish market. Their coal came in by sea until the 1980s, but then was brought in by road. They did not renew the lease in 1985, and a century's activity came to an end.

Another coal yard on land belonging to Cattedown Wharfs is rented by Pascoe Fields of Swansea who bring in a shipload at a time, store it on the quay and sell it to their local customers.

In 1875 a national company, Powell Duffryn, asked the Admiralty for permission for ships needing bunkers to anchor close inside the Breakwater. They had, they claimed, problems in coaling vessels in bad weather; recently the barge had damaged the ship it was bunkering and a number of porters had been injured. The Admiralty would have none of it, inside the Breakwater was a naval mooring and they felt that a squadron of smaller warships might need it in a hurry in bad weather. The Queen's Harbourmaster assured Powell Duffryn (inaccurately) that Jennycliff Bay was the most sheltered place for their purpose.

But bunkering went on: in 1896, for example, over 10,000 tons were supplied to foreign

CHAPTER FIFTEEN

THE DEAD HAND OF THE ADMIRALTY

At the opening of Victoria Wharfs its builder, Cornelius Duke, was scathing about the lack of interest by the Town Council in the Cattewater. But they were already developing ideas, buying land at Prince Rock. The Council at that time was riding high on a wave of progressive enthusiasm. The Liberals had won power in 1890 and a group of radicals led by the solicitor, J.T.Bond, was in the van. Two years earlier the borough had appointed its first fulltime town clerk, J.H.Ellis, under the new local government reforms, and he too was a driving force for improvements.

1897 AMBITIONS

The town was pushing ahead in all directions, for a new water supply from Burrator, for electric trams, for slum clearance and for housing for the working classes. It was also aware that the liner trade was increasing rapidly, and that Millbay could not dock the new large liners. So they engaged an engineer of international repute, Sir J. Wolfe Barry, to produce plans for developing the Cattewater. In 1897 they prepared a comprehensive Bill which not only aimed to take over all turnpikes in the town but to wind up the Cattewater Commissioners, transfer their powers

to the Council, extend Batten Breakwater, and line the Cattedown waterfront from Queen Anne's Battery to Laira Bridge with berths. They were going to widen and deepen the shipping channel up to Laira Bridge, and build deep water quays which would take the largest liners afloat. At first everyone approved, even the Cattewater Commissioners, although it would extinguish them. But then opposition grew. The Tories on the Council grew suspicious, and declared their opposition to the Council becoming involved in trade, in competition with private industry. Joseph Bellamy, a leading shipbroker and later Mayor, vigorously opposed 'municipal socialism'. A ballot of ratepayers was taken which produced 8,778 people in favour of the Bill, and 5,993 against.

Then, in 1898, came a letter from the Admiralty, which under the Dockyard Acts had authority over the whole port. In their view the scheme would increase commercial traffic, which would be to the detriment of the Navy. What is more the extension of Batten Breakwater would put both the naval traffic for the Hamoaze and commercial traffic for the Cattewater into one overcrowded channel. They would only allow it if the Mallard and the Winter shoals, in the Sound approaches to the Cattewater, were removed. Imposing such conditions killed the idea stone dead.

PARTY BATTLES

So the Town Council dropped all the Cattewater clauses in their Bill, and the Admiralty accepted it. Soon afterwards Turnchapel Wharfs were built, in 1898, and Victoria Wharfs completed. A scheme was put up by a new company called Plymouth Wharfs to build liner docks on the south side of the Cattewater which would not require any extension of Batten Breakwater, and this the Admiralty approved.

There was indignation all round. Even the Tory leader, John Pethick, who as Mayor opened the completed Victoria Wharfs in 1900, said that he had always strongly supported the Council's Cattewater scheme. At the celebratory dinner in the Corn Exchange after the opening the Town Clerk said that Victoria Wharfs had 1ft 4ins deeper water alongside its quays than either the new Empress Dock at Southampton, or the Manchester Ship Canal. If the town had been alive to its interests 70 years earlier there would have been no Southampton.

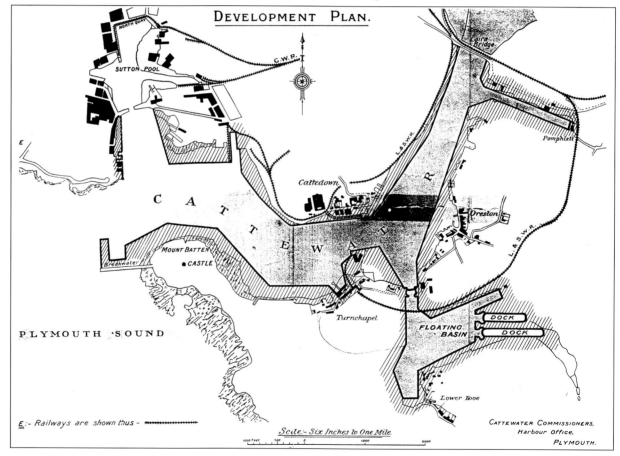

One of the many plans put forward for improving facilities in the Cattewater. This is from the 1922 proposals, and includes the idea of making Hooe Lake into a floating basin with dry docks in Radford duck ponds.

In 1901, at the Charles Ward Liberal Party's annual general meeting, J.T.Bond expressed his fury. Why did the Admiralty give permission to a private individual which they had denied to the Corporation? But then Plymouth Wharfs failed to raise the finance on the London Money Market, and it became known that the Conservative Joseph Bellamy was a director, and this annoyed the Liberals even more..

At the end of 1902, when the Liberals had regained power after three years in opposition, they decided to go ahead with building the Corporation Wharf at Prince Rock to serve their electric power station. Alderman Bond put the case in the Council, J.Y.Woolcombe and William Munday led the Opposition. Bellamy was still attacking municipal socialism. Another poll was taken of the town, and this time 9.059 voted for the wharf, 4,840 against it. When the Bill was presented to Parliament, it was opposed by Burnard & Alger, Devonport and Stonehouse councils, and both the Great Western and London & South Western railways. The Government said they would allow the Bill if the Borough of Plymouth would agree to a regular check on its books by a government auditor. This Plymouth would not accept, and the Bill was dropped.

ADMIRALTY IN THE RIVER

In April 1903 the Admiralty bought the four-year old Turnchapel Wharf. The old suspicions rose again, and when next year the Navy made new orders concerning the Cattewater, there were fears that they might be taking over the whole river. The Admiralty upset the fishing fleet by banning anchoring under Batten Breakwater, where trawlers had regularly waited, and disturbed commercial interests by demanding that a channel 50 fathoms wide be kept clear all the way from Fisher's Nose to the Breakwater Quarry. In 1904

Mr Duke, by now a leading Liberal on the Council, delivered a withering attack on a rising Conservative, W.L.Munday (who later became a leader of his party and Sir William) in yet another Corporation Wharf debate.

QAB PLANS

Two years later Mr Duke put up yet another scheme for development in the river. He planned to add Queen Anne's Battery to his Victoria Wharfs complex, and there build deep-water quays 850 feet long which would accommodate three large liners at the same time. The wharfs would have covered the whole area of the present marina. He also wanted Batten Breakwater extended, but now by turning the extension to point at West Hoe, instead of extending the existing line. In the same month there were fears that the Admiralty would close the lakeside road from Hooe to Turnchapel Station, and Turnchapel village as well.

In 1907 the Cattewater Commissioners approved the Queen Anne scheme, and Mr Duke with his solicitor went off to see the Admiralty in Whitehall. They received a letter dated 28 April 1907 in which the Admiralty were 'unable to give sanction to any scheme that would have the effect of encouraging merchant vessels, and especially large steamers and Transatlantic liners, to use Plymouth as a base'. A *Western Daily Mercury* headline declared 'Cattewater Scheme Vetoed by Admiralty'. Another letter from their Lordships dated 5 June 1907 plainly stated: 'The Admiralty resolutely decline to permit any development of Plymouth which will tend to increase the commercial traffic of its harbour'.

Plymouth was furious yet again. The *Western Morning News* and the *Mercury* fulminated against their lordships over endless columns. The Chamber of Commerce wanted to send a deputation to Whitehall, with the now knighted Joseph Bellamy in the lead. In a letter they recognised the necessity of maintaining national safety, but claimed the right to carry on their trade without interference from the Admiralty or any other Government department. In a speech J.P.Brown, another future Mayor, said that the Admiralty was throttling the commercial development of Plymouth.

WEMBURY DOCK

Plymouth resolved to get around the Admiralty by putting up a development plan outside the dockyard port limits. On 20 November 1908 both the *Morning News* and the *Mercury* published a detailed advertisement of proposals to create an ocean dock at Wembury. The proprietors and subscribers included the Earl of Morley, the Mayors of Plymouth and Devonport, the chairmen of Stonehouse Urban Council, Plymouth Chamber of Commerce and Plymouth Mercantile Association, and all the other major names in the Three Towns, among them Sir Joseph Bellamy and Henry Almond. Full details. plans and drawings were published in December. An extension of the Yealmpton railway branch would come down the little valley which ends in Wembury Beach, in front of the parish church. There would be a breakwater from Wembury Point to the

An artist's impression of the liner dock plan put forward in 1908 for the mouth of the Yealm. The breakwaters would take in the Newstone and a railway run down to Wembury beach. The drawing is signed by the young Borlase Smart, then working as an illustrator for the Western Morning News; *after World War I service in the trenches he became a leading member of the St Ives art colony.*

Mewstone, another reaching east from the Mewstone and a third reaching out from Yealm Head. A broad quay would be built across Blackstone Rocks and cover the whole beach area, leaving the entrance to the Yealm clear to the east, and on the west a basin of 235 acres with 48 feet of water at low tide and 11,600 feet of berthing space alongside.

It looks a pipedream now, more a cock-a-snook gesture to the Admiralty rather than any serious plan. The railway was going to be served by electric trains and it would be the deepest harbour in the world. It was going to cost nearly £3million. A Bill went before a committee of the House of Lords in 1909, opposed by both railway companies (who of course had their own ambitions for the liner trade). A mass of expert witnesses brought completely differing views on the possible success of the scheme, and the financial estimates. It was this in the end which scuppered the Bill; it was rejected over concern about excessive costs and the threat of bankruptcy.

THE LAST DOCK SCHEME

Not until 1922 was another plan proposed, as ambitious as the Wembury scheme. This was put up by Sir Joseph Bellamy and would have lined the whole of the Cattewater with quays, up one side and down the other, even penetrating Pomphlett and Hooe lakes. Hooe Lake was to be a floating harbour behind lock gates, with two graving docks at the top reaching over the Radford duck ponds. Laira Bridge was to be replaced with a transporter bridge, and the Laira converted into accommodation for the largest liners afloat, such as the *Olympic* (sister ship of the *Titanic*) of 46,000 tons. The Embankment was to be widened and a mile of landing berths constructed. On the other side Chelston Meadow was to have more docks and workshops.

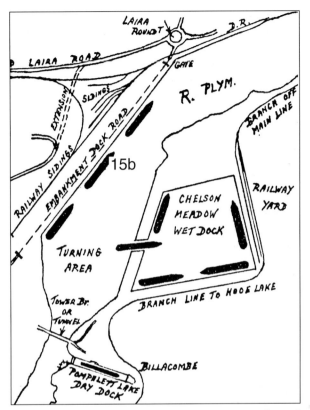

The 1922 plans included the development of the Laira, with Chelston Meadow as a wet dock and tower bridge or tunnel replacing Laira Bridge.

Railways would run around the water's edge of all the docks.

A meeting was called to listen to Sir Joseph's plans, attended by the King's Harbourmaster, Lovell Dunstan (a Cattewater commissioner and chairman of the Chamber of Commerce), R.J.Fittall the town clerk, Canning Bailey the editor of the *Morning News* and RAJ Walling the editor of the *Independent*. Plans were published and circulated by the Cattewater Commissioners. This too died the death, and no record of it going any further has come to light.

A MARSH MILLS DAGENHAM?

There is a strong folk memory, for no written evidence of the story has come to light, that the

Ford Motor Company had ideas of building a car factory beside the Cattewater at this time, but settled instead for Dagenham. So many people know the story in some detail that it is difficult to doubt it, and certainly Ford were looking for a site at the time. They had established an assembly plant in Manchester in 1911 but were running out of space. They also had a factory at Cork producing engines, but with the creation of the Irish Free State this was running into import duty problems.

So a site of a hundred acres was being sought, with good rail and sea facilities. Sir Percival Perry, Ford's representative in Britain, had contracted for two potential sites at Southampton. But Perry had fallen out of favour, and in 1923 Edsel Ford ordered a search for a new site. Particulars of thirty-seven sites were obtained, offering between fifty and a hundred acres.

The Plymouth belief is that one of these sites was beside the Plym, and at least two people believe it was above the Laira Bridge. This ties in with the Bellamy plan of 1923 to develop not just the Cattewater as a dock area, but the Laira as well. One local belief is that the factory was to be at Marsh Mills. But Henry Ford came to England and settled on Dagenham, where building started in 1929. It was to make tariff-free cars for the British market, and engines for all Europe. It was to employ 20,000 people and be the largest car factory in Europe.

The Plymouth belief is that Ford dropped the Plymouth idea because of Admiralty opposition. The car industry has notoriously all its life been a high wage business, and the Admiralty were afraid that it would breed discontent in the Dockyard and push up wages there.

Whether all the Plymouth talks with Ford were *sub rosa*, whether the newspapers of the day respected requests not to publish such backroom discussions; why no written record of this has come to light; the questions are endless but the memory remains. Perhaps it was never realised how important the opportunity was. Certainly no one at the time could have envisaged a future such as developed at Dagenham, which at one time employed 23,000 people. One can only observe that the alleged behaviour of the Admiralty is quite in keeping with what is known of them in those years.

POST WAR PLANS

In 1968, the year after Plympton and Plymstock had been brought into Plymouth, the City Council toyed with plans to develop Hooe and Radford Lakes for vessels of moderate draught, with lock gates. Soundings were made which found that there was between 50 and 100 feet of mud and clay above the rock.

The road system into Cattedown remained inadequate for a century. Both the old roads over Cattedown, now resting on ridges of unquarried stone, are closed to traffic, although the western road, up Breakwater Hill, can still be walked. The early dream of extending Commercial Road right around the waterfront to Cattedown Wharfs, the 'low level road' over which there has been so much debate, has never materialised. The Council finally reached the conclusion that Victoria Wharfs had been built across the possible route, and forgot the plan.

After 1950 Macadam Road has been cut between the Corporation Works Depot and the Shell/BP tank park, but even this meant that driving from Coxside or Cattedown Corner one had to go out to Prince Rock and then turn back to reach the waterfront. Not until 1994-5 was the road system finally improved.

CHAPTER SIXTEEN

SHIPPING SINCE 1850

There is no port in the English Channel between London and Land's End where so great an amount of business is done as at Plymouth, and where so much shipping is employed.

So recorded White's Directory in 1850. In fact until 1870 Plymouth ranked sixth in order of importance of British ports, for trade handled. But the difference in tonnages handled between the four or five major ports and the remainder was enormous. As the size of vessels grew, so Plymouth fell further and further back in importance nationally. Nowadays it is grouped in the annual statistics under 'small ports'.

The opening of Millbay Docks in 1857 saw its newer facilities immediately dominating the port. Until then the bulk of trade had passed over the Sutton Harbour quays, even though much of the goods had been off-loaded into lighters from ships moored in the Cattewater. The coming of the railway to Cattedown in 1879 saw the Cattewater rise in importance but not until Cattedown Wharfs were opened in 1890 did the Cattewater begin handling more ships than Sutton Harbour. In that year Millbay handled 2.921 ships, Cattewater 1,443 and Sutton Harbour 958. Millbay's dominance is shown even more in the size of the ships; the Millbay average was about 200 tons, while Cattewater and Sutton Harbour was only about 100. In 1890 a ship of 3,000 tons came into the Cattewater, by 1901 that size had doubled. A century later tankers of 20,000 tons were commonplace. although they could only come in carrying 15,000 tons.

Of the 1,609 ships entering Cattewater in 1896 only 94 were steamers; even Sutton Harbour had 332 steamships out of her total 990 vessels. But the pattern of Cattewater trade was already forming, 30,000 tons of china clay exported, 10,000 tons of petroleum products imported.

Trade ran along fairly steadily until the 1914-18 war reduced figures considerably. Not until 1923-4 did the Cattewater begin to pick up, only to fall away again in the slump of the early 1930s. A clue to the changing pattern of shipping is given by the sale in Hooe Lake, November 1929, of barges formerly engaged in lighterage. The *William, Mizpah, MMR, Hector Cundy, Macadam* and *Mary Edwards* all came under the hammer. They fetched between £20 and £50, although the 104 ton *Hector Cundy* only made a fiver. They all had cargo winches, anchors and cables; two hulks without gear were sold for £1.

Coast Lines vessels
Western Coast *(left) and*
Southern Coast *in*
Victoria Wharf in the
1930s. They carried
passengers as well as
cargo; one went
westbound around the
British Isles and the other
eastbound.

Always a problem in Plymouth is the loss of records through bombing in World War II, and the Cattewater is no exception. Both commercial wharfs were hit and the Commissioners office burnt out. It is fortunate that records did survive from the mid-1930s, and are shown in the table on page 81.

As might be expected, they reflect the needs of the city and rural areas behind the port. Plymouth has never had a large manufacturing base nor has it any manufacturing hinterland. Its trade is limited to the export of raw materials, stone and china clay, and the import of local needs, petrol, coal, timber and raw materials for the fertiliser firms. Imports have always exceeded exports. In 1935 the imports over 10,000 tons were petrol, 109,000; coal, 67,000; general (the groceries and so forth brought in by Coast Lines), 61.000; phosphates (for the fertiliser firms), 25,000; timber (for the building trade, plus the Plymouth and

Oreston's railway sleepers and telegraph poles), 18,000; and pyrites, 11,000. Exports were just china clay (35,000) and general (10,000).

1936 and 1937 saw considerable jumps in exports, largely due to F.J.Moore stepping up their export of lime and stone from under 7,000 in 1935 to 27,000 in 1936 and 41,000 in 1937. By 1939 the Cattewater was handling more traffic than Millbay as well as Sutton Harbour. During World War II imports maintained something like three-quarters of their prewar volume, but exports fell away very badly, down to 4,000 tons in the year of the Plymouth blitz and under 3,000 in 1943-4. The export of china clay was under a thousand tons in 1941-42, stopped completely in 1942-3 and was not resumed until 1948-9.

The huge leap of exports in 1944-5 to 118,000 tons is explained by the armed forces of the United States shipping out 44,000 tons of stores from their Cattewater bases, and the remarkable figures of re-exported petroleum products of 23,000 tons and 37,000 tons of water. Perhaps it was all going to support the U.S. armies in Normandy?

Fresh water turns up once or twice again in the export figures; 78,000 tons for instance in 1957. This all came from Burrator, surplus to the city's requirements (a comment on people's water consumption forty years later) and was shipped out to the Gulf states in tankers otherwise returning empty.

In 1949 both import and export figures begin to climb. with the total of 400,000 tons that year reaching 600,000 the next year and breaking the million in 1963. The post-war demand for petrol was of course a major factor. In the years of peace the figure went up from 77,000 tons in 1946 to 173,000 in 1950, 216,000 in 1958. 477,000 in 1960, 651,000 in 1965 and 788,000 in 1975. By 1994 petroleum imports were over the million ton mark, out of a total import of 1,128,000 tons. The

An oil tanker alongside Cattedown Wharfs. Two of the discharge arms are engaged pumping out the cargo.

surge in imports to over the million ton mark in 1970 is partly explained by the oil being imported for the Breakwater gas-manufacturing plant; at the same time South-West Gas ceased importing coal for its old plant and the Cattewater's gain was Sutton Harbour's loss. But under the pressure of North Sea gas these oil imports began to fall off in the middle 1970s and finally stopped in the mid 1980s. The insatiable demand of the motor car made up for this loss. Oil, from being a quarter of the total imports in 1945-6, was nine-tenths in 1995.

The total import-export figures for the Cattewater grew steadily through the 1950s and 1960s. The million mark was passed for the first time in 1963 and reached an all-time high of 1,625,000 tons in 1973. Since then they have fluctuated but by 1995 were over the million and a half. Imports fell off in the 1970s and 1980s, with even oil falling, due to the arrival of North Sea gas and the reduced need of gas manufactured from oil in the Breakwater plant. Exports grew during this period, keeping the total figures steady. Clay grew to fill two-thirds of the exports in 1978-9 but since then has fallen away, from that peak figure 395.000 in 1979 to 114,000 in 1995. As clay has fallen so stone has grown in volume, 169,000 in 1982 to over 200,000 tons a year in 1992-3-4. It overtook china clay as the major export in 1994.

Fertiliser was a growing import, from 37,000 in

1990 to 102,000 tons in 1995. Coal imports had fallen away, to under a thousand tons by 1995. The closure of the coal-fired power station was a contributory factor here: coal imports had risen from 115,000 tons in 1950, the year that the B station had opened, to 293,000 tons in 1957. When the power stations switched to oil fuel it was pumped ashore at Cattedown Wharf and piped to the station; 350,000 tons at peak. The final closure of the power stations was a real blow to Cattewater imports.

One perpetual problem was the steady transfer of coastal trade to the roads. Coast Lines, which had brought in so much by sea, stopped their weekly calls in 1967.

Even so, by the 1990s, when Millbay was handling very little more than the holiday-makers' cars and the lorries on the roll-on-roll-off ferries, from Roscoff and Santander (16,000 lorries in 1991), and Sutton Harbour was only handling fishing and yachts, the total quantity of commerce passing through the Cattewater was greater than all three harbours had handled at the start of the century. But it was different cargoes, with greater use of machinery meaning less dock labour. In the whole of Plymouth the number of dockers had fallen from a thousand in 1911 to a hundred in 1981.

SHIPS IN TROUBLE

There have been casualties. Much of the Cattewater business was done in small craft, the barges and so forth taking building stone and limestone for fertilising around the coast of Devon and Cornwall. The craft which plied outside the Sound were always prone to trouble; many were lost in winter gales. But even the inside craft were not immune, like the barge *Independent*, carrying stone from Oreston, which in March 1874 was run down by a government provision boat off Stonehouse.

In 1925 the *Swanston* from Cardiff carrying 450 tons of zinc plate struck the rocks off Queen Anne's Battery and sank; at high water only her funnel, masts and bridge could be seen. In the 1970s an Icelandic trawler fitted for salvage work and commanded by Captain Silas Oates sank at her moorings in the Cattewater; when she was raised Davies & Cann broke her up.

STATISTICS EXTRACTED FROM RECORDS
OF CATTEWATER COMMISSIONERS (TONNAGES)

YEAR ENDING	IMPORTS	EXPORTS	TOTAL				
March				1970	1,216,571	333,350	1,569,921
				1971	1,292,965	360,216	1,653,181
				1972	1,239,191	314,441	1,553,632
1935	328,756	70,869	339,625	1973	1,185,622	439,464	1,625,086
1936	364,035	108,647	472,682	1974	987,022	488,237	1,475,259
1937	366,755	101,154	447,909	1975	848,598	438,800	1,287,398
1938	370,723	94,312	465,035	1976	720,002	324,436	1,044,438
1939	389,400	86,180	475,580	1977	777,870	418,215	1,196,085
1940	379,401	97,028	476,429	1978	839,282	490,622	1,329,904
1941	285,366	41,011	326,717	1979	855,133	601,705	1,456,838
1942	268,529	4,215	272,794	1980	865,122	694,998	1,560,120
1943	289,398	13,420	302,818	1981	751,490	575,811	1,327,301
1944	362,827	2,759	365,586	1982	657,455	599,636	1,257,091
1945	285,574	118,268*	403,845	1983	661,486	550,737	1,212,223
1946	290,268	21,272	311,540	1984	743,068	546,807	1,289,875
1947	362,565	12,026	374,591	1985	769,975	578,179	1,358,154
1948	324,875	8,106	332,981	1986	737,778	438,230	1,176,008
1949	381,028	50,436	401,464	1987	741,140	661,117	1,402,257
1950	438,833	161,636	600,469	1988	758,162	488,726	1,246,888
1951	483,719	82,375	564,094	1989	926,370	540,757	1,467,127
1952	519,003	104,426	623,429	1990	1,005,380	353,348	1,261,688
1953	498,567	82,436	581,603	1991	961,961	328,043	1,290,004
1954	667,354	99,141	766,495	1992	972,779	373,920	1,346,499
1955	645,373	109,190	754,563	1993	1,024,818	414,913	1,439,731
1956	646,657	121,330	767,987	1994	1,128,201	353,431	1,481,632
1957	639,762	209,399	841,161	1995	1,203,524	299,348	1,502,872
1958	644,614	139,636	784,250				
1959	611,319	105,169	716,488				
1960	644,047	145,404	789,451				
1961	801,297	197,365	998,662				
1962	736,307	168,851	905,158				
1963	830,983	226,528	1,057,511				
1964	771,901	260,479	1,038,380				
1965	855,116	259,127	1,111,243				
1966	958,390	345,914	1,304.304				
1967	881,738	359,123	1,240,361				
1968	945,825	358,951	1,304,776				
1969	989,396	332,455	1,321,851				

COMPARATIVE TRADE FIGURES
Total goods handled, imports and exports
(No. of ships)

	MILLBAY	SUTTON HARBOUR	CATTEWATER
1890	(2,921)	(958)	(1443)
1891	325,610 (2,962)	108,582 (907)	165,922 (1,383)
1896	374,510 (3,007)	124,057 (990)	171,350 (1,609)
1901	605,000 (2,885)	95,000 (677)	169,000 (1,527)
1969	171,000	97,000	1,453,000
1974	241,000	68,000	1,457,000

CHAPTER SEVENTEEN

THE PLYMOUTH PILOTS

Plymouth pilots came from two villages, Turnchapel and Cawsand, for most of the nineteenth century. The first pilot that can be traced in Trinity House records, Andrew Glinn, was living at Cawsand when he was licensed in 1812, under the Outports Pilotage District Acts of 1808. His uncle was the Customs boatman shot by smugglers in Cawsand Bay in 1798, but in due course Andrew was dismissed from the pilotage service for smuggling himself. His brother Thomas, also a pilot, was drowned when boarding a vessel in 1837.

If Andrew left Cawsand as a result of his smuggling it would only have been to find employment. Smuggling was a major industry in Kingsand and Cawsand in those days and there was certainly no shame in being involved. But when Andrew's sons, William and Edward, were licensed as pilots in 1845 they were both living at Turnchapel. Four of Andrew's grandsons, John (licensed 1853), Richard (1862), Philip (1873) and Edward (c.1870). also lived at Turnchapel. John's sons Jack, Henry and Jim were all licensed in their turn and pensioned in 1917, about the last of the Turnchapel pilots. Only one of these Glinns. Richard, licensed in 1862, lived at Cawsand. The others were all Turnchapel men.

An 1830 directory lists thirty-three pilots in the port, five living at Devonport, nine at Cawsand, and the rest in Plymouth, based in the Cattewater. The 1891 census lists a dozen pilots living in Turnchapel, four of them Glinns. Henry Glinn was living at Pinch's Cottage, two other Glinns in The Row. More members of the family were boatmen, employed as crew of the pilot cutters. The other Turnchapel pilots in 1891 were Philip Cullis (retired) living at Wellfield Villas, John Pascho at Mountainside Cottage, Thomas Staddon, two Skeltons, Ridgeway at Watch House Cottage, a Tucker and a Skilton. Directories of the period also name Charles Rodway as a pilot.

The leading Cawsand pilot families were the Chapells, Eddeys, Hancocks, Hoopers and Parfolds. The Chapells even kept an inn, the Pilot Boat, in Cawsand Square, which backed on the beach.

PILOT CUTTERS

The Plymouth pilots were the last to cruise offshore waiting for customers. Their normal station was about five miles offshore and they would cruise between Looe and Start Point. In the early days just a pilot and his crewmen would be

Three liners in Plymouth Sound at the same time in the 1930s, seen from a tender bringing passengers ashore. The liners provided a great deal of work for the pilots in their day.

at sea, fishing while they waited for work. As merchant shipping built up during the century so did the need for pilots. The establishment of Plymouth as a mail port in 1850 and the steady growth of the number of liners calling led to more and more work for pilots.

From about 1850 larger cutters were at sea, averaging 60 tons gross, 70 feet length and 14 feet beam. Ships would recognise them by the letter P (for Plymouth) on the sail followed by their number, and by the red and white 'I have a pilot' flag at the mast head. By night a blue flare was burnt every fifteen minutes. They carried two crewmen - 'strappers' - and up to five pilots. They had to be good, sturdy sea boats to keep on station in all weathers, and fast because the cutters would

race among themselves; the first one to get a pilot aboard a ship won the work. In good weather they would go right alongside the incoming vessel to put their pilot aboard, in rougher conditions they would use a rowing boat to put the pilot across, and in really bad weather lead the ship inside the Breakwater and there transfer the pilot.

A cutter would stay on station until all the pilots had a ship. If the boat was being used the last pilot would row himself across; kick the boat clear when he leapt off, and the two strappers left in the cutter would have to pick it up.

Pilotage at Plymouth was compulsory for vessels over 3,600 tons and for ships regularly voyaging outside Home Trade limits. A breed of 'mud' or harbour pilots, originally unlicensed, would take over from licensed pilots off Devil's Point or Mount Batten and take the ships to their berths. Before World War I the port had seven mud pilots, local men appointed by a committee consisting of the Collector of Customs, and the harbourmasters of Sutton Harbour and the Cattewater Commissioners. Between the wars there were two groups of mud pilots, three based at West Hoe and four in Sutton Harbour. Jack Balkwill, a Sutton Harbour man, always handled the tankers berthing at the Corporation Wharf.

By about 1880 there were only two cutters working from Cawsand and four from Turnchapel. The last four Cattewater cutters were *Drift*, No 1, owned by John Pascho; *Allow Me*, No 2, W.H.Brooks; *Leader*, No 3, John Glinn; and *Verbena*, No 4, J.B.Williams. A hooker, the *Dorothy of England*,was also owned by the Glinns and used by them in conjunction with the *Leader* and would replace her when the cutter was in for refit.

There was of course considerable competition between Cawsand and Turnchapel men, but even men from the same village would race to get a ship. Until 1914 the Glinns in the *Leader* and the Staddons and Skiltons in the *Drift*, all Turnchapel men, were in fierce competition. It was not really eased by the linking of the families in marriage in 1902, when James Glinn married a Staddon daughter whose mother was a Skilton - thus uniting three families. On the day itself both family cutters were dressed overall with all the flags available. But old habits die hard!

Sailing cutters survived until after 1918; the last, the *Alarm*, fitted with a paraffin engine, acted as a standby for the regular steam cutters of the early 1920s. *Drift* was sold in 1918 into French ownership, bringing Breton onion sellers to England. *Leader*, reputedly the fastest Plymouth cutter, especially to windward, was sold by the Glinns in 1926 and became a houseboat in Hooe Lake. She survived there until 1984 when, having collapsed with a broken leg twice in bad weather, she was cut up for scrap.

TRINITY HOUSE

Until the end of the nineteenth century pilots were licensed by the Marine Department of the Board of Trade. Then, after about 1910, it was taken over by Trinity House. The work was shared between Turnchapel and Cawsand men. After 1918 pilots no longer cruised offshore but had their headquarters ashore in the Exchange in Woolster Street, across the road from the back of the Custom House. The pilot cutter was a steam launch and the one on duty took four pilots out and rode to a buoy inside the Breakwater until a ship was expected. With the end of the liner trade in 1966, all pilots were based ashore.

Ships were getting larger and ship handling ability was as important as local knowledge. Until 1914 pilots had first to be apprenticed to Trinity House pilots; after the war apprenticeships were forgotten but pilots had to have foreign-going master's tickets with square-rigger experience. The last British ship at sea which fulfilled these demands was the barquentine *Waterwitch* of Fowey. Cliff Sherlock and Frank White were among the last Plymouth pilots to have served in her.

The new breed of pilots, in their Trinity House uniform, were not necessarily local men, although Frank White (who was the No. One pilot for the French Line vessels) was the last to live at Cawsand. The rest lived in Plymouth, though they still owned their cutters in equal shares, a new man having to buy his share from the retiring man he replaced. After 1946 they had a series of motor cutters. The Exchange had been bombed out in 1941 and the pilots base moved to the Seamen's Bethel next to the Admiral McBride on the Parade, where it still is. Numbers were reduced from twelve to ten in the 1950s, eight in the 1970s and four by 1980. Ownership of the cutters passed to Trinity House in 1979, and in 1987 a new Pilotage Act transferred responsibility for pilotage to the local harbour authority. There are three such authorities in Plymouth (apart from the Royal Navy, which has always provided the pilots for its own ships). The Cattewater Commissioners were already sharing the former Seamen's Bethel with the pilots, and they were elected the responsible civilian authority for Plymouth.

RESCUES and DROWNINGS

Inevitably a business entailing many hours at sea in all weathers led to pilots being involved both in tragedy and in rescues. William Glinn of Turnchapel was given a silver medal by the Netherlands Government for rescuing the crew of a sinking Dutch freighter in September 1859. In February 1872 Edward Glinn (William's brother) together with his son, another Edward, were rowing a third pilot, George Phillips, to the West India liner *Nile*. *Nile* ran down the cutter, *Surprise*, No 5, and crushed the boat between the two. All three pilots were drowned and only with difficulty and the aid of five men from the liner was the *Surprise* kept afloat. The tug *Volunteer* towed her into the Cattewater where she was beached. Father Edward was the senior pilot; both his son and George Phillips left large families at Turnchapel.

In November 1899 in what was described as 'the worst storm experienced for thirty years' the sail freighter *Shamrock*, anchored in Batten Bay, dragged her anchor and finished up on the rocks. The coastguards at Batten repeated her distress signals. The tug *Sleuthhound* tried to help but could not get near the *Shamrock* because of the

rocks. While she was steaming to Millbay to tow out the lifeboat (dependent on her oars and sails) the pilots and crew of the cutter *Drift*, No 1, took their boarding boat to the Cattewater side of Batten. With the aid of spectators they dragged the boat across Batten field and relaunched it on the seaward side. The coastguards had already set up their rocket apparatus but did not want to use it; with the *Shamrock's* masts gone the men would have had to be dragged through the waves and the rocks. The pilots managed to pull their boat clear of the rocks out to the ship, in the teeth of the gale, take all five of the crew aboard, and get them safe back to shore - ten men in a 16 foot boat! All five rescuers, pilots John Pascho, Tom Staddon and Harry Skilton, and their crewmen Robert Frood and Bill Skilton, received watches and medals from the Royal Humane Society. It was John Pascho and the *Drift* who in World War I brought the first German prize into Cattedown Wharfs, the S.S. *Schliessen*.

Pilot Desmond McLindon boarding the Sir Galahad *in Plymouth Sound.*

The Polish brig Frederic Chopin *in the Cattewater in the 1990s, one of the more unusual vessels for the pilots to handle.*

In December 1890 the Peninsular & Oriental liner *Nepaul* tried to enter the Sound without a pilot, by the eastern entrance. She struck the Shagstone, but her distress flares were seen by the pilot cutter on station, which took off the passengers due to land at Plymouth. Later the tenders had to take off the rest of the passengers, mail and crew, and the *Nepaul* was a total loss.

When the Grimsby schooner *Fair City* was wrecked on the Breakwater in January 1919 the Turnchapel cutter *Alarm* was on station. She sent her boarding boat (by that time fitted with a petrol engine) to land on the inside of the Breakwater, fought the waves breaking over the top to be able to shout to the wrecked men to jump for it, and dragged them on to the Breakwater and so into their boat.

Similar stories of heroics and tragedies can be told of the Cawsand men, and of the pilot service since the days of the sailing cutters. But the end of the cutters saw the end of the Turnchapel men as pilots.

CHAPTER EIGHTEEN

COASTGUARDS AND THEIR AUXILIARIES

The long arms of the sea which ran out from Plymouth Sound provided wonderful routes for the smuggling fraternity. The lonely pubs at various points on their shores made excellent bases. When two men were executed in 1732 for murdering the Plymouth tide-surveyor (local head of the anti-smuggling land forces), their bodies were hung in chains at Crabtree. It was 'about the running of brandy'.

It was usual for these gibbets to be sited at the scene of the crime; so it requires no great stretch of imagination to see the Crabtree Inn as the place of the murder. It was away from most of the houses at the bigger Crabtree, beside a main route across the sands out of Plymouth, and thus well placed for distributing the 'trade' to customers. And who could suspect a pub so far from the main shipping anchorages of being involved?

Nor is it hard to imagine the feelings of the traveller reaching the slightly hazardous crossing of the Ebb Ford on the edge of dark, with the tide making, the wind rising and the bodies swinging in their chains above the point on the Plymouth shore where travellers climbed on to firm land. As a setting for a lonely pub it leaves Jamaica Inn stone cold.

At the end of the Napoleonic wars there were ships and seamen to spare, and time to pay attention to defeating the smugglers. So in 1822 the Board of Customs set up the Coastguard Service. It was to have cutters patrolling at sea and groups of ex-naval men based on shore at regular points, literally to 'guard the coast'. As Kingsand and Cawsand had been the headquarter of the whole business throughout Devon and Cornwall, some of the first shore stations were set up around Plymouth Sound. Cottages were built at Cawsand (on the road leading to Penlee Point), Bovisand (looking down to the beach) and Polhawn (on the clifftops by the fort) in 1823. Mount Batten cottages (on the seaward side of the cliffs at the point) were probably built not long after. The neat rows of cottages, whitewashed and enclosed with their small gardens by a low wall, were always built away from the community, to avoid the men becoming too friendly and in the pocket of the men they were supposed to be watching.

There is mention of a rescue in Bovisand Bay by coastguards in 1828, and a 'coastguard galley from Bovisand' was used in an 1838 rescue. There is no mention of Mount Batten until White's Directory of 1850 lists a coastguard lieutenant and another coastguard in the parish. Land was leased for

Wrecks strew the foreshore of Batten beach after the storm of November 1865. The coastguard cottages can be seen in the background.

The Mount Batten lifesaving team operating the rocket apparatus at a competition in 1945.

coastguard purposes at Mount Batten in 1855, but this was probably a renewal. By 1850 smuggling in the old-fashioned sense of running goods ashore on lonely beaches had been virtually suppressed. Coastguards were now guarding against shipwreck and in 1856 the funding and responsibility for the service passed to the Admiralty. In 1923 responsibility changed again, this time passing to the Board of Trade.

The Mount Batten team had a hut on Dunstone Point (between Batten and Jennycliff bays) in which a bad weather watch was maintained. After a lifeboat house was established on the west side of Millbay Docks in 1861 it was the practice for the Batten coastguards to fire a rocket if the lifeboat was needed. There were two such calls in November 1865, within three days of each other, and another rocket call in January 1867, all of which saved lives.

Rocket apparatus as a form of lifesaving was beginning at the time the coastguards came into being, and Manby rocket apparatus was established 'in Plymouth', says the first annual report in 1825 of the early Royal National Lifeboat Institution, without specifying where it was set up in the port. From 1854 onwards the Board of Trade equipped coastguard stations with the Boxer apparatus. The first mention of rockets being used by Mount Batten was in November 1872, when the Coastguard rescued four men by this means from the brigantine *Eliza*. Eight vessels were wrecked in Batten Bay that night, and in all sixty lives saved. When the lifeboat herself was holed on the rocks the coastguards fired lines which then helped the ship's own boats to get ashore. The original Mount Batten Rocket House holding the apparatus stood close to the Batten cottages, but at the end of the nineteenth century it was found more convenient to have the gear in a position whence it could move along the coast more efficiently. So a new Rocket House was established on the hill above Turnchapel. It was built to the standard pattern, and the oak runners of the rocket gear are still under the present concreted floor. It housed the cart carrying the gear, which would either be drawn by manpower or by horses (obtained on contract with a local farmer) to the nearest point to the casualty.

Five men were based at Mount Batten, in the five cottages, and they were not enough to man the apparatus. So a Coastguard Auxiliary (such auxiliaries were started in 1865) was formed. About the turn of the century the Mount Batten station was discontinued and an auxiliary team formed to handle the rockets. The first man in charge of the Mount Batten Auxiliaries was William Demellweek of Turnchapel, a fisherman who had become the water bailiff for the Tamar and Plym. William Demellweek had 25 years service with the crew, and handed over to his son Alfred when he returned from service in World War I. After a couple years Alfred was killed in an accident in the docks, where he worked (the auxiliaries were almost all dockers). His young brother Ronald took over.

All told by 1968 seven members of the family had put in 150 years service. Ronald Demellweek fell into the hold of a vessel being unloaded in the docks during World War II and badly smashed one thigh. It was two and a half years before he got back to work but when he retired from work in 1960 he went on in charge of the Mount Batten team. Ron Demellweek finally retired from the Coastguard Service in 1975. He had 48 years service with the auxiliary lifesaving team, 35 in charge.

Eric Burridge took over. His great-grandfather had been a regular coastguard at Bovisand as early as 1854, and his grandfather and father were in the rocket team before him. Eric joined in 1949, took charge of the look-out section in 1955, and full charge in 1975. By this time the company had high-speed rockets (the equipment had been steadily improved over the years) and the tractor which had towed the gear was replaced by a Land Rover. Mr Burridge of Hooe was the engineer in the Oreston Steamship company's *May Queen* and other vessels; he retired in 1984 with 35 years coastguard service and the Queen's Medal,

awarded in 1969, plus a long service bar. Keith Dare-Williams became the auxiliary-in-charge.

The Mount Batten crew had a remarkable record of proficiency. They were the first crew in the country to make a time under four-minutes for setting up the life-saving apparatus. In 24 competitions in the Southern Division and the Brixham district they won 17 cups. The men all came from Turnchapel or Hooe (the two villages always worked together), and their normal meeting place, and where they kept their trophies, was the Victoria Inn at Hooe.

Their biggest rescue came in 1955 when the cruise liner *Venus* dragged her anchor in a south-westerly gale and went ashore on the rocks under Mount Batten. They helped save 93 members of the crew, including women, some with the rocket apparatus, some by the men getting out on the rocks and hauling on lines from the ship's lifeboats to bring them alongside the rocks. Ronald Demellweek was awarded the BEM in the next Honours List.

Ronald Demellweek, longtime leader of the Mount Batten team, receives a trophy from Mrs Allen Hicks, wife of the honorary secretary of Plymouth Lifeboat in 1957.

One of the Mount Batten team's biggest rescues; the cruise liner Venus *on the rocks in Batten Bay in 1955.*

As it happened, this was the last time this apparatus was used. With the increased sophistication of helicopters the rockets were abandoned in 1983, though equipment is still kept at Brixham and can be sent by helicopter if needed. In the next year bad weather watch huts were given up. In 1994 the old rocket house was converted into a two-storey building, the heated ground floor becoming a garage for a four-wheel drive vehicle in which the cliff search and rescue gear is housed as well as a generator to operate a searchlight, and first aid gear. When bad weather watches are needed the Land Rover is driven to the nearest accessible point on the stretch of coast where there is trouble, and the watch kept from the vehicle.

Under the 1995 set-up the sector officer for the Tamar Section of H.M.Coastguard, which covers from Mothecombe to Seaton, is Ian Baker, based at Torpoint. He has three auxiliary teams in his sector, Yealm at Newton Ferrers, Mount Batten at Turnchapel, and Tamar (the former Rame team now based at Torpoint).

CHAPTER NINETEEN

YACHTING AND WATERSPORTS

People who work in boats have always been happy to play in boats. In the nineteenth century, when yachting for gentlemen led to their creation of regattas, the working people were not far behind. Every waterside community soon had its own regatta, although their races were for fishing boats, ranging from big trawlers down through the smaller luggers to rowing and sculling (with one oar over the stern) events between the working boats. Later on special 'flash' boats were built, purely for racing, and there were comic races with crews of rowing boats on their knees paddling with bottom boards.

Sutton Harbour Regatta was a major event, but every village had its regatta. Turnchapel, Hooe, Oreston, Cattedown, even Laira, all had their day. Crews would come from the rival communities like Cawsand, Mutton Cove and further up the Tamar. Rivalry ran high, much beer was drunk, and it was not unknown in the early days for crews to end races standing up in their craft and swiping at each other with their oars. When sailing clubs started they too raced - at the Sutton Harbour regattas the dinghies would have one turning point right inside Sutton Harbour, which meant some nippy sailing. Cecil Atkey says that in his time he has been first through the pierheads,

and then the last to come out again. Typical of the spirit which prevailed at these events is the story of the Breakwater Quarry men.

They took stone out from Oreston to maintain Plymouth Breakwater; when they were not transporting the massive blocks of stone in dockyard steam craft, but just working out there, they would row out and back in their ex-naval eight-oared cutter. In bad weather the row could take two hours. They became such practised oarsmen that one year they had a proud record of fourteen regatta wins in seventeen starts. When they competed at Looe Regatta they would row down in the morning, race, and then row back in the evening.

The only rowing club in the Three Towns before 1914 was at Devonport. This collapsed in 1914 with the onset of war, and apart from the friendly rowing clubs which every church in Plymouth seemed to have for its young men, there was nothing between the wars. Even the church clubs died out by World War II.

PLYMOUTH AMATEUR ROWING CLUB

In 1948 the Lord Mayor was Heber James Perry, who had rowed for Devonport Rowing Club for

the last six years before 1914. He was a guest at Bideford Regatta where he saw other West Country crews in competition, rowing not the old style whalers and flash boats but the shells normally associated with rivers and above all the Oxford and Cambridge boat race. He came back determined to found a Plymouth Club, publicised his intention and called a meeting. Among the people interested was Frank Sanders, who had rowed for the Dartmouth club before 1914, and Major John Startin, who was an old Etonian 'wet bob'. Early in 1949 an inaugural meeting was held in the Swarthmore Institute on Mutley Plain, in March that year the first shell was ordered, and three old shells were given by other rowing clubs. Laira Sailing Club, whose racing base was the quay at Arnold's Point, with a store in a shed

across the road beside the cottages, offered a base.

The first invitation regatta was held on the Laira in July 1949. Plymouth was able to enter three men's crew and a ladies' crew in the four four-oared race, against crews from the clubs at Bideford, Dartmouth, Torquay, Paignton and Exeter. In 1950 in Plymouth's first championship regatta under West of England rules on the Laira, there were eight visiting clubs. The course was a straight mile, the full length visible from the Arnold's Point base. By 1954 the club was calling itself 'The Henley of the West' on its programme.

Arnold's Point was in a sad state. The sea wall was falling down and the surface a mass of grassy mounds. By 1951 the jetty lease was taken over from the sailing club and planning permission obtained to build a club house there. An early recruit who became a driving force in the building was A.E.K.Rodgman, owner of the garage beside the Morley Arms. By 1956 the jetty had been repaired and the two storeys of the clubhouse completed. A bricklayer who directed operations, David Macleod, is still a vice-president of the club.

By 1958 Plymouth was winning the cup for the club scoring most points in the regatta. By 1965 350 rowers were taking part. By 1968 Plymouth School of Navigation and the Royal Naval Engineering College at Manadon were competing. The only other rowing club in the port in the 1990s is that at Torpoint. In 1995 the club had between forty to fifty members. It not only owns its clubhouse but has one eight, eight fours and one coxless pair. A number of single sculls are privately owned by individual members.

SAILING

With the end of working sail came an end to the old village regattas. Plymouth fishermen still race their motor trawlers around the Sound once a year; but regattas now are more decorous affairs, run by the various sailing and yachting clubs. With the greater affluence after World War Two, more leisure and the availability of cheaper mass-produced yachts, so ownership of decked sailing craft with their bunks and galley came more widespread; they were no longer the playthings of the well-to-do. Existing yacht clubs opened their doors to more humble people and grew in membership, and new clubs came into being.

PLYM YACHT CLUB

The first Cattewater club proper, born in a waterside community out of a need by local people, was the Plym Yacht Club at Oreston. It started in 1970 when some members of the Parent-Teachers' Association of Plymstock School were

The start of a race in Plym Yacht Club's 1990 regatta.

anxious that their children should learn to sail. A meeting was called at the school, at which the local city councillor, the late Rodney Easton, took the chair. This meeting elected a steering committee, which had its first meeting in a room at the Plymstock Inn; a second meeting was held in the school that April, and it was decided that the best way forward was to form a Sailing and Powerboat Club.

The driving force in these early days was Tony Reeves, who became the first secretary, and the original steering committee included Barry Chapman and Don Burbidge, who were to become the first and the second commodores, in succession. They bought an old bakery, the 'forlorn and semi-derelict' Lang's House, on Oreston Quay, and a group of volunteers set to work to turn it into a club house. For this purpose they received grants from the Sports Council and Plymouth City Council, and made a tie-up arrangement with the brewers, Courage. It was opened at the end of 1971, and the interior completely refurbished in 1994-5.

In the early days there were only two or three members with sailing experience, but the club was given permission to use a famous old craft, the *Temptress*, for instruction. It had been owned by Edward Allcard, the rather eccentric single-handed sailor who had sailed *Temptress* around the world. The man he had sold it to was getting old and stipulated that, when the yacht was used for training, he could sail as a passenger.

As members became experienced so more and more bought yachts, and the club hired thirty moorings off Oreston from the City Council. Members started cruising in company, first to Cargreen, then the Yealm and eventually to Fowey and Salcombe. A programme of weekly races was started. In 1971 49 craft competed in the first regatta, held off Mount Batten, where the members were invited to use the Watersports Club as a temporary base. They had their first rescue boat. The club has not looked back. Friday evening racing from April to September has become a standard fixture, with dinghies as well as yachts competing. Since 1981 the club has had a fairly steady membership of just over 200 members. It could claim the biggest Division II (a yardstick handicapping system) fleet in the port. For racing these are divided into five groups; one for the bigger faster craft, one for the medium yachts and three for the cruisers. There is also a small dinghy section. In 1995 the club celebrated its 25th anniversary with a jubilee regatta with racing in three Yardstick divisions.

CLASSIC BOAT RALLY

One of Plym Yacht Club's achievements has been the staging of a series of classic boat rallies, popularly known as the 'old gaffers' from the prevalence of gaff-rigged craft in the assembled fleet. The first was held in 1981, the fifth in 1995 was jointly organised by Plym Yacht Club, Cattewater Cruising Club and Clovelly Bay Marina. It was supported by Plymouth City Council and Plymouth Development Corporation, who lent a marquee for the green in front of Plym YC's clubhouse at Oreston.

An 1881 dipping lugger from St Ives, taking part in the 1988 Plymouth Classic Boat Rally.

Over a hundred entries from England and France gathered for the week-end, including an 1898 fishing yacht, a 1900 lugger, a 1902 racing gaff cutter, another gaff cutter built in 1902 as a Solent day boat and a 1908 schooner. The Sunday afternoon parade of yachts along the front of the Hoe made a magnificent spectacle. The event was so timed that participants could cruise on to Fowey and then Falmouth to join in similar rallies. These rallies, which attract old-time sailing craft and modern reproductions, draw together all the clubs and facilities on the south shore of the Cattewater.

CATTEWATER CRUISING CLUB

The other local product is the Cattewater Cruising Club. It was formed in November 1989 when owners of small boats based off Turnchapel became alarmed at the marina developments, and to protect their interests formed the Turnchapel Area Cruising Club. Essentially they were people who sailed from Turnchapel and took their shore pleasure in the Boringdon Arms.

Very quickly the present name was adopted, and the 'Bori' is still the headquarters of the club. The principal point of its constitution is the encouragement of water-borne pursuits. The original 27 members have increased to 208, who own between them about a hundred boats. These range from a 70 foot motor barge and a 45 foot MFV to 14 foot day sailers and a number of sailing dinghies. Nowadays relations with the marina company are harmonious and most members' boats are berthed there.

Cruising is still the main activity; apart from local waters members have crossed the Channel to north-west France, cruised individually to Ireland and the Azores, and the commodore, Mike Clarke, has sailed single-handed to Australia and back.

ROYAL WESTERN YACHT CLUB

Founded in 1827 as the Plymouth Royal Clarence Regatta Club, this was renamed the Royal Western Yacht Club of England in 1833; it is now out and away the senior club in the port and only four or five other clubs in Great Britain and Ireland can claim to be senior. Millbay was its original base, when it was a simple bay with only the Royal Marines Barracks on the western shore. The clubhouse was at the northern end, looking down on the water.

Since then it moved to imposing premises next to the Grand Hotel on Plymouth Hoe and, when that was destroyed during the war, moved into the clubhouse of the Royal South Western Yacht Club at West Hoe. The South Western had broken away from its parent Western in 1890 to encourage local sailing; the two became one again in 1965. The club moved from West Hoe into its present clubhouse in Queen Anne's Battery Marina in May 1989, and was opened by the Princess Royal.

It can claim to be the cradle of ocean racing; the first offshore event ever, in 1925. The race from the Solent around the Fastnet Rock and back to Plymouth, was in part run by the Royal Western, and over dinner in the club while that first Fastnet was still being sailed the Royal Ocean Racing Club was formed. It has been organising the finish ever since. In 1960 when Blondie Hasler proposed a single handed west-east race across the Atlantic he asked the Royal Western to run it. The club still does, as well as a two-handed Transatlantic race and a two-handed Round Britain and Ireland Race. Sir Francis Chichester started and finished his trail-blazing single-handed voyage around the world in 1965-6 at the Royal Western.

These fixtures, which involve the club in a major ocean event every year, are run from the marina and the visitor's basin in front of the clubhouse is filled before the starts (or after the finish in the case of the Fastnet) with the cream of the world's ocean racing yachts.

The club has a membership of about thirteen hundred, not all of them local by a long chalk, and a number from overseas. Between them they own over four hundred craft. Apart from the ocean racing, the club has annual offshore races to France and along the English coast, as well as a programme of racing series in spring, autumn, and even an 'Icicle' series that finishes in December. Its cadet section flourishes.

The yachts get away in the 1964 Single-Handed Transatlantic Race. Blondie Hasler's renowned junk-rigged Jester is seen to the right of the motor boat in the foreground.

ROYAL PLYMOUTH CORINTHIAN YACHT CLUB

The third club whose yacht and dinghy races start at the mouth of the Cattewater is the Royal Plymouth Corinthian, whose headquarters west of Fisher's Nose are just outside the Cattewater boundaries. Founded in 1877, and Plymouth's second senior club, its yachts race on Sundays and dinghies on Wednesday evenings. It too has a long record of organising national and international events.

HOOE POINT SAILING CLUB

The Hooe Point Sailing Club is a branch of the national Civil Service Sailing Association and of the Civil Service Sports Club based at Beacon Park. Its 120 members are drawn not just from civil servants in local employment but also from Post Office and local government officers. Dinghies, cruising yachts and a few motor vessels make up the club fleet. The club is based on land rented from the Ministry of Defence at the entrance to Hooe Lake, alongside the Royal Marines base at Turnchapel Wharfs.

This area provides ample space for winter boat storage ashore. It is very much a 'do-it-yourself' club, with members having set up the club house and resurfaced the slipway built in Sycamore Bay to handle landing craft in World War II. It has an annual programme of dinghy racing on Monday nights and yacht racing on Tuesday nights, both starting off the end of Batten Breakwater. Until the Royal Naval Engineering College closed down, the Manadon Rowing Club was also in adjacent premises.

MAYFLOWER SAILING CLUB

When the Mayflower Sailing Club was started in 1922 its name was obvious; Plymouth had only a year or so earlier celebrated the 300th anniversary of the sailing of the *Mayflower*. Legend has it that old boys of the St Andrew's Church sea scouts got together and formed the club under the leadership of 'Grandad' Hocking, who leased a number of the old warehouses then fronting Commercial Wharf (between Mayflower Pier and Phoenix Wharf). Mr Hocking became the first commodore, and the original club was a store in the old warehouses rented from Hocking. There was no question of class racing; members raced in whatever small sailing craft they had, under handicap.

In 1924 the old warehouses were pulled down to make way for the widened road which links the Barbican with Madeira Road under the Hoe. Stores were built under the road and one of these became the club's base. After 1945 the club reformed under the leadership of Jimmy Kingdon, a nephew of old Mr Hocking. It took over No 13 store as its headquarters; during the war it had been a National Fire Service base and then an officers mess for the American troops based in the Cattewater. The club flourished; K.R. Skentelbery of the boat building yard above the Laira Bridge designed the Mayflower one-design dinghy for the club and a number were built. They were normally kept on moorings off the Skentelbery yard and he would tow them down on Tuesday evenings for the weekly racing.

Other one-class dinghies followed in the post war dinghy boom, and when the City Council converted the cleared area of the old Elphinstone barracks into a dinghy and car park, the Mayflower moved to its present headquarters in the house at the back of Phoenix Wharf. Today the club has a membership of about a hundred; not as strong as it was, but has remained faithful to dinghy sailing. Hornets, which the club has sailed since their inception in the 1950s, still race as a class, but members also compete in handicap races with Phantoms, Lasers, Scorpions and the new Assimetric high performance craft. The

Old-timers sailing out of the Cattewater and past the Royal Plymouth Corinthian Yacht Clubhouse in the 1995 'Classic Rally of Sail and Steam'. Since 1988 the yachting organisations on the left bank of the Cattewater have organised this weekend rally annually (with one break). Such gatherings of old craft and modern replicas have already grown to become important events in Brittany, while English ports and their associated yachting clubs are catching up.

Above: *Plymouth River; this view of the Plym estuary from the Hoe and Mount Batten to above the Laira Bridge shows how the modern city enfolds the river. Radford duck ponds and Hooe Lake at low tide are on the left.*

Below: *The Citadel dominates the Cattewater entrance, with the 1993 extensions reaching out over Lambhay Hill. On the waterfront are dinghy and car parks stretching from Fisher's Nose to Mayflower Pier. Mayflower Sailing Club's base is between the slipways on either side of Phoenix Wharf. The Cattewater Commissioners' office is in the tall building facing the pier.*

Mount Batten cleared for its new life by Plymouth Development Coporation. The new main road snakes across the site from St John's Road. New offices for the Cattewater Commissioners are planned to go just left of the base of the pier. Enclosing the pier is the 'armour' of massive stone blocks dropped to guard against storm damage.

Above: *Mark Gatehouse, who has raced two-handed round Britain and in the Single-handed Transatlantic race, seen at the mast-head of his monohull, Queen Anne's Battery Marina. Mark was originally joint-owner and developer of the marina, and now owns Victoria Wharfs.*

Left: *Queen Anne's Battery Marina in June 1996 with the big trimarans alongside other entries for the Single-handed Transatlantic race. The club-house of the Royal Western Yacht Club is the L-shaped building right, and the University of Plymouth's Sailing Centre is the square white building just left of the clubhouse.*

Victoria Wharfs in 1996 with the new red-roofed office block left and the new white transit sheds right. Left of the sheds are the recently-installed circular grain silos.

Turnchapel Wharf, with the pontoons to facilitate the landing craft and small vessels of the Royal Marines. To the left is Sycamore Bay with its Normandy slipways and Hooe Point Sailing Club. Behind the wharf is the old village built on the quarry floor; the quarry face is clearly shown behind with modern housing on the plateau above. Above the right-hand edge of the village is the new car park at the Mount Batten entrance. Across the field (where houses are being built) is the white roof of St Luke's Hospice, in front of Staddon Fort, now a leisure centre with caravans parked inside the walls. Plymouth breakwater can be seen behind Jennycliff Bay.

Opposite: Cattedown Wharf seen across the Cattewater from Turnchapel, with an oil tanker and a white cruise liner alongside. Over the bows of the liner can be seen the Shell oil tanks.

Oreston village: the foreground projection is Al Brotherton's boatyard with (behind) the area around the Anglican church. Beyond that the ruler-like embankment running to the left is the altered waterfront of the 1960s which created the green in front of the old quay road, lined with houses. From the foreground of the green the road to Plymstock runs at right angles to the waterfront, passing the Methodist church. In the background are the modern developments sited in Breakwater Quarry.

Below: the varied craft of Seastructures, the marine engineering and salvage firm now employing over fifty men in Breakwater Quarry. In the background is the loading ramp of Pomphlett stone jetty.

The last waterside quarry, supplying the limestone and shillet to make cement in the Blue Circle plant behind. The main road to Yealmpton runs to the left of the quarry, and to the right is the desolation of the tip covering Chelston Meadow.

The Plymouth pilot cutter Leader, *based on Turnchapel, built by Shilston in Sutton Harbour in 1880, sold in 1926 to become a houseboat in Hooe Lake, broken up 1984. She was reputedly the fastest cutter on the station. Ship portrait by Percy Dalton, in the possession of the author. Inset, the modern cutter* Mallard, *photographed by the pilot, Desmond McLindon.*

Cattewater-built: (above), the topsail schooner Richard Hill *entering Palermo. She was built at Oreston by Richard Hill in 1829 and kept in the family ownership until 1841; she ended her seafaring life in 1877 after being damaged in a gale. The portrait was discovered, restored and is now owned by Judith Godfrey, who has since become the authority on Hill's shipyard. Left, the launch of HMS* Clarence *from Turnchapel in 1812, probably the biggest ship ever built in the Cattewater. An oil painting by John Rogers, in Plymouth City Art Gallery.*

Mount Gold and Lipson, a peninsula until the building of the Embankment. The now filled-in Tothill Creek, right, is bounded on the right by the railway to Friary, on the left by Lanhydrock Road, and ends where trees encircle the playing fields. The former Laira Lake, on the left, is bounded on the left by the Great Western main line into Plymouth and on the right by the line of houses; it ends in Lipson Vale. The green area centre left is Freedom Park, passed on the right by Lipson Road, the main road to London in pre-embankment days.

Laira and Efford; in the foreground the mud of the Laira at low tide, the main railway line and the main road into the city. Laira Green is the group of houses immediately above the road-rail crossing; the grassy area backed by trees top right was the demense of Efford manor. The house was at the top of the path.

Marsh Mills, with the Devon Expressway (A38), the main road from London striding across the Plym and the old marshlands to the Parkway, and so to the Tamar Bridge and Cornwall. Beyond A38 the Plympton road is still on the line of the old turnpike, crossing the Plym on an up-dated 'New Bridge'. 'Longbridge', the causeway across the marshes, ran from the left-hand side of the bridge, under the roundabout to the Marsh Mill inn and Travel Lodge which replaced the old Rising Sun in 1995. Sainsbury's store and car park is in the left foreground. On the other side of the road can be seen the warehouse and industrial establishments filling all the flat ground.

From Marsh Mills to Plympton; the old arm of the sea which once took ships to Plympton has been dry land so long that the main railway line runs down the middle and nearly all the flat ground is taken up with more warehouses and factories. The Tory Brook is confined between walls and even separates the traffic lanes of the Plympton road for part of the way. In the right foreground are the sewage works which so annoy the neighbours; left of the railway is Tavistock Junction marshalling yard.

Cattewater vessels; above, *a fully-laden oil tanker sails up to Cattedown Wharf;* right, *the* Montania *loads stone at the Pomphlett jetty.*

Left, *the Conoco oil refuelling craft tops up a Brittany ferry;* right, *the Commissioners' 1996 purchase, the tug now renamed* Plym Echo.

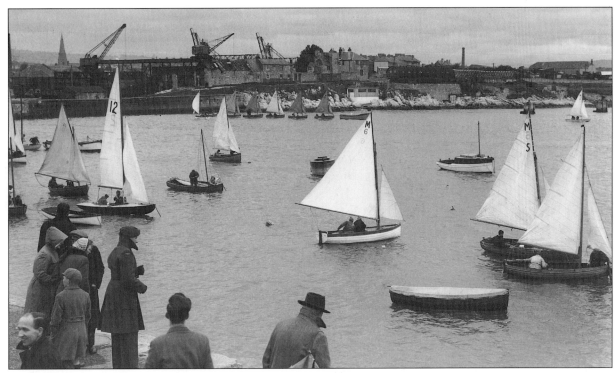

The Mayflower Sailing Club prepares for its regular Tuesday evening races, back in the 1960s. In the background are the dinghies based in the Laira, regularly towed down for the weekly racing.

healthy cadet section has the use of four club Toppers and two Wayfarers for their Friday evening sessions.

It is a club of wide repute. Most years it runs national dinghy championships; in 1995 there were three, two lasting four days and the third a week. There have been a number of world championships as well and all these events can produce starts of a hundred and more craft. It has its dinghy racing starting from Fisher's Nose on Tuesday evenings from April to September, and Sunday afternoon racing from April until a week before Christmas.

WEST HOE SAILING CLUB

For years the West Hoe Sailing Club had its headquarters in the old Western clubhouse at West Hoe. When the Western moved to Queen Anne's

Battery in 1988, the West Hoe moved as well, but kept its old name. It started in 1936 as a dinghy club but while it still has a few Dolphins its members, getting older and needing more comfort, have graduated to yachts. It is the one club in the port which has always had level rating racing; with no handicapping.

At present its sixty-seventy members race in three classes on Thursday evenings, in J twenty-fours, Carissmas and Fox Terriers; four classes if the Dolphins are also out.

UNIVERSITY OF PLYMOUTH SAILING CENTRE

Plymouth University has taken over as its Sailing Centre the building constructed at QAB as the Seamanship centre of the former Plymouth School of Navigation. It is located between the dry dock of Pope's shipbuilding yard and the green slopes of Teat's Hill, and was opened by the Duke of Edinburgh in 1967. Training was carried out for various certificates required by Merchant Navy officers: efficient deckhand, lifeboatman and the survival course. A number of cutters and whalers were based there which could be hoisted on davits in front of the instruction block. From 1964 until 1980 the school owned an old trading ketch, the *Tectona*, normally kept on moorings at Turnchapel.

The School of Navigation became part of Plymouth Technical College which became the Polytechnic; then the University took over, cadet training dwindled and finally disappeared and the school became the Institute of Marine Studies, part of the University.

WATERSPORTS

Also based at the other end of QAB today is Plymouth Sailing School, founded in 1958 by the late Donald Gaskell-Brown with a club in Vauxhall Street, at the back of Little Vauxhall Quay. The club became enormously popular with the bright young things of Plymouth and is still *in situ*; the sailing school was sold separately in 1977 and moved eventually to Queen Anne's Battery. It offers full courses, residential or weekly, in all forms of skills from dinghy sailing up to the Yachtmaster's Certificate.

But yachting in the Cattewater is not just a modern development. As long ago as 1897 a review of the year in the river bemoaned the fact that in the past year only 264 yachts had come into the Cattewater, compared with 632 the year before.

Sailing today is well organised but all kinds of watersports are enjoyed. An area off Chelston Meadow is set aside for wind surfers. Wind surfers, water skiers, jet ski enthusiasts all enjoy their sports from QAB, and divers operate from both QAB and Commercial Wharf under the Citadel. Bodies such as Plymouth Hospital Trust also have boats based on Commercial Wharf, and Devon Education authority has moved its marine-based activities from Sutton Harbour to Mount Batten.

The eight clubs actually based on the shores of the Cattewater and the Laira have over 2,500 members, and probably double that number take their recreation on the water. The formal clubs organise racing every week in the summer from Sunday mornings to Friday evenings; nearly all starting in the Cattewater. These amateur sportsmen have now replaced in numbers the men who earn their living afloat or in sea-related jobs on the river.

CHAPTER TWENTY

MARINAS AND BOATYARDS

With the tremendous growth in yachting since World War II the demand for moorings has increased enormously. Glass fibre hulls mean that boats can be left in the water all the year round, but many owners still like to have them ashore for the winter months where repairs, maintenance and painting can be done more easily. So there has also been increased demand for winter boat storage. The first marina in the port, in Sutton Harbour, grew from 70 berths in 1972 to 200 within two years. It now has 275 berths, plus room for visitors. Another marina, Mayflower at Mount Wise on the Hamoaze, opened in 1972 and is now owned by Sailport PLC, a co-operative of berth holders. This too has about 275 berths. In all, Plymouth can offer nearly a thousand alongside marina berths.

QUEEN ANNE'S BATTERY

The first marina established on the Cattewater is at Queen Anne's Battery, but the marina is only part of its activities. It caters for every kind of water sport, not just yachting but dinghy sailing, canoeing, diving, water surfing, jet ski-ing, angling (there are a couple sea-angling boats berthed in the marina, and fishing competitions are run at times from the breakwater. It all started in 1984, when the then Conservative City Council resolved to create a watersports centre.

Its final shape and location was determined by the chance arrival in the port of Mark Gatehouse. His father is a gold medallist of the Royal Institute of Navigation and a founder of Brooks & Gatehouse, internationally-renowned in marine electronics, based at Lymington. Mark himself is a civil engineer. He formed a company and set up a regional office for construction work in Exeter. He had the contract to remove sludge from South West Water's sewage plants in Plymouth, and designed the specially-built vessel for the job, the *Douglas McWilliams*. For this purpose he was looking for a Plymouth office, and took over the property of the bankrupt Tamar Boat Enterprises. This company had been building yachts on Pope's slipways at QAB.

The new arrival by now had the familiar name of Dean & Dyball, and Mark was managing director. He entered into discussion with Plymouth Corporation, and in the end it was agreed that his company should build a water sports centre at QAB, with a subsidy from the Council. A special Act of Parliament had to be obtained.

Entries in the 1996 Single-Handed Transatlantic Race assembling in Queen Anne's Battery Marina in front of the Royal Western Yacht Club house.

There was opposition (led by David Owen, then MP for Devonport) from those concerned about people who would lose their cheap boat moorings. These were pacified with buoys in a trot off Commercial Wharf

Work started on the new marina in 1985, with a thirty per cent grant being sought from the European Union, and hopes that the new centre would bring an extra £500,000 a year to the city. It was planned to be protected from the sea by a double wave screen, a series of girders faced with greenheart timber, and surmounted by a £100,000 promenade. Dredging to remove 10,000 cubic metres of mud began that November.

By March 1986 trouble had started; initial boreholes into the mud had missed a deep chasm in the rock bed right under the breakwater. Eventually this had to be overcome with extra deep piles; the longest one used was 176ft; higher than the tallest building in Plymouth, the thirteen-storey Civic Centre. Eventually the Corporation had paid £3.5 million to the engineers; after going to law they had to pay the engineers an extra £800,000.

But the marina was opened just in time for it to serve as the base for the Carlsberg Two-Handed Transatlantic Race in 1986, run by the Royal Western Yacht Club. Now, ten years after, the marina has berths for 300 yachts and a basin reserved for visitors. In May 1989 the Royal Western moved into their clubhouse overlooking the visiting basin, which ever since has been the starting base for all their ocean races. Mark Gatehouse finished third in the 1989 Round Britain two-handed, with Anthony Boalch, who runs a yacht-rigging service at QAB, as crew. Since then Mark has competed in most of the offshore and ocean races run from the marina, and his forty-foot yacht, *Queen Anne's Battery Marina*, has widely advertised the base. The whole watersports centre is now jointly owned by Marine Development Co Ltd of Southampton

Apart from the yacht club, the marina has a bar and restaurant, with a bookshop, a number of ship chandlers, brokers, insurance companies and suppliers of every kind of service, from spar-makers to electronics and hull maintenance. There is a twenty-ton slipway hoist and ample dry berthing space. The marina is also the base for Plymouth Sailing School, and now offering every kind of instruction from five-day yachtmaster courses to evening classes for beginners. They have yachts and dinghies.

CLOVELLY BAY MARINA

In 1989 various boat owners at Turnchapel were getting fed up with the standard commercial marinas, and the idea developed that they would form their own, on a co-operative basis. The driving force was Jim Gill, who had been resident in the village since 1970, when with Alan Bax he had set up the diving school at Fort Bovisand. Twenty years on, this was the biggest diving school in Europe with a staff of seventy.

So two Clovelly Bay companies were formed, one holding and one managing, with Jim Gill as managing director. Jim had two 740 feet tubes constructed on the Hamoaze, and towed each one

across the Sound. They were the longest things ever to cross that stretch of water, longer than the biggest aircraft carriers. Off Turnchapel they were anchored to serve as the floats carrying the decks of the marina pontoon, with a link to the shore. The licences from the Cattewater Commissioners allowed 180 berths, and that number was created, 120 of them in deep water. All shareholders in the holding company have concessions on the cost of berthing their craft. At the base of the shore link, alongside the beach in the village, a concrete base was established with the offices and attendant stores and workshops grouped around.

Jim Gill, the originator of the Clovelly Bay Marina, boards his old-timer motor yacht Cordelia, *which he rescued and restored.*

BOATYARDS

A.S.BLAGDON & SONS

The yacht yard of A.S.Blagdon & Sons off the Embankment is probably the oldest established business of its kind on the river. The first Arthur Blagdon, a boatbuilder, started on his own about the turn of the century, at Arnold's Point. He had the little quay there from which he hired out

Part of Clovelly Bay Marina, in front of Turnchapel village.

Blagdon's Boatyard at Crabtree, in the stretch of water between the road and the railway embankments, all now under the six-lane highway to Marsh Mills. Getting in and out through the tunnel (right front) under the railway required a precise judgement of tide height.

rowing boats. In time he moved the business to Laira, where there were stretches of water between the railway embankment and the old main road. It was reached by a tunnel under the railway where there had to be enough water to float the boat, but not so much that the superstructure would not clear the roof. Here Arthur Blagdon was joined by his son, Arthur Stanley, who was always known as Stan to avoid confusion. In his younger days Stan and his sister would row around to the dockyard and tow back the boats that father had bought in the sale: they too became champion rowers at local regattas. In time Stan was joined by his two sons, Peter an engineer and the younger Arthur, also a boatbuilder, who continued running the business after the death of their father.

In 1970-71 their base was destroyed by the creation of the dual carriageway from the end of the Embankment to Marsh Mills. Spoil from the road widening was used to recover a stretch of foreshore between Arnold's Point and Laira Bridge, and Blagdon's eventually took over six acres of this reclaimed land to create a yacht yard. Nowadays it has a store supplying all kinds of boat and yacht needs, a workshop, a travelling crane for lifting craft out of the water, and a large area where boats of all descriptions are stored and where their owners can paint, repair and convert their craft. Business grew steadily all through the 1980s, but rather stagnated in the recession that followed, an experience common to most boatyards.

One reminder of the boating activity in this area is given by the ribs of a long derelict sailing trawler built in 1906, the *Antelope*, which stick out of the mud off the former Crabtree yard. This was bought by a Blagdon after 1945 when timber was scarce; the mast and what timber could be used again was salvaged, and the rest left to rot.

At the other end of Plymouth is Alec Blagdon, also a boatbuilder with a yacht yard on Richmond Walk. His grandfather and the first Arthur Blagdon were 'some kind of cousins'.

SKENTELBERY

K.R.Skentelbery started a boatbuilding business in Cremyll Street, Stonehouse in 1921. In 1949 he moved to the other side of the town, buying the lease of a boatyard at Chelston, just above Laira Bridge, from A.E.K.Rodgman. Rodgman, who owned the petrol station beside the Morley Arms on the main road, was a boatbuilder who had turned coachbuilder and behind his petrol station repaired and built bus and coach bodies.

When Skentelbery took over the boatyard they had moorings for rental in the Plym and also stored boats on the hard, as well as their boatbuilding. In 1986 when their lease was up for renewal, they bought the site from Plymouth Corporation, who had acquired it when they bought Chelston as the tip. Then in 1992 the Crown Estates, who owned the fundus of the river, vastly increased the charge for moorings (the fundus had belonged to the Duke of Bedford as lord of the manor of Plymstock, but when he relinquished the river rights they reverted to the Crown.) So the Skentelbery sons, John and Paul who by now had taken over from father, cut out renting moorings and boat storage and concentrated on boat building. The recession was biting into that business, so at the same time they had to pay off their work force of half a dozen men. Since then the pair of them carried on the boat building. Originally they built in wood, now it is glass fibre hulls. Since 1976 they have turned out thirty-one 40-foot yachts, and twelve 36 footers.

Tragedy hit the yard in 1995 when the building was destroyed by fire, along with a 36 feet yacht mould and a completed yacht. A car restoration garage next door was also burnt out, and arson was suspected. The brothers, however, had a yacht under construction in an undamaged building which kept them in business until a new 3,200 square foot unit was completed in twelve months.

RICO POWER BOATS

Tucked away at the end of Breakwater Road, alongside Pomphlett Creek, a new company called Rico Power Boats exhibited at both the 1994 and 1995 Southampton Boat Shows. In 1995 they sold two of their £77,500 Marlins, with more 'orders in the pipeline for both that and their £42,500 Mirage'. They aim to have another two models available for the next show.

RON GREET BOAT SERVICES.

Ron Greet has been on the old coal wharf (possibly a Westcott yard) at Turnchapel since 1965, when he bought out a boatyard being run there by Plymouth Sound Boat Services. He offers maintenance, repairs, all services in fact, and regularly has a full yard. When he started he had a few moorings off the yard, but with the advent of Clovelly Bay marina he happily gave up his moorings to them.

AL BROTHERTON

In 1965 the late Al Brotherton, a renowned rally motor cyclist, took over what had been the Lucas boat-building yard in Oreston, at the end of

Paul Skentlebery alongside the first craft completed after the fire in their Chelston yard.

Marine Road. The newly formed Plym Yacht Club was just doing extensive work on gutting and rebuilding its clubhouse at Oreston, and all the waste and rubble was dumped in front of the boatyard, to create the little quay that is still there. Here Mr Brotherton established a boat storage yard where people could do their own maintenance. After his death his widow continued the business, which still flourishes.

ROCKY PINDAR

English Clays Quarry Division built Pomphlett stone jetty in 1969 and gave up using the stone wharf in Pomphlett Creek. Davies & Cann had already bought the old Cole Brothers timber yard at the entrance to the creek, and very soon they had taken over the eastern side of the creek as a scrap metal yard. Then Derek Wood, whose father had bought the yard, cleared the scrap and turned the long thin stretch of land between the creek and the main road into a boat storage yard. After three years he sold up.

Enter Rocky Pindar! Born in Watford, trained as an industrial chemist and as such employed in Surrey and Sussex, Mr M.B. (Rocky) Pindar changed direction in 1979. He came to Plymouth and bought the petrol station next to the old Barton Motor Company building at the end of Mutley Plain, opposite the Hyde Park Hotel. But

The pontoons off Shore Store's boatyard at Laira Wharf.

he had always had a boat, and in July 1994 bought the Pomphlett boat yard. He rented the other side of the creek from Camas Aggregates and has boat moorings now on both sides. The yard is a boat storage area and the base of Plymouth Boat Sales (which is also Pindar), who act as agents in buying and selling. This kind of yard is popular with owners who want to work on their boats themselves, but engine and hull work can be done (by sub-contractors). In 1995 the yard opened a chandlery.

Mr Pindar has close links with Plym Yacht Club, of which in 1995 he was treasurer.

SHORE STORE

Martin's Wharf, or Laira Wharf, just south of Laira Bridge on the Plymouth side, was abandoned as a scrap yard by Davies & Cann when they ceased trading in 1992. The company sold the wharf to two young brothers, Andrew and Ian Sleep who then embarked on the herculean task of clearing the abandoned scrap metal from the quay and the mudbank in front of the quay; when that was done they started in business as Shore Store, offering marine services and boat storage.

Bit by bit they repaired the quay wall, built a slipway down to the water, and set up a couple lines of pontoons offshore for mooring purposes. Portacabins provide office and workshop space; opposite the entrance they have a flagstaff with an interesting collection of scrap found on the site, including a borough boundary stone inscribed '1873, Alfred Rooker, Mayor'. They have a mobile crane to lift craft from the water, and in the winter of 1994-5 had 140 boats laid up, filling just about all the space available. Like their friend Rocky Pindar across the river, they can supply a certain amount of servicing and sub-contract whatever else is needed.

THE PICKLE YARD

One of the the biggest yacht storage areas in the Cattewater is at the old Bayly's timber yard in Oreston, always known locally as the Pickle Yard. Here J Boston & Sons (Shipping) Ltd, run by Captain Nigel Boston (whose father had the scrap yard at Shapter's Field, Cattedown), opened in the early 1990s. They offer diving services, pumping and salvage, moorings laid, surveys and repairs, hull cleaning, boat hire, towage and a wide range of other services. Nigel Boston is also engaged in research for universities and similar bodies, work involving diving, underwater robots, sonar, hydrography and marine biology. Labour is hired as required.

The quays at the turn of the river into Hooe Lake are occupied with an old puffer from the west coast of Scotland which Nigel Boston restored to working order and a few old coasters and similar craft laid up. In the large expanse of the old yard is ample room, well used, for yacht storage. A number of the old sheds of the timber yard remain, typical in their wooden construction. One houses a firm called Outboard Engine Services, another a shipwright company, Rockrun Yachts.

PART THREE - MAN ON SHORE

CHAPTER TWENTY-ONE

THE WATER MILLS

Mills driven by water power, that is by the force of a stream or the tide, is one of the oldest forms of mechanism in the world. There is none on the Plym mentioned in Domesday Book, but they were not then common in Devon, and those that did exist were concentrated in south and east Devon.

Although many mills in Devon went over from grinding flour to making woollens, the Plymouth mills all remained as flour mills serving their local communities.

PLYMPTON

There were mills on the Tory Brook, on the Newnham estate, but these are above the tidal area. Lower down there were two, Earl's Mill and Priory Mill.

Earl's Mill, or the Manor Mill, first recorded in 1155 is probably the older and served the original manor. It took its water from the Longbrook (which flows down the valley south of Plympton St Maurice's Fore Street) by means of a leat which curled around the lower edge of St Mary's Churchyard and the playing fields on the other side of Ridgeway. A stretch of the leat is still visible behind the police station at the corner of Station Road and Earl's Mill Road, and the water after driving the mill flowed into the Tory Brook.

The mill stood on the corner of Tory Brook Road and Earl's Mill road. opposite the police station. Mill and weir were both in decay in 1705, and the mill was rebuilt in 1714.

By 1793 it was again 'in decay, dilapidated' and by 1894 the building was serving as a furniture factory for Price & Clatworthy. It has since housed Plympton's first electricity supply and the town's first cinema: been Russell's pickle factory, Widger's mirror silvering establishment, and the first home of Chaplin's DIY store. There is believed to have been a tall chimney attached

J. R. F. BRADFORD
EARL'S MILLS, PLYMPTON,
Motor and General Engineering Works
All Kinds of Machinery Repairs Executed on the Premises
Commercial and Private Cars Completely Overhauled by Skilled Mechanics
Any Make of Solid Tyres Supplied and Fitted on the Premises
Stockist of Brake Linings
Separate Lock-up Garages for Hire
Accumulators Charged
Phone : Plympton 9, Day or Night

A 1930 advertisement for Earl's Mill in the South Devon Times.

which suggests that at one time it turned to steam power. No trace of the building remains. Priory Mill, just above Market Road, is the younger establishment and was probably built to serve the Priory. It was fed by a mill pond which also took its water from the Longbrook, and was filled in about 1990 to provide the site for the Priory Mill housing estate. The miller in 1850 was Samuel Heal.

The three-story mill had an overshoot waterwheel, and the miller's house was alongside. It has now been cut down and parts incorporated into a a private dwelling house called the Old Mill House. The warehouse in front, now called Priory Mill, was originally a malt house.

MARSH MILL

A flour mill stood close beside the Longbridge and its name indicates the kind of area in which it was situated. Until there was some kind of dry ground in the area it could not have been built; it was close beside the road from Longbridge to Plympton (its actual site was in the angle between the road and the railway bridge, and is now under the B&Q car park).

Its water supply came from a leat taken from the weir still above Cann quarry, made by Lord Boringdon in the early eighteenth century. In 1830 this leat was deepened and widened to form the canal which brought slates down from Cann Quarry to join the Plymouth and Dartmoor Railway. The canal was abandoned in 1835 but still served the mill; within living memory the water driving the mill was discharged into the Plym, when the mill was not working the water was into the Tory Brook.

In 1850 the mill was owned by Daw and Frean, who also ran the big Drake's Mill at Sherwell in Plymouth. George Frean, who had a big house in Skardon Place looking down on Sherwell, was a partner at one time of Serpell and associated with that family's biscuit bakery at the foot of Lambhay Hill. Later Frean went to London as a partner with a Peek son of the Devon family by then established as coffee dealers in the city. Together they set up the biscuit making firm of Peek Frean.

Marsh Mill was still working in 1927, owned by Mr Boswell Harris. The family lived in the Mill House alongside, but a Plymothian who took tea there as a small boy remembers a tall chimney, confirmed by a photograph. The mill had at some time gone over to steam.

LEIGHAM MILL

Leigham Mill stood on a side creek of Forder Valley, just above the traffic lights at the foot of Forder Hill. It was on the stream that flows through the small valley beside Novorossisk Road, somewhere in front of the school. The miller in 1850 was John Cornish, and the mill was still working in the early days of the this century.

EFFORD MILL

At the head of the other branch of Forder Valley, now traversed by the Parkway, was Efford Mill, built to serve its manor as was Leigham Mill. It was just above the bridge where the old Egg Buckland to Higher Compton road loops over the dual carriageway. The building was probably destroyed when the Parkway was built, though it had ceased working as a mill much earlier.

LIPSON MILL

Another manorial mill stood in Lipson Vale, just north of the railway embankment and west of the point where the railway bridge crosses Laira Road. Its mill pond was higher up the valley towards Lower Compton., in what is now the little park called Trefusis Valley. It has not operated since World War I, but the 1850 miller was John Ryder.

RADFORD MILL

The mill at Radford, one of the oldest on the Plym, is mentioned in 1303 as belonging to the manor of East Hooe. It stood between the present adventure training centre and the ruins at St Keverne, on the south side of the duckponds. The waterpower came from a leat taken under the road in a tunnel which launched the water into the wheel, finishing in a spectacular waterfall. It has long disappeared, but was sketched by the Rev John Swete on his tour of Devon in 1793, and is mentioned in the particulars of sale of the Radford Estate in 1917.

TIDAL MILLS

Another source of waterpower was the tidal mill. In this a dam was built across the head of a creek to cut off a mill pond. In the dam was set two swing gates. so constructed that the incoming tide pushed them open, and the ebb tide shut them. Then the water was allowed to escape through a channel cut under the mill, to drive a water wheel. There were a dozen tidal mills around Plymouth, but only one on the Plym. On the Henry VIII defence map only one western creek of the Laira is shown. Across it is a structure which looks like a tidal mill, but there is no reference known to such a mill and it remains a mystery

POMPHLETT MILL

There was however, a tidal mill at the head of Pomphlett Creek, on the right of the road to Plymstock where it leaves Pomphlett Roundabout. It was originally built by Tavistock Abbey, lords of the manor of Plymstock, as the grist mill for the manor. Accounts for the mill survive in the Bedford papers from 1392 to 1521. In 1532 it was leased to Nicholas Rede. After the dissolution of the monasteries it passed to the Russell family (who became the dukes of Bedford). They kept it in hand until in 1683 it was leased to Ellis Long, a ropemaker of Oreston, 'lately modified and rebuilt'. (When the mill was demolished in 1969 the earliest surviving parts of the building were dated as sixteenth century by James Barber.)

In 1892 the Duke of Bedford sold the mill to William Mitchell. It was described at this time as 'an excellently well-built freehold tide-water grist mill'. It was of four stories, with the water driving a 27inch turbine which could generate 50 horse power and had a driving shaft up to the second floor. The corn store alongside was of three storeys. There were was also a coal store, wharf, dwelling house and stabling. Milling had stopped before the 1914 war. and the buildings were used as stores. In 1923 William's son, the celebrated Billy Mitchell, uncrowned king of Plymstock who

A 1794 drawing by the Rev. John Swete of Radford Mill with its overshot wheel. The boathouse, which still survives, can be seen on

bought Radford House at about this time, rented it to Plymouth Co-operative Society. Two years later the Co-op bought the mill. and used the place as a general store until it was pulled down for road widening. In its time the mill stood on the creek side of the road which leaves the Elburton road for Plymstock and Oreston; in the wall across the present head of the creek can still be seen stonework surviving from the mill.

CHAPTER TWENTY-TWO

THE QUARRIES

Plymouth is built of the limestone quarried from the shores of the Cattewater. It has been used for centuries either as fine squared ashlar, rough-hewn blocks, or just random stone. St Andrew's Church, the Prysten House, the Citadel, all are in the nearly white limestone. 'Plymouth marble', it has been called, and C.W.Bracken used to explain that marble was limestone subjected in geological time to great heat and great pressure. Plymouth limestone did not quite reach the necessary height of heat or pressure, and that is all that prevents it being true marble.

Even the old street pavements are laid with it, and particularly after a shower the fine coloured veins glisten in the stone. In the sunshine, seen from Mount Edgcumbe or any other vantage point, Plymouth shines like a white city.

Quarries cut into the cliff faces on either side of the Cattewater yielded building material that could easily be transported by water to the growing town. Quarries, mainly run by small men, opened from Deadman's Bay to Prince Rock, from Mount Batten to the edge of Chelston Meadow. The Journal of the Rev John Swete mentions Pomphlett, Hooe Lake and Radford quarries in the eighteenth century, and they are shown in the 1780s watercolours of William Payne. The Rogers painting of the launch of the

Clarence in 1812 quite clearly shows how Cattedown had been quarried away, even by that time, right up to the line of the road across the hill to Coxside.

A writer, 'J.P.', in the *South Devon Monthly Museum*, wrote in the first volume, January 1833, 'Limestone...whether we regard it as yielding at once the material and cement for building: as a manure almost universally applicable...we see the whole breadth of Cat Down, Turnchapel, Mount Batten, Teat's Hill...all presenting a source of perpetual activity...The quantity burnt into lime, in the quarries themselves, is probably not less than 300,000 bushels annually. The lime fetches at the kiln 10d a bushel, and the stone exported 1s per ton at the quarry...The number of men employed may be averaged at 350, the gunpowder consumed in blasting the rock at 89,600 lbs annually.'

At the start of the nineteenth century the quarrying on the Plymouth side was in one area, from the Bear's Head to Prince Rock, and had not bitten very deeply into Cattedown. But then Plymouth started to grow; its population rocketed from 16,000 in 1801 to 107,000 in 1901. Stonehouse and Devonport were growing as well, but they had their own supplies of limestone for building. It was the tremendous demand for Plymouth

This 1831 drawing by H. Worsley of Laira Bridge was made from Laira Wharf when it was handling granite from Dartmoor. The white cliffs across the river shows how the limestone cliffs dominated so much of the river.

housing all through this century that brought the major growth to the quarries, and the opening of new ones. Random limestone is behind the stucco fronts of all those terraces which cover the northern slopes of the Hoe and climb over the hills from King Street and Cobourg Street and Exeter Street. When the 'by-law housing' under the new Health Acts of the 1890s demanded back access to new houses, the cobbled back lanes were all lined with six foot garden walls of random limestone. It all came from the Cattewater shores.

BREAKWATER QUARRY

The building of the Breakwater took 3.5 million tons of stone, and the bulk of that was limestone shipped out from the Cattewater. In 1812 the Government bought 25 acres of land from the Duke of Bedford. It was already being worked as a quarry, reaching back a hundred feet into the cliff. By the time the Breakwater was completed, in 1841, the quarry stretched from just north of Oreston to the mouth of Pomphlett Creek, and reached back to the road from Pomphlett to Oreston.

The quarry is also notable in that it contains the second railway ever built in the area, and the stone was shipped out on the first ever train ferries. John Rennie the engineer, laid rails from the waterside to the quarry face in 1812 and kept them moving forward as the stone was dug out. Ten specially-designed barges were built, flat-

The two-decked barges used to transport truck-loads of stone from Breakwater Quarry at Oreston to construct Plymouth Breakwater; it has claims to be the world's first train ferry.

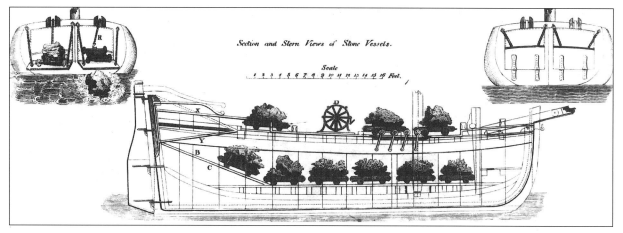

bottomed craft with two decks both equipped with a stretch of railway track. The lower deck was loaded by running the trucks carrying the heavier blocks aboard, and then an internal ramp enabled trucks carrying the lighter blocks to be run to the upper deck. Each barge could carry eighty tons. At the Breakwater site the stone could be tipped overboard, and later on the trucks were run ashore on to rails laid along the top of the work. Another 45 vessels, each capable of

carrying 45 to 50 tons of stone in blocks of up to two tons, were loaded by crane and discharged by sheerlegs.

The 1812 railway was of 3 feet 6in gauge and parts are still buried under rubble. The rails visible today on the quaysides here are of a much larger gauge. Breakwater Quarry was an industrial complex on its own, complete with pitch works, cement works and a lime kiln. On the corner of the creek was a boat house and slipway, with a small dock on the main river. The Breakwater Office was to the south, on the shore, and then came a small dock capable of handling two barges abreast, with two railway lines leading to the head of the dock. A long building entitled Government Works, to the south again, contained a carpenter's shop, mess house, coal house and smithy.

The quays are remarkably intact today, with the two docks partly filled in. Of the office block only the gable ends remain, but the Government Works are remarkably intact. A new Plymouth marine contracting company, Seastructures, has taken over the buildings and converted them to provide a base. The blacksmith's shop on the northern end still has its immense forge with chimney to stimulate the blast of air. The mess house next

The Breakwater Quarry blacksmith's shop in the foreground still has its original forge; the remaining 'government works' have been converted to offices and stores for Seastructures.

door provides offices, with the remainder of the building used as stores and workshops. The company's diving and salvage vessels and tug still berth alongside the quays.

Back at the 1812 start of the Breakwater: within eleven months over 43,000 tons of stone had been dropped in place and the structure began to appear above the water at low water springs. In 1814 vessels were able to anchor in its shelter, and in 1815 the prisoner Napoleon aboard the *Bellerophon* was an interested observer of the work.

The Admiralty continued to maintain the Breakwater with stone from the quarry, but later large concrete blocks were cast in a small corner of the complex, and shipped out to the Breakwater as required. The quarry was sold to Devon County Council in 1967 for a mere £3,500. The concrete block-making was moved to the Clovelly Bay end of RAF Mount Batten, but moved back again to Breakwater Quarry with the arrival of Plymouth Development Corporation.

SPARROW'S QUARRIES

When much of eastern Plymouth, from the Friary and Teat's Hill out to Prince Rock was included in a sale of part of the Manor of Sutton Pill in 1820, the occupants of Cattedown Quarry were shown as Messrs Symonds and Sparrow. The lot was described thus: 'Three FIELDS called by the name of Catdown together with the Limestone Quarry thereto adjoining, and the old Lime Kiln Buildings and Wharf erected thereon. These FIELDS have a good South Aspect and the Soil very good. Much Business may be done at the QUARRY, if managed with skill and spirit.'

The names of Sparrow and Simons (different spelling) crops up even earlier; as early as 1813 they were leasing part of Hooe Lake Quarry for £20 a year. Other lessees of Hooe manor quarries were Rowse & Barker, Shepherd, W.Pearce, James

The face of the long-worked-out Deadman's Bay quarry at the back of the Conoco quay. The walls of the road from Coxside to Cattedown can be see right on the edge of the quarry top.

Butland (who was also the tenant of West Hooe Farm), and Skardon, Prinn & Wakeham (who had the biggest stake). Several of the quarry owners had built quays in front of their quarries and, says an 1813 report, 'levelling the space for house building has always been contemplated by the proprietor (Sir John Rogers), but the quarries having been opened only a few years, sufficient room is scarcely accomplished for this purpose'.

The senior member of Sparrow & Simons, Benjamin Sparrow senior, lived at 6 Brunswick Terrace, the fine redbrick terrace of Regency houses built about 1811 on the eastern outskirts of Plymouth and inhabited by well-to-do merchants like the Baylys, moving out from the increasingly congested areas closer to Sutton Harbour. Sparrow's son, another Benjamin, lived at the original family home close to the quarries in Cattedown. When St John's Church was being planned but not built in the 1840s, a room in the Sparrow house at Cattedown was licensed for worship, to hold 38 people. From 1852 until 1863 a series of Sparrow children were christened, probably at first in this room because the church was not consecrated until 1855. In 1855 Benjamin Sparrow, an adult, was baptised, presumably Benjamin junior. When the last child was christened the family was living in Caer Badden

Terrace, North Road East. They appear as a substantial family because they were also the senior partners in 1852 in Sparrow Hodge & Co, in Sutton Road, Coxside, manufacturers of sheet and pipe lead, manure and superphosphates.

Their quarries at Cattedown worked steadily back into the hill, and in 1878 a lease was taken by Benjamin and Louis Sparrow, stone and lime merchants, from Lord Graves. The old quarry floor, about forty acres, was described on the accompanying map as rubble bumps, and the new lease allowed quarrying further north into the hill, on the land now occupied by the Works Depot of Plymouth Corporation. Louis Sparrow, incidentally, excavated the cuttings required by the building of the railway from Plymstock to Turnchapel. Sparrow was still at Cattedown in 1900 but by 1905 he is described as just a stone and lime merchant; by 1910 the name disappears from the directories.

F.J. MOORE & CO

Sparrow's quarry business was eventually taken over by F.J. Moore & Sons Ltd. The first Moore, Thomas, was originally in the Dockyard but he became the manager of a quarry. His son, Frederick John, leased Prince Rock Quarry and in 1885 leased Battery Hill from the Earl of Mount Edgcumbe. His name first appears in the directories as being the agent at Battery Hill Quarries, Stonehouse, in 1890. By 1900 Moore is recorded as a quarry owner at Prince Rock; by 1914 he was operating both Prince Rock and Cattedown. The family understanding is that the Moores bought out the Sparrows, but the business really took off when the Duke of Bedford sold up his Plymstock estate in 1911. F.J.Moore bought five quarries, quays and land for £3,000. He now owned Cattedown, Prince Rock, Radford, Hooe Lake, Moorcroft (at Billacombe), Billacombe black and Billacombe white (so named after the colour of the stone they produced) and Hexton quarries. To handle all the stone from the former Bedford quarries Moores had their own railway siding and loading bay at Oreston Station. Their offices were in Quay House, Cattedown, right opposite Sparrow's Wharf. Moores owned two barges, named the *EMM* and *FLM*, after his two daughters, Edith Matilda and Frances. The barges brought sand from Par and Pentewan, and the wharf became known as the sand quay.

Frederick John continued running the company while his son Frederick Herbert was in the Army in World War I, but the son never came home: he died of the influenza epidemic in a German prisoner of war camp. The old man continued running the company until his death in 1922. Frederick Herbert's son, Frederick James, was only six or seven years old when his grandfather died so his aunt, Edith, ran the company until the boy came of age to take over. Edith, a strong character held in great respect by both staff and customers, was the only woman quarrymaster in the country. After Quay House and the adjoining houses in Cattedown were demolished, the office was moved to Hamilton House in Tothill Road.

On the Plymouth shore first Cattedown and then Prince Rock were worked out by this time, and the centre of activity moved across the river. Moores established a cement works, Stoncrete, beside the Elburton Road, just beyond the head of Pomphlett Creek. Frederick James went to Camborne School of Mines and qualified in 1938. When World War II broke out in 1939 he joined the Royal Engineers, and was away until 1946. Edith ran the firm all through the war; when her nephew came home they ran the company jointly.

In 1945 the firm had a number of quarries in production, Hooe Lake, Radford, Saltram, Hexton, Billacombe black and white. Most of the quarries went out of production as time went on, either they were exhausted or were getting too close to housing. Blasting was the only way to move the stone, any houses close could be shaken or damaged and caused endless disputes. Nowadays big machines can claw out the stone without recourse to explosives. But in the decade after the war the climate was turning against small quarry companies.

Moores first of all amalgamated with other limestone quarry owners in the westcountry. The Moore name has disappeared by the 1951 directory. The amalgamated company eventually sold out to the Quarries Division of English China Clays, which in 1994 was hived off from the parent company and became a self-contained company, Camas Aggregates. Their Plymouth headquarters were established at Moorcroft, just behind the site of the former Billacombe Station, and this quarry and another adjacent, which became one, were extensively worked for roadstone.

AGRICULTURAL USE

Limestone was also used to make slaked lime, used to improve the farmers' fields. As early as 1594 there were kilns on Lambhay where the stone could be burnt to produce the powder for spreading on the fields. This use of lime received a considerable impetus in the agricultural revolution of the eighteenth century and enormously increased in the nineteenth. John's Directory of 1823 records that vast quantities of limestone were shipped out from the Cattewater to parts of Devon and Cornwall.

Water transport was the easiest way of getting the lime to the farmers; and the only places on the south coast of both Devon and Cornwall where limestone reached tidal waters were Plymouth and Torbay. So Plymouth boats provided the stone for the south coast of Cornwall and along the Devon shore as far as Salcombe; beyond that

point it came from Brixham and Berry Head.

There were some kilns close to the quarries: the eighteenth-century twin kilns which survive on the western shore of Hooe Lake obviously fed the farmers right out to Wembury. There were more limekilns by the ruins in Radford Lake and in Cattedown Quarry. J and T Harry had a kiln at Deadman's Bay in 1852 and their kiln was still there at the turn of the century. But it was generally easier and safer (wet lime is highly caustic) to ship the unburnt stone to kilns high up the rivers and creeks, close to the farmers who needed it.

There were for instance five kilns at Crabtree, not far from the Cattedown quarries but until the Embankment was built lime could only be moved by road from Cattedown by travelling right through Plymouth. So it came up by barge. These kilns fed the Egg Buckland farms which were the market gardens of Plymouth, and were so busy as to raise complaints about the amount of traffic on the Crabtree roads. The Laira Green kiln stood

A barge loading stone from Radford Quarry at the head of Hooe Lake; the building behind is the 'castle' on the duckpond dam.

where now Old Laira Road meets the embankment, the Great Kiln was between the two Crabtrees, and three more kilns were close together, at higher Crabtree.

The Parkers of Saltram owned the Great Kiln, and probably the others; accounts of bills for stone, and wages occur in the Saltram papers from 1787. Some of this was used to fertilise the Saltram fields; the Parkers preferred to have the burning done on the other side of the river, away from their house! Business was improved when the Dartmoor railway was built beside the kilns in 1823 and the lime could be carried to Roborough Down and Princetown. The next railway, the South Devon, cut these kilns off from the river and they are not mentioned in White's 1850 Directory; probably out of business.

The transport of the stone gave employment to many little sailing barges which could penetrate to the highest points that the tide could reach. Probably these barges, like the little quarries, were individually owned by small men. Sparrow and Son built up a fleet of barges to carry the limestone: their ships dominated the lime trade to Salcombe.

GRAVESTONES

The monumental masons of Plymouth also made use of the best quality limestone as 'marble' for their gravestones, and decorative purposes .

This 1787-8 drawing by William Payne is entitled 'A stone and marble quarry near Plymouth'; the workmen in the foreground are using a saw on the block of stone.

Different quarries produced different grades; Kitley produced Kitley Green which was used in the ornamentation of Brompton Oratory in London, Radford Red was mainly used for inlaying and columns for pulpits and fonts, and Pomphlett Black was also used in church work.

THE QUARRIES

A list can be compiled of the main quarries, based principally on notes written by F.H.Evea in 1896 and in the West Devon Record Office. They were:

DEADMAN'S BAY, or BAY QUARRY

The quarry on the seaward side of the Coxside-Cattedown Wharfs road was worked out by the 1850s. The main quarry, entered by the lorry entrance off Breakwater Road, now carries the name although it is on the back side of the hill facing Deadman's Bay. It now houses the storage oil tanks for Esso. Early in the nineteenth century Sparrow & Simons were the owners, but the two limekilns predate these partners. At the south entrance there was a deposit of good clay (which may have helped the pottery off Cattedown Road opposite the Shipwright's Arms, (originally the Shipwright and Potters) Much of this clay was shipped to the Hamoaze to make the dam which kept the tide back from the building of the Keyham Extension Yard.

CATTEDOWN QUARRY

Sometimes called Middle Quarry (it is between Deadman's Bay and Prince Rock quarries), it extends from the back of Cattedown Wharfs to Maxwell Road. In its heyday it produced a first-class white stone. Quantities were carried to Southampton by two 80-ton smacks the *Emu Flower* and the *Wheat Ear*, which brought back cargoes of flour. Early cargoes were extracted by two brothers, William & Frank Joslin, and John Hornfield, and later on by Sparrow & Simons. Mr Sparrow built himself a house which his son was living in during the 1850s. The oldest part of the quarry became the Wallsend Industrial Estate, the newer area is occupied by the tanks of Shell-Mex and BP, and the Corporation works depot.

PRINCE ROCK

The third major quarry stretched from Oakfield Terrace Road to Laira Bridge Road. There were a couple limekilns here, and it was being heavily quarried when the railway arrived in the 1850s.

MOUNT BATTEN

Probably quarrying here is as old as anywhere in the Cattewater; it is likely that the stone was used to build the tower about 1666. Lord Morley was letting leases of quarries to a number of small men in the 1820s. Quays and slips were built on the foreshore to ship out the stone.

Peter Simons had control of all quarrying here by 1841, and he sold large quantities of 6-ton blocks for the building of the Steam Yard in Devonport Dockyard, which began in 1844. The work kept four barges working. Quarrying was eventually stopped close to the tower in 1848 because the tower foundations were undermined. By 1864 quarrying had also stopped on the south side to protect the coastguard cottages.

HOOE LAKE

This very old quarry stretches around to the back of Turnchapel, which is built on the quarry floor. Boringdon Terrace in the village is early nineteenth century, which suggests that quarrying had already finished by that time. The lime kilns

beside the lake are eighteenth century, which also gives an idea of the quarry's age. The main quarry, facing Hooe Lake, was owned by Taylor & Wright, but eventually taken over by F.J. Moore. By the limekilns at the entrance is Billy Hart's Quay, still being used to load stone in the 1930s. At the end of the quarry entrance opposite the quay is a dilapidated structure of crumbling concrete and corrugated iron sheets flapping in the wind, originally a limestone crusher.

SAWMILL AND LANGSHILL

Opposite Hooe Lake Quarry, across the water, are the smaller quarries, Saw Mill (behind the timber yard) and Langshill. They were worked in the 1840s by various people; a couple went bankrupt and one was drowned. In 1870 the owners of these Oreston quarries were J.& E.Goad. Mr Bayly, owner of the timber yard, finally stopped work on these quarries to save Larry's Hill as a recreation field for the Oreston people

HEXTON

A small quarry on the south side of Hooe, just east of Hooe village. This is unusual in that it was not worked from the waterside and a tunnel links the workings with its quay on the south shore of the lake. A little group of industrial buildings on the quay, complete with a factory chimney, still dominates this side of the lake. F.J. Moore bought it from George Hart. It had gone out of business by 1932, when the material removed from the widening of Hooe Lane, from opposite the school to the corner of Belle Vue Road, was tipped into the quarry.

RADFORD

In 1848, when this quarry was leased by a Mr Toll from the Duke of Bedford, plans were submitted to the Admiralty to build a quay at the head of the lake. Later it was worked by Thomas Gill & Company, who were developing the Millbay and West Hoe quarries. They used the stone in their kilns at Morwellham. Sparrow took it over in 1872 and worked it into the next century. Sparrows built more quays at the head of the lake to serve the Tamar barges carrying the lime.

BREAKWATER

Often known as the Government Works, it had docks and wharfs along the water's edge, with the Breakwater Offices between two small embarking bays.

BEDFORD

It lay at the top of Pomphlett Lake, a deep narrow cut stretching back from the lake shore to Thorneycroft Lane. Its floor is now filled with light industries.

POMPHLETT MILL

This quarry, on the southern side of the road to Elburton, just past the roundabout, was worked by a mason, John Davis, who went bankrupt in 1841. It was then taken over by the Scott brothers, Edward and Robert. In fact these brothers took over all the Earl of Morley's quarries in 1843.

They are said to be of the Scott family who owned the Star Brewery in Hoegate Street, which they bought with the prize money they acquired as naval officers. Hence they are relatives of Scott of the Antarctic, whose father Robert was the senior partner in the brewery. A *Western Daily Mercury* report of 1869 refers to Emmanuel Church, Mannamead, being built of stone 'from J.A.K.Goad's quarry at Pomphlett'.

POMPHLETT

These quarries on the north side of the Elburton road, opposite the lake, were also run after 1841 by the Scotts. Benjamin Sparrow went in as manager, and from then on these quarries and Cattedown were run in conjunction. It is probable that this quarry provided the limestone for the first Laira Bridge. On the floor of the worked-out quarry, now owned by SWEB, are the warehouses and industries which line the northern side of the road from the Laira Bridge to Pomphlett roundabout

MOORCROFT QUARRY

Originally owned by F.J. Moore, Moorcroft Quarry is the other side of Billacombe, with its approach road past the former Billacombe Station. Moores sold it about 1950 to English China Clays. It is now worked by Camas.

CHAPTER TWENTY-THREE

THE RAILWAYS

THE PLYMOUTH & DARTMOOR

The first railway reached the shores of the Cattewater in 1825, the horse-drawn Plymouth and Dartmoor. This was the brainchild of Sir Thomas Tyrwhitt, sometime secretary to Prinny (the Prince of Wales) and the Duchy of Cornwall. He was an MP for Plymouth, creator of Princetown and its prison, and had a vision of turning Dartmoor into a blooming and fruitful countryside. His magic wand was simple, a railway which would link Princetown and the port of Plymouth. This would transport lime (as fertiliser), coal and timber to the Moor, and pay for it by bringing back granite, peat and the eventual farming products from his improvements. His first Act of 1819 empowered him to build his terminus at Crabtree, his second extended it to Sutton Harbour. It was opened in 1823

The line approached Plymouth above the right bank of the Plym, reached Forder Valley through a tunnel, came around in front of Crabtree on the water side of the road to a bridge under the Embankment. Thence it came down on the landward side of the Embankment and swung to the right at the end. The present Gdynia Way and the new approach road to Sutton Harbour follow

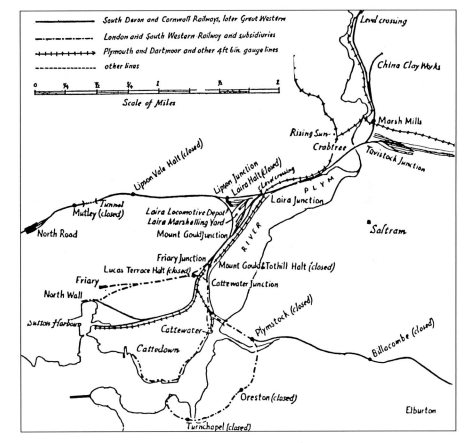

A sketch map of the railways of eastern Plymouth, showing the cat's cradle of lines alongside the Laira and in Cattedown.

its track. A spur went on beside the railway to just past Laira Bridge and so carried it to the shores of the Cattewater. Here Laira Wharf was built, the first one on the right bank of the Cattewater.

Lord Morley wanted a branch built from the railway to his Cann Quarry, and this was eventually completed by 1829, running from Crabtree along the northern side of Longbridge and crossing the Plym by an iron bridge which still survives. Then the firm of Johnson & Bryce, which had contracts to provide granite for the new Plymouth Breakwater, Laira Bridge and London Bridge, built a siding from the wharf on Cattewater around the bluff of limestone into a quarry floor now occupied by various stores across Laira Bridge Road from the bus depot. Here they set up works to process the Dartmoor granite, which in turn was shipped from the riverside wharf. Johnson was soon the virtual owner of the railway.

In 1833 an extension of the Cann Quarry branch was built, from Marsh Mills to Plympton. The raised bank which carried the railway can still be

A train of china clay trucks crossing the road in front of the Rising Sun at Crabtree; this was the main road to Exeter and London and the only warning to traffic was the man with the red flag, seen right. This crossing right was not forfeited until 1960.

seen alongside the road west of St Mary's roundabout. Lord Morley's china clay from Lee Moor was being brought to Plympton by packhorse, where it was transferred to the railway and taken to Laira Wharf. Part of the Plympton branch was bought out by the South Devon Railway (later the Great Western Railway) in 1847 when they were bringing in the main line, and closed down.

LEE MOOR TRAMWAY

In 1853 a branch was built from the Cann Quarry line, reaching from Plym Bridge to Lee Moor, using two inclines to deal with the change in heights. For decades it carried china clay to Laira Wharf, its trucks being hauled above the incline by steam engines (one can still be seen at Saltram) and by horses below Plym Bridge. This line had to have a level crossing over the main Plymouth-London road in front of the Rising Sun inn. There were no gates, just a man with a red flag who stood in the road and stopped traffic.It continued to be the main form of transport of china clay until 1927, when a pipeline brought the clay to new drying works at Marsh Mills. Here it was transferred to main line trucks in the Tavistock Junction goods marshalling yard, either for the rest of Britain or for the specially-built china clay harbour at Par in Cornwall. The railway was still kept working, however, although it was virtually closed during World War II. After 1945 a short section was kept open between Marsh Mills and Maddock's concrete works (now Heywood Pavings Ltd) on the Embankment, carrying sand. This closed finally in 1960. It was kept open for so long just to guard the railway's right to the road level crossing at the Rising Sun, and a crossing of the main GWR railway line at Laira.

The china clay trains, made up of five trucks and hauled by a pair of horses, the driver sitting on the leading truck and a brakeman perched on a following truck, were a familiar sight to generations of Plymothians. They plodded alongside the main road at Long Bridge to the Rising Sun level crossing. Now all this area is under the vast road roundabout and fly-over. From the Rising Sun the train left the road on its own track, briefly re-appearing opposite the Crabtree pub and running between the Embankment and Laira railway yard.

THE GREAT WESTERN

Originally the South Devon Railway Co (which was taken over by the Great Western Railway in 1876) built a main line linking with the Bristol and Exeter, and so with the Great Western to London. It reached the northern end of the Embankment at Laira in 1849. The first Plymouth railway station was opened there and served the town until 1851, when the line into Plymouth was completed.

For a large part of the nineteenth century the Great Western Railway, created by Bristol merchants, and the London & South Western - originally the London & Southampton - fought for control of Plymouth shipping. The GWR originally planned to follow the line of the Embankment north of the Laira and to reach Sutton Harbour. But at the last moment it changed its mind and switched to the new dock at Millbay (Thomas Gill, the man who had built Millbay Pier and started the docks there in the first place, was also chairman of the South Devon Railway).

The GWR did get a route to Sutton Pool in 1851, using the route of the Plymouth and Dartmoor line from Crabtree to Sutton Pool. But as the GWR had a wide gauge rail laid outside the P&D width, and the line mixed both horse and steam as traction power, it was never very satisfactory, and quickly became just a GWR line. It remained in service until 1975.

LONDON & SOUTH WESTERN

The LSWR reached Friary in 1878. By the following year the LSWR had laid a line from Friary to North Quay, in Sutton Harbour, and the GWR., already on Coxside Creek by the old Plymouth & Dartmoor route, built a spur to reach North Quay as well.

The LSWR now saw hopes of competing with the GWR for Plymouth's seaborne trade. In 1879 they had built a line from their Devonport Station down the side of Stonehouse Creek (opening that up) to a deep water quay at Richmond Walk, Ocean Quay, to compete with the GWR at Millbay for the liner traffic. That year too they opened a branch line along the Cattedown shore. It reached the Passage House Inn in 1879 and a year or two later was down to Deadman's Bay.

THE TURNCHAPEL BRANCH

By 1887 the LSWR had built a railway bridge across the Laira, alongside Morley's road bridge. The railway bridge always looked a drab affair against the elegant Iron Bridge: it is described as 'the now familiar LSWR lattice girder bridge...each of the six sections butted together on five pairs of cross-braced tubular steel legs'. That year they opened a station at Plymstock. and by 1897 had extended the line to Oreston and Turnchapel, with a bridge across the entrance to Hooe Lake.

This had two latticed sections running out from either bank, and a central span pivotted in the centre. The central span, when opened, rested on dolphins on either side. It was operated by the Turnchapel signalman who, after telling the signalman at Plymstock, walked out on the bridge and opened the bridge by hand cranking. Regulations stated that he must always have in his possession a red flag, a hand signal lamp and fog signals. The bridge had to be closed half an hour

The Cattewater branch; a train of Esso trucks in the days before Conoco took over the Deadman's Bay waterfront from Esso.

before a train was due, and it was not allowed to be opened if it might delay a train. At night a signalman had to be on duty from one and a half hours before high tide, to one and half hours after, in case a vessel required passage (The lake was too shallow for any sizable craft to move except close to high tide).

GWR TO YEALMPTON

But the opening of the bridge across the Laira by the LSWR threw a panic into the GWR, who feared that their rivals would reach out across the South Hams to harm the GWR line to Torquay and

Dartmouth. So they got running rights across the Laira railway bridge to Plymstock Station and by 1898 had extended the line as far as Yealmpton. This line was an early victim of bus competition, and was closed in 1930. It reopened from 1941 to 1947 to help wartime traffic. All this meant a cat's cradle of railway lines beside the Plym, as the map shows.

END OF THE LINES

Apart from the main GWR line, all these ventures are now dead. Plymstock Station, which was

An engine emerges from the tunnel under the old Cattedown road close to Cattedown Wharfs; all the engines had spark guards on the funnels as the railway line passed through three oil tank farms.

actually just above the roundabout at Pomphlett, on the left-hand side of the dual carriageway from Plymouth, was shaped like a V, one wing serving the GWR line with a typical GWR canopy, and the other facing the LSWR Turnchapel line with no canopy. It was partially destroyed by a bomb in 1941 but roughly rebuilt. Turnchapel Station was completely destroyed when the oil tanks alongside were set ablaze in 1941. It too was restored.

During the war years the Yealmpton branch had its Plymouth terminal in Friary because the GWR bridge over the Embankment had been removed

(it had been too low to permit much road traffic underneath; its removal opened the Embankment as the main road into PLymouth, instead of the Laira-Alexandra road route previously used.]

But the Yealmpton branch died in 1947, and Turnchapel four years later. It was actually closed by a shortage of coal in January 1951, and when it was re-opened in July it had lost so many passengers to the buses that it closed altogether in September of that year. Hooe Lake bridge was demolished in October 1963. Laira railway bridge continued for a few more years to carry coal to Pomphlett cement works, and then butane gas for the Breakwater plant, but that died with the gas plant. No more trains crossed Laira rail bridge. Stamps Bridge, across the main road to Yealmpton, was demolished in May 1963 when the dual carriageway from the rebuilt Laira Bridge was constructed. The Pomphlett roundabout is now on the site of the bridge. Friary Station closed to passenger traffic in 1958 and the Tavistock line in 1963. The clay line finally died about 1950

KILLED BY THE BUSES

The passenger lines across the Laira were killed by the bus services which came in after World War I. In 1923 Devon Motor Transport Company started running to Plymstock. In 1928 there were bus services as far as Hooe, run by three more companies, Palace Saloons, Eddystone Motors and Hopper & Berryman. The latter took over Eddystone Motors in 1928 to become HB Buses; in 1929 Palace was taken over by the Western National, and in 1930 HB Buses were swallowed by Southern National. The 1930 Road Traffic Act required all bus services to be licensed, much of the old and quite often vicious competition between rival firms was ended, and in 1931 Western National took over Southern National. So they remained in a monopoly position. During World War II a joint service was provided with Plymouth Corporation, which in the 1967 boundary extension took control of both banks of the river.

But the important railway in the Cattewater story is the LSWR's line to its waterfront. It reached as far as the Passage House Inn in 1879-80. and Deadman's Bay by 1882. It was the spur to the building of quays on Cattedown waterfront, and a new surge of trade.

CHAPTER TWENTY-FOUR

FERTILISERS AND CHEMICALS

Apart from the sea and its associated trades, shipbuilding, sailmaking and ropemaking, Plymouth has no natural industries. But in the nineteenth century two sprang up, both with a chemical base. Soap-making first began in Millbay where Thomas Gill was quarrying the limestone and realised that it could be the source of the alkali used to produce soap. Then the interest of farmers in chemical fertilisers was aroused by the publication of *Elements of Agricultural Chemistry* by the Cornish chemist, Sir Humphry Davy, and the formation of the Royal Agricultural Society. The need for phosphates and nitrogen to encourage the growth of plants, began to be appreciated. An early source was guano, the droppings of seabirds on remote islands off the coast of Peru.

In spite of the growth of steamships, the long voyage around Cape Horn for guano and back was far more economical made in sailing ships, and Plymouth became a source of supply to the farmers of the West Country. Then Liebig published his book, *Organic Chemistry in Agriculture* and it was realised that these vital chemicals could be produced artificially.

NORRINGTONS

In both cases the Plymouth pioneers were farmers' sons. Charles Norrington was born on a farm at Lamerton, near Tavistock, and was quite young when he became interested in these new sciences. In 1846 he set up a factory on Commercial Wharf at Lambhay. He soon outgrew the cramped warehouses of the old victualling yard, and started a new factory at Cattedown. Norrington built his new factory on the floor of the quarry, alongside the old Cattedown quay. His factory site is now occupied by the Wallsend Industrial Estate. In 1859 the company was described as the Devon and Cornwall Manure Works and Patent Steam Bone Mills, supplying superphosphate of lime, bone dust, sulphuric acid and manure salt. They had agents at Cotehele and Morwellham.

Norrington was mayor of Plymouth three times, in 1863, 1864 and again in 1879. When his son died in 1877 he gave a carillon and Westminster chimes to St Andrew's Church; four years later when his wife died he built a fountain on Plymouth Hoe in her memory; where it still stands although long since dry. He was dogged by

Charles Norrington, from the Comet *of 1893.*

Robert Burnard, from the Comet of 1893.

tragedy; his second son died in 1881 and in his memory he gave an aisle to the church of St John Sutton-on-Plym. He himself survived until 1900 when he was described as one of Plymouth's greatest philanthropists. Fittingly enough his home in Seymour Road, Abbotsfield, is now a Salvation Army home.

BURNARD LACK & ALGER

Charles Burnard was another farmer's son, from Laneast on the edge of Bodmin Moor. He had begun making fertilisers at Millbrook in 1840 as a manager for Thomas Gill, the soap pioneer at Millbay. In 1854 he formed a partnership with J.W. Lack and the two started their own works at Lambhay Hill, as Norrington had done. In 1860 the firm was moved to Shepherd's Wharf on Coxside Creek. A plant for making sulphuric acid was established in 1872 at Cattedown, on the bed of the worked-out quarry behind Hill's shipyard. Then the partners began to build a new works alongside their acid works, just east of the Norrington plant and at the foot of the hill. This was finished in 1880 and the Coxside works abandoned.

In this time Mr Lack had been bought out and a new partner brought in, Mr W.H. Alger - the company was known as Burnard Lack & Alger before eventually becoming Burnard & Alger, or

the Plymouth Chemical Works. Ground up bones had long been used as a fertiliser but was slow working; treating with sulphuric acid produced the much faster-working super-phosphates. The supply of casked beef to the Royal Navy from Plymouth victualling yards had for a long time been a good source of bones in the town; now these new fertiliser factories had mills for grinding the bones and could make their own acid. Not that old sources of fertiliser were abandoned, for the company had a large guano warehouse and imports went on until World War I.

Burnard & Alger also undertook copper smelting, serving the great nineteenth-century copper mines of the Tamar Valley. Gold, silver, lead and zinc were also smelted - again using the firm's acid - and day and night shifts were worked. The 152 feet chimney of the smelter was a landmark. The firm was small beer alongside the giant smelters of Swansea, but they served a local need and in 1891 were producing basic slag, super-phosphates, and sixteen different kinds of fertilisers. In 1894 they were highly regarded as one of the earliest firms in chemical fertilisers, and had gained over five-hundred prizes all over the world.

Once the firm was established at Cattedown, Charles Burnard left management to his son Robert and to W.H. Alger. Burnard senior had been elected to the Town Council for the Sutton Ward in 1879, and was mayor in 1882. Now he concentrated his attention on local government work from his Mannamead home at Chatsworth, and also bought a house at Huccaby, on Dartmoor. Incidentally his partner, W.H. Alger, although not on the borough council, was invited to be mayor in 1885, and was so successful as to be invited to stay for a second year. Alger lived at 8 The Esplanade, on the Hoe.

A third acid and fertiliser plant was built between the other two, by James Gibb and Co.

A drawing of the fertiliser and acid works of Burnard & Alger from the Commercial Directory of the 1890s.

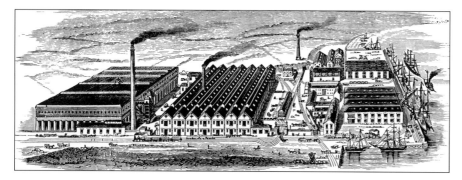

This was a large company with other works on the Thames River, at Bristol and at Cymbran. The Plymouth plant was established by 1870, with a manager.

FISONS

The Anglo-Continental Guano Company bought Gibbs in 1918 and Burnard & Alger a year later. Norringtons continued independently until 1934, when it was bought by National Fertilisers Ltd, a subsidiary of Fisons Packard & Prentice. In 1937 Fisons took over Anglo-Continental. So all three works came under one control. All the works were heavily damaged in the Blitz, and after the war the damaged buildings were all demolished and a new factory built on the Norrington site.

It was opened by Sir Clavering Fison in 1957, and by 1969 the output had been increased to 100,000 tons a year, employing 114 people. Partly-processed materials were imported from Immingham and Avonmouth, involving two or three ships a week and producing about one-third of the cargoes handled by Cattedown Wharfs. Then in 1981 Fisons decided to close three of its smaller works, including Cattedown, and 120 men were thrown out of work. The site was bought by Wallsend Properties, the buildings knocked down and within four years 75 per cent of the 13 acres had been let to fresh industries. who developed it as an industrial estate.

A separate firm, Independent Fertiliser (Solent) Ltd moved into Cattedown about 1989, renting units seven and eight from Cattedown Wharfs and beginning manufacture there. In 1993 they took over the former factory of Blight & White, and in 1994 were producing about 60,000 tons of fertiliser a year.

Across the water at Mount Batten is a limestone building with brick quoins, which carries the date 1834. Certainly this was employed towards the end of its life making fertiliser from fish.

A tinplate advertisement for Burnard & Alger's products, seen in 1996 in the Beamish Mining Museum in Co. Durham.

CHAPTER TWENTY-FIVE

CEMENT, SAND AND TIMBER

Building requires more than stone or brick. Also needed is cement, which is made from a mixture of limestone and shillet, both of which were found in the quarries on either side of the river, sand which used to come from the bed of the Laira, and timber which was imported over the Cattewater quays.

CALDWELL & ALMOND

When the waterside quarry in Deadman's Bay was worked back to Breakwater Hill and could go no further, the bed of the quarry was used for industry. The first factory set up was a cement works, where the eastern arm of Victoria Wharf now is. Under Caldwell & Almond, who were in business as early as 1850, this plant grew into a considerable factory. As the sea wall alongside the works was a retaining wall with no real depth of water, it could not be used to any great extent as a wharf. So they shipped their products from Millbay Docks, and later from Lockyer Quay in Sutton Harbour. In 1882 they had offices in Cambridge Street.

They had grown large enough by the 1890s to take the contract to supply all the cement used in the building of the dam at Burrator Reservoir.

Eventually they ceased manufacturing but remained merchants, bringing their cement in by sea. Their Deadman's Bay works became empty sheds, and in the early 1920s the tall chimney was blown up as being dangerous. After World War II Caldwell & Almond's simply became builders's merchants, with a base on North Quay, Sutton Harbour, on a site now occupied by Jewsons. They were finally taken over by M.A.C (Bristol) Ltd.

SALTRAM CEMENT WORKS.

This, the biggest industrial complex on the shores of the Plym, and worked by Blue Circle, is based on the extensive quarry on the Saltram side of the limestone ridge. The quarry has been opened in the last fifty years. It stretches from the back of Pomphlett Quarry (separated by a narrow ridge of untouched stone) nearly to Colesdown Hill at Billacombe. The western, worked out end is occupied by the cement works, and it is not intended to extend the quarry either towards the main road or Billacombe. The untouched fields on the road side have been given to the Billacombe Residents Association. On the Chelston Meadow side the quarrying is moving from limestone into

The Blue Circle Cement Works at Pomphlett in the 1970s, with the quarry which supplies its raw materials stretching out in the background.

shale, which provides both the requirements of cement. Quarrying will go on that side towards the Meadow, and it will also go deeper. The quarry was thought in 1995 to have a further life of 25 years, when the works will be dismantled, the site landscaped and the quarry allowed to fill with water to make a recreational feature. Blue Circle has a good record of restoring worked-out areas.

The Earl of Morley first sold the 208 acres of Pomphlett Farm to the Amey Roadstone Corporation. It was bought by Associated Portland Cement, now Blue Circle, in 1953. They built the cement plant in 1958-61. In 1963 a railway branch was built off the Turnchapel Line, just short of Plymstock Station, taken through a deep cutting specially cut in the quarry wall. At the same time the railway bridge over Embankment Road had to be replaced, to provide adequate strength to carry the bulk cement traffic. Originally a two-kiln plant, it was reduced to one, more efficient kiln in 1981.

40,000 tons of coal are used each year. Until the coal strike of 1984 it all came by rail over the bridge; now it arrives by road. Because the limestone is highly alkali, 100,000 tons of bauxite is shipped in each year from France, over Cattedown Wharfs. From this the 50-acre quarry produces 420,000 tons of cement a year, supplying the whole West of England by road and by sea to the Channel Islands. 130 people are employed.

A fire in the plant in 1993 caused £350,000 damage but the company responded by investing £3.8 million to repair the damage and improve efficiency. By the end of 1995 a total of £6m had ben spent on refurbishment. An export drive had increased sales by nearly 20 per cent. In May 4,000 tonnes of clinker was sent to the North of England, followed by 3,800 tonnes of cement for Ulster, and a regular cargo of 3,000 tonnes of cement began to Spain.

When the Prime Minister, John Major, opened a new control complex which brought the complete manufacturing process into one central remote control, in 1996, he was told that the works produced two to three million bags of cement each year.

CONCRETE

W. Maddock started making concrete blocks by hand in a yard off De la Hay Avenue, between Stuart Road and Alma Road. In 1945 he moved to a piece of empty ground off the Embankment, between the main railway line to Friary Station, the branch to Turnchapel and the end of Lanhydrock Road. When Mr Maddock died the business was taken over by Messrs Moon & Maynard. In 1973 they sold out to Amey Roadstone Corporation. They in turn sold the works in 1983 to Heywood Pavings Ltd of Newton Abbot.

Over the years machinery had been increasingly introduced until the yard was only turning out pre-cast concrete for making garden walls and pavings of all kinds. Heywoods now have a staff of 22, including Len Goodman who started there in 1953 in Maddock's day.

ARC, when they left the Embankment yard, set up a premix concrete works in Breakwater Quarry, on the western side of Pomphlett. They had been there since 1960, making concrete blocks, a business which had been started in the quarry by Plymstock Concrete. At one time ARC employed over thirty people; in 1995 they were only making concrete blocks and with improved mechanisation only employed ten.

SAND BARGES

Almost forgotten are the sand barges which once found a free supply on the banks in the Laira exposed at low tide between Crabtree and Saltram. These barges would sail up the river on the tide, anchor over the bank, and go aground as the tide dropped. Then the crew would clamber over the side with shovels and load the barge with sand washed down from the china clay works at Lee Moor.

When they had filled their craft, about twenty-five tons, the barge would sail down the river on the next high tide and into Sutton Harbour. There they would moor over the Sand Hard, behind the China House in Coxside Creek. As the tide fell, horses and carts would be driven to the side of the barge and the sand shovelled into the carts. It was used by local builders.

Lecturing in the Athenaeum in the 1890s, Robert Burnard estimated that fifty to a hundred thousand tons of sand had already been removed from the Upper Laira for building purposes. The practice did not end until the 1920s, when a couple of barges were still engaged in this business.

The sand barges which have loaded from the sand banks of the Laira unloading in Sutton Harbour. They would anchor at high water so that, when left high and dry by the retreating tide, horses and carts could come alongside and the sand be shovelled into the carts. A drawing by G. W. Cook.

TIMBER

The Plymouth & Oreston Company was founded by the Bayly family, the first member of which, John Bayly came as a boy of 14 to join his uncle Brabant, a merchant, and live with his family in Island House on the Barbican. That was in 1737; he eventually inherited Island House and a descendant still owns it and has a home there, over the information bureau, in the only Tudor house on the Barbican.

John Brabant Bayly went into business like his uncle. By 1771 he was also a timber and builder's merchant in Coxside. The family archives survive from that year, the oldest set of business records in Plymouth. He was rapidly supplying timber to most of the shipbuilders in the neighbourhood;

Isaac Blackburn of Turnchapel, Moore of Sutton Harbour, Banks of Stonehouse and Pope of Turnchapel, as well as to customers like Shepherd the woollen merchant on the other side of Coxside Creek and his brigs, the *Nancy*, the *Fleece*, the *Lily* and the *New Lamb*.

The Baylys dealt with Rosedew of Beechwood, who hired out the stage coach horses on the Exeter road, as well as Lord Morley and Boger, Lord Mount Edgcumbe's agent at Plympton. Their customers ranged far and wide, from Banfield in the Isles of Scilly to Chepstow (they once sent a cargo of St Petersburg deals there). Other customers were the local gentry, like Morshead of Widey, Bulteel of Flete, Henn-Gennys of Whitleigh, and people at Topsham, Modbury, Yealmpton, St Germans and Lostwithiel. In the

A photograph taken to show the LSWR passenger train crossing Hooe Lake Bridge to Turnchapel. It is also a graphic view of the Plymouth & Oreston Timber Company's timber yard behind the bridge.

long French wars the Baylys were making money by renting cellars at Coxside for storing cargoes from French prizes, like brandy from *L'Esperance* and the cargo of a Dutch East Indiaman. In 1787 they were buying mahogany from the wreck of the ship *Hector*, as well as timber from the wreck of the *Lady Edgcumbe* and from French prizes.

The wharf at the head of Coxside Creek still bears the name of Bayly's Wharf: the multi-storey car park serving the new fish market is now on the site. A surviving letter from the first John's son Robert, dated 3 August 1831, reports that his son John had just landed a cargo of American timber, and was that month receiving a cargo from Memel.

By 1844 the Baylys had timber ponds in Hooe Lake where logs for sleepers to be used on the South Devon Railway were seasoning. A Fox had

become a partner - the Plymouth Foxes, an offshoot of the important Falmouth family, were by now linked with the Baylys by marriage. Bayly & Fox in 1872 were asking the Queen's Harbourmaster if the Oreston end of the ferry to Turnchapel, which had gone straight across the entrance to Hooe Lake, could be moved nearer to Oreston village. This cleared it of the area where the partners were developing another timber yard.

In 1875 the business was renamed the Plymouth & Oreston Timber Company. The Oreston yard stretched from the southern houses of Oreston village along the waterfront into the narrow mouth of Hooe Lake and around to the shores of the lake. The Fox partner left the business in 1891 to start another timber yard in Millbay Docks with an Elliot. In the 1890s another Robert Bayly, now head of the family and playing a leading part in the public life of Plymouth, resolved the Council arguments over the site of a new water supply for the town by giving the land at Burrator on which the dam was built, and supplying the stone for its construction from Langshill Quarry, in which his yard was situated. The family was given to good works; Mary Bayly was the first woman magistrate in Plymouth and a granddaughter of the third Robert was Dame Agnes Weston, who founded the Sailors' Rests in Devonport and Portsmouth.

Ships bringing in timber from Scandinavia, Russia, Canada, and Brazil would pick up a buoy on the tier in the Cattewater. The timber would be secured in rafts and towed into Hooe Lake. Later quay walls were built at the entrance to Hooe Lake and smaller craft could lie alongside to unload. Rafting continued for the larger vessels, operated by stevedores called Skilton and Haskel. So much softwood was kept in the Hooe Lake timber ponds that at times boys would walk across the timber from one shore to the other.

Oreston became the main timber yard and sawmill of the company, with Coxside operating mainly as builders' merchants. The yard became a very big centre for treating softwoods with preservatives or pressure-treated creosote. Scandinavian spruce was treated in this way for telegraph poles, and all the railway sleepers for the Western Region of British Rail came from the yard. A special railway cutting from the Turnchapel line came into the yard, bringing in the iron chairs which were fixed to the creosoted sleepers, and then taking the finished sleepers out. The railway trucks also carried the creosoted telegraph poles. The railway link was not closed until October 1961.

In its heyday the yard employed over seventy men, and the Baylys were very paternal employers. A house opposite the end of Bayly Road, which leads from Oreston to the yard, is still

Rafts of timber left to season stretched from the 'pickle yard' of the Plymouth & Oreston Timber Company nearly across Hooe Lake to the village; an unofficial playground for neighbouring children as the pictures shows.

called the Library, and used to house the books which employees could borrow for a penny or so a week.

In 1919, at the end of World War I, the company was put up for sale. The published details said its Oreston Quay had a frontage of 830ft, was spread over ten acres with another six acres of foreshore used as timber ponds, and another six acres of cottages, gardens and pasture lands. Its main business was said to be railway sleepers, and at Oreston they had the only creosoting works within fifty miles. A 21 year lease was offered for £2,600 per annum. No sale seems to have been effected, and the company kept in business. In 1957 the company was merged with an expanding North Devon timber merchant to become Bayly Bartlett. Now that name has disappeared, the company has been taken over by Meyers, the parent company of Jewsons, and the Oreston yard was finally closed in 1992. Old people in the village still call it the Pickle Yard, because so much of the timber was pickled with creosote.

COLE BROTHERS

The other main timber firm in the Cattewater was Cole Brothers Ltd, whose offices and main yard were in Elliot Road, Cattedown. The firm was founded just after World War I by two brothers who are believed to have been connected with Fox Elliot, the timber merchants of Millbay Dock and Richmond Walk.

When my school friend George Burr (now of Solihull, whose memories provide much of the following information) joined the firm in 1932 there were three directors, Owen Cole of Chaddlewood and Stanley Cole of Plymstock, sons of one of the founders, and Mr W.J.Morgan. He had been secretary and was made a partner when the father of Owen and Stanley died, because of their youth..

Some timber from Archangel came in large vessels into Millbay. The Plymouth timber importers would share out the cargo, and Cole Brothers share would be loaded into coal trucks and moved by rail to their yard in Elliot Road, where they had their own siding. Most, however, came in over the firm's own wharf at Pomphlett, long known as Cole's Wharf. It was just behind the Morley Arms and close to Laira Bridge. There was just enough water at high tide for small ships

to berth, and very little at low tide: constant dredging was needed.

Every year eight or ten ships would arrive in the summer months, having sailed 'first open water' (when the ice cleared) from Sweden and Finland. They would bring in 450-500 tons of softwood, each vessel heavily laden with deck cargo. Nothing was packaged by size and each piece of timber had to be individually handled into crane loads for transport. When a ship berthed the company stevedores would engage the men to offload. They had heavy leather pads on their shoulders and would compete with each other as to how many pieces of timber they could carry, spring bouncing themselves down the gangways and up the planks to the top of the stacks. They had a slate at the Morley Arms for their beer (it was thirsty work) and would settle their score on being paid off when the ship was cleared. Then the captain would politely visit the office to receive his 'new hat', his tip for the load.

Originally the timber was transported across Laira Bridge to Elliot Road by horse-drawn pole wagons, not replaced by lorries until 1936-7. Once in the yard the cargo would be counted and sorted into stacks. There it would wait until wanted, in the saw mill or moulding mill, both in the yard. George Burr also remembers buying mahogany from a ship being broken up in Castle's yard.

After World War II, when air raids caused many fires in Cattedown, Cole Brothers were taken over by Reeves-Fox Elliot, which after another amalgamation became Graham Reeves and eventually disappeared from Plymouth.

CHAPTER TWENTY-SIX

GAS, ELECTRICITY AND OIL

By the 1820s the new factories of Plymouth had filled up the Coxside shore to the end of Sutton Road, the head of Coxside Creek. So later industries had to spread further out, towards Deadman's Bay, and the thoroughfare was called Commercial Road. One of the new industries was making gas.

Both a Plymouth Oil Gas Company in Woolster Street and a United Gas Company in Mill Bay were started in 1823, but in 1845 they were replaced by a Devonport company and the Plymouth & Stonehouse Gas Co. which set up business on the shore side of Commercial Road.

For over a century this plant was to supply Plymouth with gas for street and house lighting, cooking, and industry. Eventually its gas holders multiplied and spread south to the entrance to Deadman's Bay Quarry and close to the bay itself.

BREAKWATER GAS

With nationalisation the Plymouth gas works came under the control of the South West Gas Board. In the 1960s, after the completion and successful operation of a plant at Avonmouth making domestic gas from oil, a similar 'oil reforming' plant was built at Plymouth by the British Gas Corporation.

Breakwater Quarry was bought from E.C.C. Quarries and Devon County Council. Twenty-five acres of quarry waste, varying in depth from twenty to sixty feet, had to be cleared - over 600,000 tons in all - as well as 2,000 tons of scrap iron in one corner, plus the blasting and removing of 60,000 tons of limestone from a promontory in the middle of the site. In November 1965 construction began of the £3 million space-age plant, and Phase One began supplying gas in 1967. This could deliver 20 million cubic feet of gas a day into the supergrid pipeline under construction to serve the whole of the board's area. Breakwater was already producing twice the capacity of the conventional gas plant at Coxside, and two more phases were planned.

The light distillate oil was delivered at Cattedown Wharfs by 10,000 ton tankers, and thence pumped by a pipe laid five feet under the bed of the Cattewater to Hooe Lake Quarries. South West Gas had bought the quarry from the Ministry of Defence (whose oil tanks on the site had been destroyed in the war) and British Rail. Another pipeline took the oil under Hooe Lake and thence along the back of Oreston to the plant in Breakwater Quarry.

More liquified butane gas was delivered by British Rail tankers to Plymstock station, at the

The futuristic plant in Breakwater Quarry which made domestic gas from oil; it came on stream in 1966 and was almost at once made obsolete by the discovery of North Sea gas. Finally closed in 1985, it was demolished in 1989.

head of Pomphlett Lake, and again piped underground to Breakwater.

By the time the plant was completed, North Sea gas had been discovered, which was to revolutionise the industry. By 1974, just eight years after it first delivered gas, the closure of Breakwater works was under consideration. But there was a need for more gas during peak hours, and so in 1975 the plant was converted to making substitute natural gas, from naphtha. The naphtha was still brought in to Cattedown Wharfs and piped under the river. There were only half a dozen such plants in Britain, and the conversion was supervised by Peter Hannah, who had originally been a shift engineer. The work completed, he became group works engineer for

both Breakwater and Avonmouth, with a workforce of about eighty at Plymouth. By 1984 Breakwater was mentioned in the Guinness Book of Records as the largest gasworks in the United Kingdom, producing 50 million cubic feet a day. But increasingly the plant was only used to boost production at peak times.

By late 1984 with more offshore gas fields coming on stream, it was really becoming re-dundant. That winter, with record low temperatures, it was needed to work at peak production for a longer period than ever before. But it finally closed at the end of March 1985.

The Breakwater plant, the gleaming, futuristic, demonstration of new technology, was demolished in 1989. That year British Gas South Western built a £5 million operational control centre for the Plymouth and Cornwall Districts on the Breakwater site, together with a major appliance store.

NAPHTHA AND TAR

Soon after the opening of the first gas works in 1845, a naphtha works was started nearby on the shores of Deadman's Bay, just south of the cement works.

Naphtha, an oil used for lighting purposes, was a by-product of making gas from coal. By 1877 the building had been taken over by William Harvey's tar distillery, making another gas by-product. Over the years the distillery grew in the strip of land, 140 feet wide and 850 feet long, between the sea and the quarry face.

When William Harvey retired his daughter ran the business for some years. Eventually it became a subsidiary of the Plymouth gas company. A report and photograph in the *Gas Journal* of 1927 shows that the works had two chimney stacks at the southern end, one of which served the steam engine supplying power. About two and a half

Plymouth tar distilleries in Deadman's Bay, an illustration from Gas Journal *of 12 October 1927. The tar was a by-product of coal gas and the company a subsidiary of Plymouth and Stonehouse Gas Co Ltd.*

million gallons of crude tar were received each year from the gas companies of Devon and Cornwall, either in railway tankers or barrels. From this was made road tar, creosote, various chemicals and some 50,000 gallons of motor benzole and white spirits. The bulk of the road tars was sent out in barrels, of which a stock of 12,000 was needed. Four coopers were employed keeping them in repair.

On nationalisation the works were taken over by the South Western Gas Board to become Plymouth Tar Distillers Ltd, a company wholly owned by the Board. J.W.Dean was one of the original directors and eventually manager of all the Board's tar companies. He was a Cattewater Commissioner and its chairman for sixteen years before he retired in 1979.

Within living memory it was possible to walk below the Deadman's Bay quay to Victoria Wharf at low tide, but there was a little dock to enable small bulk tankers to land supplies.

The distillery was eventually taken over by yet another national company and then closed down in 1970-1. The whole waterfront occupied by the tar works and quay was taken over by Esso, who used part of the plant to manufacture bitumen, the modern road-surfacing material made from petroleum.

ELECTRICITY: THE POWER STATION

In the twentieth century electricity was to challenge gas as the main source of light, heat and power, but its introduction to Plymouth came for another reason. The Three Towns had had horse-drawn trams since 1872 but in the 1890s there was a new fashion for go-ahead towns: electric trams. Plymouth Corporation got its Act of Parliament to introduce them in 1896; in 1898 they began building a power station on the shores of the Cattewater, just south of Martin's Wharf and a four-road car shed to house 28 trams nearby, in River View at the corner of the new council house development. This was to remain the main tram depot until 1922.

The electric trams started service on 22 September 1899. Rails linked the depot to the Prince Rock terminus - where the Exeter road leaves Laira Bridge Road. The first electric tram service in the Three Towns then ran along Embankment Road, Tothill Road, Beaumont Road and Ebrington Street to Drake Circus and Market Avenue - the rest of the route to Derry's Clock - or Theatre, as the main terminus was always called - had not been finished. (A standard query in Plymouth was 'where is THE ATRE?' from the destination board on trams. And Devonport trams later on were said to go to FOREST.)

Electric street lighting followed almost at once for the main streets, and on the Hoe one can still find the original standards (similar to those which carried the overhead wires for the trams) with the date 1898 on the base. Most streets in the town remained gaslit, attended by the lamplighter with his pole, until the 1930s.

The power station came into action the first day the trams ran, supplying them with 550 kilowatts direct current. It could initially supply 200 kilowatts alternating current for lighting and power. Over the years this was steadily built up,

The electricity power station at Prince Rock first opened in 1899 to drive the electric trams, steadily increased in size and capacity over the years and finally closed in 1974 as being uneconomic.

all output changed to a/c, and in 1935 was joined up with the national grid. By 1945 the supply was up to 64,000 kw., and Station B. was started in 1948. The building of this was taken over by the British Electrical Authority when the system was nationalised in April 1948, and was finally commissioned in 1951. Its initial capacity was 90,000 kw. By 1952 the output was up to 100,000 kw., and by the time the second phase was completed in 1960 reached 220,000 kw. A far cry

from the designed output in 1899 0f 800 kw. Coal and later on oil to drive the dynamos came in both by sea and by rail. The redbrick buildings with their two chimney stacks - Station B was 300 feet high - were a local landmark.

But such was the march of technology that both Plymouth stations, after being steadily run down for a number of years, finally closed in 1974. They were kept on standby for some years, then finally phased out in 1981 and demolished early in the

1990s. For just a few years the two new power giants, the electricity station with its giant chimneys and the gas plant with its high-tech super-modern appearance, stood opposite each other on the banks of the Cattewater. By 1992 both had completely disappeared.

PETROLEUM PRODUCTS

As early as 1875 the Admiralty agreed that petroleum could be landed at Cattedown, but insisted that only 250 gallons at a time should be handled. Petrol was controlled by the Explosives Act and was regarded as dangerous. But natural security barriers had been created by the two roads across Cattedown. Quarrying had gone right up to the edge of the roads on either side, so that they had a perpendicular cliff face on both sides which formed natural walls to serve as enclosures.

In 1893 Cattedown Wharfs established two oil tanks behind their wharfs, so that oil could by pumped ashore from tankers as well as landed in barrels. That year the first oil company established in Plymouth, the Anglo-American company, had an oil store in Deadman's Bay Quarry. In 1900 the first motor bus to challenge the new trams was the short-lived Plymouth Motor Company, running from Derry's Clock to Salisbury Road, serving the new and fast-growing suburb of Lipson. The first private car was brought to Plymouth by F.H.Pearce in 1901..

Early on Shell were bringing in their white spirit supplies by rail, and selling it in two-gallon cans. In 1898 the steamer *Potomac*, drawing nearly 25 feet of water, was the first large vessel to use the newly-dredged Cattedown berth to unload 5,000 gallons of oil. By 1901 Cattedown Wharfs were also quoting wharf rates for unloading oil per barrel. By 1911-12 petroleum imports through the Cattewater reached 16,000 tons a year. Soon after

The various grades of petroleum products are all piped ashore from tankers at Cattedown Wharfs and delivered to the companies concerned, Esso, Shell, BP and Conoco. The pipes are conveyed across the roads by gantries, illustrated here.

World War I the total was 23,000 tons. In the late 1920s the major oil companies reached an agreement whereby Cattedown Wharfs became the major oil terminal for Plymouth. In 1929-30 the wharfs modernised their pumping system, which could now deliver 2,500 gallons an hour. Esso built a pipe line into Deadman's Bay Quarry, tunnelling through the protective rock screen, and both Shell and BP linked their storage tanks in the same way. Nowadays each company has several pipelines carrying the different grades of petroleum products.

By 1931-2 Shell Mex could store 7,900 tons of oil, BP 8,300 (another 5,000 was added in 1938) and Anglo-American 10,600. Imports increased all through the 1930s. In 1939, the last year before the war and petrol rationing, 135,541 tons of petroleum products flowed over Cattedown Wharfs, an increase of 850 per cent since 1911.

The wharfs in 1972 created a deepened berth at the west end for tankers, with a complex of five marine discharge arms erected to produce the most speedy clearing of tankers. The major oil companies have modernised their plant over the years, and all now have reduced the dangers of evaporation and fire by introducing floating roofs to their tanks. Supplies come from Shell's refinery at Shellhaven and BP's from the Isle of Grain

Industries old and new' petrol tankers parked in front of a limestone quarry face.

refinery, both on the Thames estuary. Esso is supplied by Fawley. on Southampton Water.

Since 1993 over a million tons of oil have been imported every year into Plymouth. Tankers of up to 20,000 tons come up harbour to berth at Cattedown, though the depth of water available limits their cargo to 14,000 tons. Petroleum products now provide the largest tonnage of any commodity moving in or out of the port, and supplies 95 per cent of the needs of Devon and Cornwall.

ESSO

Anglo-American, a company formed in 1888, was the first foreign affiliate of Standard Oil, the American giant created in 1870 by John D. Rockefeller. Anglo-American was in Plymouth within a year after the formation of the company. There had been a petroleum store in the quarry in 1877, and the company still uses a tank built there in 1898 to store diesel. Other firms had petroleum stores in Plymouth at the time, Thomas's in 1888, Bear Creek and James Brothers the next year.

Anglo-American had been retailing petrol for road vehicles since 1896 as Pratts (named after a founder member of the company). In 1934 the petrol brand name was changed to Esso, although Pratts was the name used for their lubricating oil until the 1950s. In 1951 the company changed its name to Esso (the phonetic spelling of the initials of Standard Oil, which by then had been broken down into a number of smaller companies, such as Texaco, Mobil and Gulf under United States anti-trust laws.

In 1995 Plymouth was the only Esso depot west of Southampton and Avonmouth. At one time it distributed its products throughout the West by rail, but now it is all moved by road tankers, through fully automated loading pumps. The Esso depot in Plymouth does supply petrol of British standard to other linked companies. Until twelve

years ago Deadman's Bay Quarry also housed the Esso records office for the whole of Britain.

Regent, marketed by a partnership of Texaco and Standard Oil, had a base in Cattedown from the 1930s until it was absorbed completely by its major partner, Texaco.

SHELL and BP

The first Shell tanker carrying bulk supplies came up the river in 1921. By 1924 Shell had established the largest of its seven depots on the Cattedown Quarry floor, bounded on the east by Oakfield Terrace Road. In 1925 they began building another depot across the road from Cattedown Wharfs. BP had built its storage and distribution centre at Prince Rock by 1927, on the other side of Oakfield Terrace Road. In 1929-30 Shell built a 5,000 gallon tank. In 1931-2 Shell and BP amalgamated for selling, storage and transport purposes, and their two depots were linked. The process was completed in 1967 when the two companies decided to to establish a joint storage and distribution centre. The Shell No One site on Oakfield Terrace was used, and over a period of three years the 30 feet high tanks were replaced with ten new storage tanks double the height, providing a total capacity of 15 million tons of white spirit (petrol and diesel oil). This opened in 1972, when work began on an another joint 8 million storage plant for black oil, just across the road from Cattedown Wharfs.

National Benzole, which used a great deal of benzine, made from coal, in its petrol, had a depot in Cattedown from the 1930s until the late 1950s, when they were absorbed by the parent company.

CONOCO

When South West Gas ended Breakwater's working life and finished importing oil for gas,

Conoco (the American-based Continental Oil Company, which supplies Jet petrol) moved into Plymouth. Early in 1970 they leased the Hooe Lake Quarry tanks.

On 9 April that year one of the underground storage tanks exploded, burning for hours and threatening the other two, as well as leaking oil into Hooe Lake. Two hundred people were evacuated from nearby houses and not for eleven days was it deemed safe to let them return.

There was violent local opposition the following November when Conoco applied to re-licence its tanks. This was eventually granted for a limited period, and in 1970 Conoco acquired part of the tar distillery waterfront on Deadman's Bay, building a number of storage tanks there. Their operation moved across the river in 1972.

BUNKERING

Ships nowadays require oil, not coal, for their bunkers, and Allantone Supplies keep a barge, the *Onward Mariner*, on call 24 hours a day in the port. She draws her supplies from Conoco, sometimes straight over the quay alongside their tanks, handling about 30,000 tonnes a year. Her services are required, on average, about half a dozen times a day, mainly to ships in the Sound.

CHAPTER TWENTY-SEVEN

IRON MINING
AND FARM MACHINERY

Almost forgotten is the existence of the shafts of an old iron mine, on the grassy area between Turnchapel and Mount Batten. For most of the century it has been inside the air station perimeter and so unknown. Spoil heaps from the shafts can be seen under the grass from across the river, and the shafts are near the cliff edge at the corner of St Johns Road, Turnchapel.

The Earl of Morley gave a licence on 1 April 1839 to William Conway of Plymouth to search for iron ore in Mount Batten field. It was not an All Fool's joke, for on 8 August the first shipment of 56 tons of ore went off to a smelting house at Neath, South Wales. Cargoes continued until 1841 but little payment came back because so little iron was extracted. Two cargoes were sent back, 'refused not being ore but rubbish'. That year it was said that there were 600 tons of ore 'of good quality' standing on the quays. Clay, taken out in open heads, was reported as being equally suitable for potting or brick-making, and several thousand tons were awaiting sale on the premises.

The mine, Wheal Morley, was abandoned in 1844, but in 1873 another optimist, Richard Moore of Plymouth, took a licence for 21 years. But Moore was dead within six months, and in 1877 his widow sold the lease to B.B.Hussey and W.D.Mann of Torquay. An advertisement of the sale in the *Miner's Journal* said that a shaft had been sunk about seven fathoms deep, 100 yards from the quay. It opened on a lode seven feet in width from which 40 to 50 tons had been brought to grass. The ore consisted of a brown haematite yielding 57 per cent of metallic iron. The plant was a 14 hp steam engine, an 8 ton Cornish boiler and the necessary drying sheds. Planning to work the property on a large scale, the new partners tried to get better terms from the Earl of Morley, but the railway was by that time proposed for Turnchapel and Lord Morley had high hopes for the area's development. Letters flowed between owner and developers from 1874 to 1893 - 'increasingly vituperative', says Owen Baker, who unearthed part of the story from the Saltram papers - and then the project ended.

AGRICULTURAL MACHINERY

A waterside site for a factory manufacturing agricultural machinery may seem a little odd. But until 1935 the site in Laira Bridge Road, at present occupied by the Western National Bus depot, housed the large factory of Davey, Sleep and Co. It was well-chosen, however, alongside the railway lines of both the GWR and later the LSWR, on the edge of a large industrial town with a considerable engineering work force trained in the Dockyard, and on the route that many farmers would have taken going to market.

The founder of these Excelsior Works, William Sleep, was born in 1837. He was an orphan at the age of ten and started work on a farm near Mevagissey. After a year or two he was apprenticed to the local blacksmith, who in those days would not just have shod horses but repaired the iron machinery used on the neighbouring farms. Sleep taught himself to read and write, moved to another blacksmith when he had completed his articles, and in their employ brought out a new pattern plough. He began applying himself to improving farm machinery.

By 1892 he had been in his factory close to Laira Bridge long enough to have won over three thousand medals and prizes for his machinery. In 1892 he won first and second prize at a trial organised at Warwick in conjunction with the Royal Agricultural Society for turnwrest ploughs. Sleep also produced improved versions of rakes, cultivators, rollers, cutters, elevators, cake breakers and whippletrees - which like swingletrees were fitted to both carriages and ploughs and gave the horse freedom to move its shoulders. All his products were designed to be drawn by horses.

After World War I the managing director of the firm was Richard Priest, who was followed in the

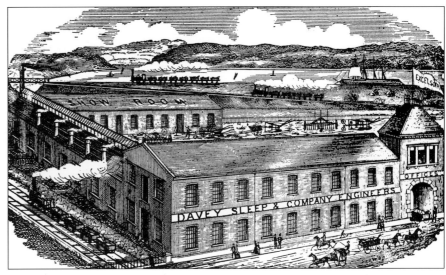

1920s by his son, W.H.J. Priest, renowned as the youngest ever Mayor of Plymouth in 1927-8. A fire virtually destroyed the factory in 1923, but it was restored.

In 1935 the business was amalgamated with that of Bickles, another engineering firm and moved to Millbay, where the new company was taken over by Willoughbys, the shipbuilders and repairers in Millbay Docks. Now both Willoughbys and Bickles have disappeared. Western National, formed in 1929, built their garage next door to the Excelsior Works in 1930 and when Davey Sleep moved in 1935, they took over the whole site and replaced the old works with their garages. The bus company is still there.

An 1890s drawing of Davey Sleep's agricultural implement works at Prince Rock; notice the three railway lines passing the factory and the farming machinery in the courtyard. The site is now occupied by the Western National garage.

A portrait of William Sleep, founder of the works.

CHAPTER TWENTY-EIGHT

CHELSTON MEADOW AND PLYMOUTH RACES

The fashionable and the unfashionable at Plymouth Races in 1885, observed by the artist of the Western Figaro.

Opened in the same year as Laira Bridge was the Morley Arms, the pub on the Pomphlett side. It was built by the Earl in fine cut limestone and it is tempting to think that James Meadow Rendel also designed it. The family did not sell it until 1923 to the Octagon Brewery (now owned by Courage).

Probably a great deal of trade was brought here by Plymouth Races. These had started at Crabtree in 1824, in the flat field now occupied by Sainsbury's store at Marsh Mills. In 1828 the meeting was moved to Chelston Meadow. It was the year after the opening of the bridge, which made an easy approach for Plymothians. As the enclosure had only been completed in 1817 the ground must have dried out remarkably quickly. Lord Morley was the moving spirit: his father had been a great breeder of horses and one of his foals, Saltram, won the Derby in 1783. The next year he gave up the sport and the Prince of Wales bought many of his horses. Either his son shared his father's interest in the sport, or he saw a way of making money to pay for all his expensive developments, like the meadow and the bridge.

The Plymouth, Stonehouse and Devonport Races were held for three days in the first week of August. An oval course running right around the perimeter of the reclaimed land was laid out. It was about a mile and a half long, with the grandstand near the Pomphlett approach. In its early days the main race was for a cup given by Queen Victoria, worth a hundred guineas. From Whitfeld's description in his *History of Plymouth* it sounds like a local Derby Day, with peers in their four-horse carriages with glittering outriders, booted grooms and powdered lackeys, and dashing equipages from nearby country houses. There was the other side, glib quacks and cheapjacks, flashy gambling tents with showy women and harpies at the door, flaring lamps, 'vice clad in a hundred allurements'. Eventually Queen Victoria withdrew her cup, and (says the Liberal and probable Methodist Whitfeld in his 1900 history), 'the meeting began to go downhill'.

Even so, in 1882, when the meeting was down to two days and raced on August 23 and 24, the chairman was Admiral Parker of Cornwood, with Mr Mildmay and Mr Bulteel among the stewards. There may have been no Queen's Cup but there were five races each day, opening with the Licensed Victuallers Plate. In 1891 the two day meeting was on September 2 and 3. The stewards now included the Earl of Morley, Mr Coryton and Mr Clark of Efford Manor, plus senior officers of the Services, and was attended by two regimental bands. Now they could boast that 'excursion trains will run'; public entrance was 6d and a carriage and four paid a guinea. A Race Day Steamer, a paddlewheel excursion boat, ran a special service each day from Saltash to the quay off the Morley Arms, calling at North Corner, Mutton Cove, Millbay Pier and the Promenade Pier (opened in 1884). Racing finally ended in 1926 (the author can remember watching a late meeting from the field then at the end of Mount Gould Road).

AN AIRPORT?

In 1923 the idea that air travel would attract business to the city was being mooted. The *Western Morning News* and *Western Independent* together arranged two experimental flights from Chelston Meadow, carrying mails which had just been landed from liners in the Sound. There was much debate about creating a municipal airfield. Sir Alan Cobham pioneered flights from Roborough, and then Staddon Heights was advocated as a site. But the polo field at Roborough was chosen in 1930, Chelston being regarded as too boggy.

USE AS A TIP

Chelston Meadow was more or less neglected until 1961, when Plympton Rural Council obtained a compulsory purchase order on the land for use as a tip. In the same month Plymouth City Council bought the land from Lord Morley for development as playing fields. The argument over ownership dragged on for a couple of years until a joint ownership agreement was reached, and tipping began in 1964. Saltram Farm on the edge of the park was still occupied, as were a row of cottages in the other corner of the meadow. The racecourse grandstand, which had survived the 1939-45 war, had gone but the winning post still stood.

In 1967 Plymouth boundaries were extended to take in Plympton Rural District, solving the ownership problem. Then in 1974, when Plymouth was reduced to district council status, Devon County took over ownership and management of the Meadow. In 1992, when the Conservative Government was demanding the privatisation of many local government functions, Devon Waste Management Ltd (in which the County Council was still the major shareholder) took over all Devon's tips. In 1995, it was estimated that the meadow, whose level had already been raised some thirty feet by tipping, had another seven years life. With landfill sites increasingly hard to find, the company began to pursue a policy of waste recycling and its biggest centre was established at Chelston Meadow. Green waste is composted; other waste such as tins, paper and cloth are separated and recycled for further use.

Private people are encouraged to use the recycling centre for their waste products, and a Visitor Centre at the entrance to the site was opened in 1995.

An advertisement in the Western Figaro *of 1885 for Plymouth Races.*

CHAPTER TWENTY-NINE

THE OPENING OF PRINCE ROCK

Anyone who walked from Cattedown Corner down to the Passage House Inn on the shores of the Cattewater in 1880 would have seen a forest of factory chimneys on his right hand, but a wilderness of bumps and humps and nearly worked-out quarry floors on his left. Industry had flowed out from Coxside for much of the century to fill the nearest areas of Cattedown, but got no further than this road. There was not even a road across the downs to the east until one got to a track leading down to Prince Rock quarries, the present Elliot Road, and this petered out at the top of the quarry face. Further east Laira Bridge Road had been built at the same time as the bridge, to link up with Embankment Road.

TOWN BUYS LAND

In February 1894 Plymouth Corporation paid John F. Soltau £23,000 for 70 acres of land at Prince Rock, on both sides of the GWR's Sutton Harbour Branch. North of the railway (now Gdynia Way) they built the town's first 'houses for the working classes' (see Chapter 26). South of the line the area reached right down to the waterfront. The next year they bought for £22,100 still more land from A.J.P.Newcombe, who had bought the Prince Rock

quarries from Lord Graves. This put the Corporation in control of all the land between the waterfront and the quarry faces, from Laira Bridge Road to Cattedown Road. There were just a few pockets in this area still in private hands, like Martin's Wharf and other odd stretches at Prince Rock.

A large part of this land was used for building the electric power station and Corporation Wharf on the foreshore. The grandiose idea was that this quay would handle coal for the power station and also be used by the new factories that would spring up on the Council land. But the other wharf owners on the river fought the Corporation over this new wharf, and eventually the Act of Parliament that authorised the wharf only allowed coal to cross the wharf, and no charging of tolls. So in 1908 the Corporation put the land up for lease.

ACHESON COLLOIDS

One of their first tenants was an American firm, Acheson Colloids. Dr Edward Acheson, an American scientist and a protege of Thomas Edison, had discovered and developed silicon carbide and a way of making graphite

Dr Edward Acheson, founder of Acheson Colloids.

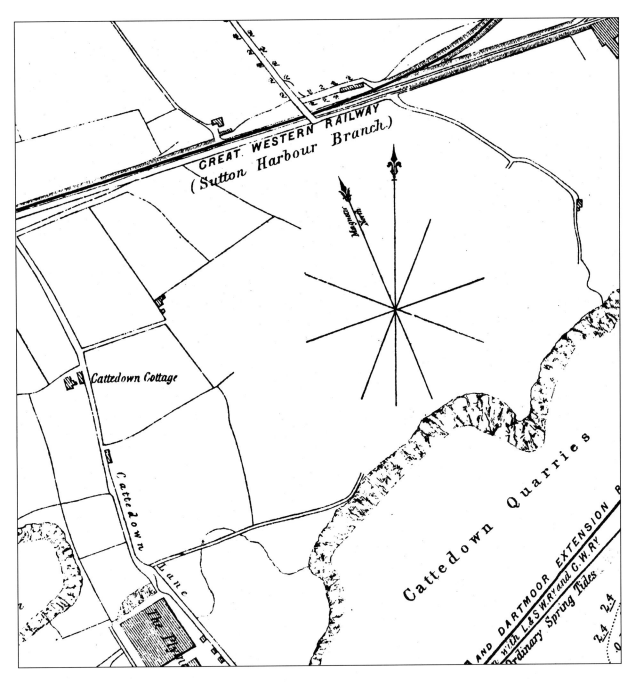

Prince Rock and Cattedown from a harbour plan of 1877, showing how undeveloped Prince Rock was at that date.

synthetically in an electric furnace. This graphite was used originally as a non- greasy lubricant, but since then a mass of new uses has been found, from coating non-stick frying pans to forging jet engine blades.

To protect his patents Dr Acheson decided to set up manufacturing bases throughout Europe, and sent over a young engineer, Fernley Banbury, to locate sites for these plants. Plymouth offered real advantages for the United Kingdom plant; it had soft water, low rates, was a Channel port and was served by two railways. What may have tipped the scales in Plymouth's favour was that Banbury trained as an engineer in Cornwall and at Bickles, in Plymouth, and married a Bickle daughter.

The Plymouth establishment briefly closed down on the outbreak of war in 1914, when all its employees went off into the Forces, but was soon back in business. Its name, Oildag, roused suspicions in the police; it had a German ring, and they came investigating. Acheson replied furiously; the *Western Morning News* wrote a leader defending the company, and all was forgotten. A young son, George Acheson, was appointed to manage the Plymouth plant and he lived with his new English bride near the Prince Rock factory. It was an experimental as well as a manufacturing plant, and by the end of the war was the only Acheson factory in Europe.

It is still on the same site, though it has been enlarged and rebuilt a number of times, and is now one of many such plants throughout the world. In 1966 it had a payroll of 120, but like most other industries, by 1995 it had a larger output although its workforce was reduced to 65. The company has three manufacturing units in Europe as well as an equipment unit, and the plant at Schiedam, in northern Holland, has replaced Plymouth as the company's biggest manufacturer in Europe. Plymouth still has a large research and development role in the worldwide company, but again the major role in this field has moved to Holland. It remains the 'centre of excellence' for products used in forging aircraft engines and turbine blades, in heat treatment for engineering purposes, and for chemical products.

In 1992-4 the Plymouth general manager was a fourth generation Acheson, Michael. He had been born in England, and his son Max was born during Michael's stay in Plymouth. It is extremely rare for an American company to remain in family hands until the fourth generation.

MORE DEVELOPMENT

By 1915 the Corporation had built an incinerator with a tall chimney just west of the power station; at times it supplied steam to the power station. It was not demolished until the late 1940s, when the new power station, Prince Rock B, needed the site. By 1920 the timber yard of Cole Brothers (see Chapter 25) was established across the road from Acheson Colloid, and soon after the glass and paint works of Newton & Andrewartha was built near the bridge over the railway line. Its rather grand facade still faces across what is now called Cattewater Road, and has become part of Faraday Mill.

By the time these factories were being built, Oakfield Terrace Road had been built at the eastern end of the terraces south of the railway line, and continued south to the waterfront. The old rough track at the end of Elliot Road had been extended between Acheson Colloid and Andrewartha to the western side of the power station, and was eventually called Faraday Road, in honour of the great English pioneer in the development of electricity as a source of power. A road was built parallel to the waterfront which linked the bottom of Faraday Road and Oakfield Terrace Road to Cattedown Road, called Maxwell Road.

In the 1920s a number of small firms had opened up in the area, a mangle manufacturer, offal works and a knacker's yard where horses were slaughtered. The charitable dog's and cat's home also opened, roughly on the site it still uses opposite Faraday Mill. One of the biggest of the new firms was Lomas Gelatine, opened on the waterfront by 1920 just west of the incinerator.

LOMAS GELATINE

Lomas was started in 1915 as a sideline in the Brown Wills & Nicholson food factory in Finewell Street (see chapter Thirty). It was a way of using up the bones left over from the making of the

various food products, and made glue among other things. It moved at the end of the war to Millbrook, but by 1920 was on the Cattewater waterfront. It was called 'Lomas Gelatine', and gelatine is a substance obtained by extraction from animal bones. Its top quality can be used in making a variety of products, from jellies to capsules for the pharmaceutical industry, its lowest quality makes glue. Lomas called its product Prince Rock Glue and marketed it very successfully.

Bones came in by lorry, train and barge. They were rendered down to remove fat and meat. The fats separated were sold as tallow to soap manufacturers (there were two soap factories in

An 1985 aerial view of Prince Rock, showing how it had filled up. The photograph was taken to show the building of Gdynia Way (which runs down the centre of the picture) on the line of the old Plymouth and Dartmoor railway.

Plymouth, one in Coxside and another in Millbay). The meaty material went as animal feed or fertilisers (and again there were fertiliser factories close by, in Cattedown). Then the cleaned bones were put under pressure in hot water, to make glue, and there were also two kilns (long demolished) into which what was left behind was calcinated to ash for use in bone china. Nothing left to waste!

In 1928 Lomas were taken over by the British Glue and Chemical Company, which was still producing glue, fats and fertiliser materials until the 1970s.

OFFENSIVE SMELLS

Between Lomas and the refuse incinerator was a collection point for pig swill, started in 1940 to save importing so much animal feeding stuffs. About 700 tons a month was collected, plus another 170 tons from Service establishments, and to this was added blood and meat offal from the abattoirs, yeast from local brewers and fish offal. At Prince Rock were the premises of Deacons, the tripe dressers and offal merchants, who also took in bones and produced sausage skins.

Cattedown could now boast acid works, manure works, guano companies, glue works, incinerators, pig swill dump, knacker's yard and tripe dressers; all sound offensive. As early as 1875 a public meeting was called in Plymouth to protest at the effluvia from Cattedown. It penetrated as far as Mutley, said some speakers, and certainly the stink was evident a mile north in the writer's childhood - the Cattedown glue works were always blamed. The Lomas works even had to have a licence under the Offensive Trades Act. The general view was that Cattedown, isolated and remote, was a dump into which any offensive or unsocial industrial activity could be pushed.

A nonagenarian who grew up in South Milton Street describes the smell vigorously: 'Tar from the works near the Breakwater pub, the choking fumes from the sulphur works, and the stench of the burning bones from the manure works, forerunners of Fisons'.

BETWEEN THE WARS

In the inter-war years the Corporation owned all the land from the fertiliser plants at Cattedown to Prince Rock, from the waterfront back to the cliff edge to the quarries. During the 1920s and 1930s the oil tank farms of Shell-Mex and BP expanded. On the waterfront there were Hocking Brothers, boat repairers; and Castles ship-breaking. The printers, Clark Doble & Brendon built an entirely new plant in Oakfield Terrace Road which they called the Oakfield Press.

In the 1920s Plymouth Oxygen Co. Ltd opened up in a site close to the railway and the waterfront. They were quickly taken over by British Oxygen, in 1928, who moved to the present site of the company in Maxwell Road in 1938.

A new factory, built on the site by A.N.Coles in 1950, is still in use. When BOC took over the Plymouth company had 400 customers to whom they delivered a very limited number of industrial and medical gases; today BOC is supplying over 7,000 customers with something like 150 different gases. It is a world-class company strongly established across Europe, the United States and the Americas, Asia, including a big organisation in China, Australia and New Zealand.

But for much of the interwar years behind the occupied waterfront, between the fertiliser plants at the back of the Cattedown Wharfs and the power station, apart from the Shell-BP petrol tanks, there were just the deserted and worked-out quarry floors.

CHAPTER THIRTY

INDUSTRIAL ARRIVALS AFTER 1945

During the war the area had its share of the bombing; the gas works, power station, bus depot, Cattedown and Victoria Wharfs were all damaged. But the area was reasonably lucky; across the rest of Plymouth many industries had their premises destroyed and had been struggling on in all kinds of temporary accommodation. The Council was also very anxious to attract new industries to the city, and the empty areas of Cattedown and Prince Rock presented opportunities. They already owned much of the land and by means of a compulsory purchase order in June 1946 they obtained all the land that had been outside their control, like eleven acres of quarry land stretching up to South Milton Street

and ten acres of allotment gardens between Oakfield Terrace Road and the present Faraday Road, the former Coles timber yard and Martin's Wharf. All Cattedown and Prince Rock was designated for industrial development. By 1953 four firms had been found sites at Cattedown, and seven at Prince Rock. Chief among these were the steel engineers, Blight & White, and the provision merchants, Brown, Wills & Nicholson.

BLIGHT & WHITE

In 1815 a blacksmith, John Blight, 'first lit his forge' in Market Street, Stonehouse. He built up a firm of iron-masters which had a shop at 36 Union Street. His son, W.W.Blight continued in the business, becoming busier with the provision of structural steelwork. He played his part in local affairs, as a member of the East Stonehouse Board of Guardians and of Stonehouse Fire Brigade. He was twice chairman of the Urban Council, in 1893-6 and again in 1913.

The present company was formed in 1923 when Frank White, who came from Bristol, became managing director on the death of Frank Blight. The firm expanded on Ocean Quay, where the Mayflower Marina on the Hamoaze now is. The

The curved steelwork of Plymouth Dome, the visitor centre on the Hoe, was planned and made by Blight and White. The Dome's designer, Robin Wade, is shown leaving the building during its construction.

premises were seriously damaged in the wartime bombing, and the old firm broke from its century-old Stonehouse roots and took a site in Cattedown, between the glue works and the level crossing.

They took over Moore's railway siding, which was right alongside their seaward side, and by 1948 had a new steel works in production. C.J.Woodrow, a nephew of Frank Blight, became the new managing director and, like his predecessors, played his part in public life as a magistrate and a long-serving chairman of the Guild of Social Service. He is one of the few Plymothians to have been High Sheriff of Devon.

Plymouth was crying out for steel to rebuild and Blight & White provided much of it. They grew steadily in the postwar years. Such well-known buildings as Dingles, the Westward Television studios (now the offices of Foot & Bowden, the solicitors) Central Park swimming pool. the Argyle stands at Home Park, the Farley factory at Tor (now replaced by Safeways), the original Tecalemit plant at Marsh Mills (also demolished now), the Bush (now Toshiba) television factory at Ernesettle, Berkertex (again vanished), Plymouth Dome, the Pavilions and the Plaza at Exeter, all had the steel work designed and made by Blight & White. They were increasingly contracting nationally, designing and supplying the steelwork for hangars at Heathrow and Luton, the centre court at Wimbledon, the Princess of Wales Conservatory at Kew, and helicopter pads at the Eddystone and Bishop Rock lighthouses, among other contracts. When the Plymouth company sold out to a national firm in 1985 they were one of the major steel suppliers in the south of England. Unfortunately their successors did work at Canary Wharf where the developers went bankrupt. As a result the Cattedown factory closed down. The premises were taken over by Independent Fertilisers in 1993.

The 1948 building of Brown, Wills and Nicholson, now taken over by Faraday Mill.

BROWN, WILLS & NICHOLSON

The food producers, Brown Wills & Nicholson, also wanted new premises for their offices and wholesale distribution. Their choice fell on Prince Rock.

The firm had a long history. William Burnell started up as a provision merchant in Bretonside in 1797, and with his sons moved in 1828 into Bilbury Street. In 1835 they took a farmer's son, Eldred Brown from Egloshayle near Wadebridge, into the business. A shipping agent, Thomas Nicholson, joined in 1846 and a partnership was formed, Burnell, Brown & Nicholson. A new partner arrived in 1854, Joseph Wills. The firm became Brown, Wills & Nicholson and moved into what is now called the Prysten House, alongside St Andrew's Church. It was then known as the Abbey. Eldred Brown, a bachelor, lived in the Abbey above the food stores. He was a sharp business man but he and his partner Thomas Nicholson were public-spirited men; they started the ragged school movement in 1848. Brown was chairman of the Reform League in Plymouth, seeking to enlarge the franchise, and an alderman of the Corporation. All three partners died within a few years of 1880 and nephews of Eldred, John and Joseph Brown, took over.

Their sons were in turn taking over after World War I, and in 1921 they sold the Prysten House to St Andrew's Church, who had been persuaded that the building had once been used by the canons of Plympton Priory, who supplied the clergy who conducted services in the church. (It is now established that the building had no ecclesiastical background, having been built as a private house about 1490 by Thomas Yogge, the merchant who gave the stone for the building of St Andrew's church tower). The firm kept the Abbey Stores, below the Prysten House in Finewell Street which they had built over the years, using it as their tea blending department (the firm produced Sunny Island Tea), office and distribution centre. Their food production was moved to a former brewery in Alexandra Road, which was renamed Beechwood (the firm had always used beech wood to smoke its bacon).

FARADAY MILL

The Abbey Stores in Finewell Street were blitzed in 1941 (Catherine Street Baptist Church now stands on the site). After various moves Brown Wills leased a site from the Corporation at Prince Rock, facing Acheson Colloids across Faraday Road. It was built in 1946-8, at a time plagued by steel shortages. So the first part was built on a steel frame; then steel ran out and the second stage was erected in reinforced concrete. Then steel became available again, and was used for the third stage.

Production remained at the Beechwood factory but the offices and wholesale warehouse were at Prince Rock. Every morning a fleet of vans would load up and distribute over a wide area. The business was sold to Aplin & Barrett in 1957; and after various new owners it finished up with Bowyers who moved out to Newnham industrial estate in 1979.

London & West Country Securities, the owners of which are Mr and Mrs Mike Hocking, bought the Prince Rock building of Brown, Wills & Nicholson in 1986, rechristened it Faraday Mill (after the name of the road) and let it out to various trading units. Eventually they added the old Andrewartha factory, which had for a spell after the war been the manufacturing base of Corona, the soft drink firm, and another building. In 1995 there were about thirty-five tenants, ranging from a sofa shop to a supplier of ski equipment.

NEW MEAT MARKET

The rebuilding of Plymouth after the war led to many problems. The old wholesale meat market stood right in the middle of where the higher part of New George Street was planned. There were three private abattoirs close by, (the writer clearly recalls cattle being herded through the streets from Plymouth Station, down York Street and along Russell Street to turn up Library Lane, not far from the present sundial at the bottom of New George Street. They were going to what we then called the slaughterhouse). By 1948 the new streets were being laid out and new shops built; as someone has remarked it would not do to have blood running into these pristine premises.

So in 1949 a new Corporation wholesale meat market and abattoir was started at Cattedown, at the western end of Maxwell Road. It was also planned to replace two other obsolete slaughterhouses in outlying districts. The new outfit was needed quickly, so the whole complex, lairages, slaughter hall, cooling hall, wholesale market, canteen and changing accommodation, offices for the retail buyers and the Wholesale Meat Supply Association, was constructed in material available, though the slaughtering equipment was all new and up-to-date. The American armed forces had not long left the area, and steel and corrugated iron cladding from their buildings was adapted.

The complex was eventually taken over by the Fatstock Marketing Corporation, the farmers co-operative, and after various changes in the parent set-up (which did not affect either plant or employees) it was taken over by Plymouth Quality Meat Company, a subsidiary of a national organisation. Nowadays it draws all its animals from Devon and Cornwall; the nearest competitors of comparable size are at Launceston, North Devon and Bodmin. Over the years the whole place has been rebuilt and now employs more than sixty hands, some of whom have been working with the company for thirty years. All waste and by-products are taken away to be handled elsewhere.

CORPORATION WORKS DEPOT

For many years the Engineer's Department of the Corporation had maintained a works depot just west of the power station at Prince Rock. In 1945 it was found necessary to build a new station to increase the output, and the obvious site was occupied by the Works Depot. Not far away was Cattedown Quarry, which the Corporation already owned. As working over the years had pushed the quarry face back, so level (more or less) land was left in front, and this was now adapted for a new works depot.

It was opened in 1950, at a time of intense building activity in the city. Apart from all the new roads being built in the city centre, there were enormous housing estates being built, from Efford to Ernesettle, and most of all this was being done by direct labour. By 1953 the Cattedown central depot (there were a number of other depots around the city) employed 150 men. The quarry was still working along half its face of 750 feet (the other half was becoming uneconomical) and

Brightening the drab industrial landscape; flowering red chestnut trees have been planted outside the Corporation engineers workshops and depot.

yielding 18-20,000 tons per annum. Quarrying was difficult because of the nearness of houses to the top of the quarry; warning had to be given of blasting by the tolling of a large bell. There was also a stone crusher which mixed the limestone with worn out granite setts from roadworks, the sand being mainly used for making concrete blocks on the site. Quarrying finally stopped about 1977, and the crusher scrapped.

There are now shops for plant and repair work, joinery, painting, and an asphalt plant. Parking space is provided for many of the Corporation vehicles, with repair and servicing bays, vehicle building, coach painting, blacksmith, tyre and battery shops to maintain the large fleet. The canteen once served as the clubhouse of the City Engineer's Department sports club, and in the early days there was a football pitch on the site, until the space was needed for the depot's expansion. A replacement pitch was found in what had been a school playing field at the Plymouth end of the Embankment.

Much of the house building and road construction over the years has been done by direct labour. In 1988-9, however, the Government required that all Councils should separate the commissioning from the execution process, and so contract services groups were set up to compete with other tenderers for the work available. Nowadays Prince Rock houses contract services groups providing building cleaning, construction, street cleaning, manufacturing, vehicle maintenance and uPVC window manufacturing. The playing field and the sports club have gone, and the working depot occupies all available space.

CRODA COLLOIDS

One result of the move into the area of food handling factories was their objection to the established factories operating under Offensive Trade licences. The major offender was British Glues, which had originally been started by Brown, Wills & Nicholson, and it is ironic that the campaign against their smells was led by Lawrence Brown, at that time running BWN at Prince Rock.

The glue works stopped production in 1955 and the bones were sent on to another British Glues factory for treatment.After a year or two an associate company of British Glues, International Protein Products Ltd, took over.

It was the time when the hopes of Africa and other starving third world nations were based on groundnuts. Of the 1,500 million people suffering from chronic malnutrition, the largest group were deficient in protein. A British Glues chemist had discovered in 1947 a way of extracting protein from the nuts. Huge tropical areas of Nigeria and other African countries were being ripped up and replanted with groundnuts, or peanuts (they are the same thing), and they were going to feed everybody. A pilot plant built in Bermondsey proved by 1959 that nuts could be turned into a powder which, marketed as Lypro, could be introduced into a wide variety of foodstuffs. So the Plymouth plant was used as the site of a new factory which was the first in the world to process the nuts on a commercial basis.

When it opened in 1962 it was going to be the prototype of worldwide factories of the future. But if the production difficulties had been solved, marketing had not. Poor countries could not afford the Lypro, and its use in infant and geriatric foods in the developed countries was not enough to absorb the output. So in 1967 the revolutionary plant closed down. It turned out to be an idea before its time; the process is used with greater success now with soya beans. But the world-leading factory in Cattedown, like the groundnuts scheme throughout Africa, came to naught.

The spray drying system developed in the factory was not wasted; in 1968 Croda International acquired British Glues & Chemicals. The Cattedown plant was then used to produce spray-dried hydrolised gelatines for use in shampoos and conditioners, and to make the capsules enclosing vitamins and other pharmaceutical products. One man who saw the factory in all its aspects was Ernie Howard, who arrived in Plymouth in 1934 in the old glue days, became assistant manager and engineer when the Lypro process started, remained at the factory single-handed after closure and continued as manager with Croda until he retired in 1971. He died in 1993. Entering the factory today from Maxwell Road, all the old buildings on the left are the original glue works, all the new buildings on the right were built for the Lypro process.

WALLSEND INDUSTRIAL ESTATE

When Fisons closed their Cattedown factories in 1981 they sold the thirteen-acre site and buildings to Wallsend Properties for £500,000. Wallsend, which carries the name of a one-time coal concern, is a Plymouth development company. They knocked the old buildings down, cleared the site, and christened it the Wallsend Industrial Estate. By 1984 three large companies and a number of smaller units had moved in. Among them was Chelton Electronics, who took over the Fisons office block on the hill overlooking the site. They had started in business in the Barbican area. and were much concerned with defence contracts. Unfortunately the contracts dried up under the post Cold War defence cuts and the firm closed.

INTERFISH

In 1985 Interfish Ltd bought a large part of the Wallsend area and built a new plant. The business

The maritime image, the office block of Interfish on the Wallsend Industrial Estate.

One of the two new trawlers built by Interfish, the Admiral Blake *at her naming ceremony in Plymouth Sound in 1989.*

to Plymouth in 1977 and started his own fish business, with offices in Millbay Docks and a freezing and smoking factory in Saltash. It did so well that his father joined him in 1979, and his younger brother Frank came in as well in 1982.

Father died in 1985, the year that David Owen, then MP for Plymouth Sutton, opened Interfish's new plant. This brought offices and factory together on one waterside site, right opposite the entrance to Cattedown Wharfs. In 1989 Interfish built two new trawlers in Holland, named *Admiral Gordon* (PH 330) and *Admiral Blake* (PH440). For six months of the year these two vessels, using the most modern equipment, land their fish in Plymouth, and for six months they work out of ports nearest the fishing grounds in season. Their white fish is sold in the local market, the rest goes by road to Plymouth. Other fishing boats under contract to the company do the same. When the boats are fishing in local waters the catches for auction are landed over the new fish quay into Plymouth Fish Market. Fish destined for the factory lands over the neighbouring Cattedown Wharfs. White fish are filleted and frozen, mackerel, herring, cod and haddock are smoked.

Most of the fish handled by Interfish is locally caught. The factory employs about eighty people fulltime, and thirty part time. Their products are exported to forty different countries, with an export value of about £6m a year.

SEVERNSIDE WASTE PAPER

Next door to Interfish on the Wallsend estate is the Severnside Waste Paper Co. A national firm, it took over Plymouth Waste Paper, which had started in Newport Street, Stonehouse, on the shores of Stonehouse Creek, in 1981. Severnside, based in Cardiff, has fifteen depots in the United Kingdom. The Plymouth plant collects waste paper from an area stretching from St Austell to

had its roots in Manchester, where Frank Colam had a fish import-export business. Some of his fish came from Holland and when he began getting train supplies suffering from coal dust, he went to see his supplier in Holland. That problem was not only amicably sorted out, but his son Gordon also married the daughter of his Dutch merchant. Their youngest son, Jan Colam, moved

Buckfastleigh. About a thousand tons a month are handled by the eleven employees; it is sorted into grades, baled, and sold on to paper mills. Eighty percent goes to the company's mill at Watchet.

COUNTERSPARES

At the far end of Prince Rock, just behind Laira Wharf, are Counterspares, vehicle dismantlers and scrap metal merchants. There are two or three similar firms in the area but this is the biggest. The business was started in 1971 by Vicky and Roy Herbert, a husband and wife team, but their Prince Rock base was in the line of the new road constructed in 1994 to provide access to Cattedown from Laira Bridge Road.

So Devon County Council, the highway authority, found the Herberts a new site just at the back of what had been the scrap yard of Davies & Cann, and in compensation helped them set up the fine new building. Their five employees operate grabs, cranes and a car crushing plant. They sell off bits and pieces from scrapped cars, and produce about 2,000 tons of scrap metal a year. This goes by road to Cardiff, to Allied Metals, for export.

Another scrap metal exporting firm, European Metal Recycling, collects up metal at Victoria Wharfs for export to Spain.

POMPHLETT

Opposite the Western National garages in Laira Bridge Road now are two 'out of town' shopping centres, and across the bridge the lefthand side of the road is lined with new establishments nearly as far as the Plymstock turning. Here are more DIY establishments, and the Sugar Mill Business Park in the former Jewsons builders yard. The Sugar Mill was the original venture of the

Hockings of Faraday Mill: it is now a similar mix of small enterprises. The Mobil petrol station was originally a Massey-Harrison tractor depot built by Mumfords, the Plymouth motor firm. Next door is Aztec office equipment suppliers.

EAGLE SIGNS

Oreston Road, which climbs the hill across the head of Pomphlett Creek, is similarly lined on the west side with new developments. Among them is Eagle Signs Ltd, a business started in 1961 by two men who had been working for an Exeter firm of sign makers. Jack Carter and Brian Manley, both experienced in making neon signs, began operations in old farm buildings near Plymstock Broadway, moved to a site opposite the Palace in Union Street, and settled in their present building in 1975. It is very much a family firm, with both men still in the business, Mrs Carter the company secretary and the sons, two Carter sons and one Manley, also on the staff.

Signs produced by the fifteen-strong work force include all on the Plymouth Pavilions (including the electronic moving message display), the Tamar Bridge, Plymouth University, and many on shop and office premises in the city centre.

Various other smaller firms line the hill, and where the road turns at the bottom along the west side of Pomphlett Creek are still more factories.

BREAKWATER ROAD

The former Breakwater Quarry is occupied by the concrete block making plant of Amey Roadstone Corporation. Further along the road, where it opens into Breakwater Quarry (hence the name of the road) the GPO has the Plymstock Letter Delivery Sorting Office. Next door are depots for Fyne Papers, and then the area is occupied by the factory producing Rico Sports Boats. a pump hire

The Theatre Royal workshops are now established in a former car establishment at Prince Rock, where everything from pantomime transformation scenery and whole stages for the Drum down to the smallest props, can be made. These heraldic beasts were used in a 1996 production.

company and Seastructures. For ten years the area included the headquarters of Denham Productions and the Quay West Studio, the independent television production company led by Chris Denham, the former Spotlight Southwest presenter, and Colin Rowe, the cameraman. But by 1994 they had outgrown the building and moved out to the old Loughtor water mill.

LUKE'S SAUSAGES

In Oreston itself is one of the leading manufacturers of sausages and cooked meats in the country, W.H.Luke and Son Ltd; a far cry from the traditional village industries. William Luke left his father, a farmer-cum-butcher at St Austell, in 1934 to set up business in Plymouth. He had a shop in Caprera Terrace, now part of North Road West where, like most butchers at the time, he made sausages and cooked meats in the back.

But in a 1940 raid the shop took a direct hit from a bomb. William Luke continued his business from his dwelling house on the other side of North Road. In 1945 he also took over Stribley's butcher's shop in Oreston, on the corner of the Quay and Plymstock Road, and lived there with his family. When meat came off wartime controls in 1952 William decided to make the 'small goods' for both his shops in outhouses at the back of the Oreston premises. Very soon he was supplying other butchers as well.

In 1958 his son David joined him in the business, and in 1964 they decided to concentrate on manufacture. They built a factory on the land William already owned behind Oreston Quay, and bought more land so that the factory now fronted on Endsleigh Road. The building, still on the same site, has had to be enlarged over the years, and now the firm distributes its sausages, hog's puddings, beefburgers and cooked meats right through Cornwall, Devon, Dorset and Somerset, and has national distribution through the various multiple stores that take Luke's products.

In 1980 it was necessary to expand, and an ice cream company's cold store and distribution plant in Oreston Road at Pomphlett was taken over. In 1995 the company employed about fifty people, and produced over five million lbs of sausages every year.

David Luke has two sons, one a production manager with Geest in Lincolnshire, the other a student at the Royal Academy of Dramatic Art. As neither son intended to come into the business so a management take-over of the company was arranged, with David Luke becoming chairman, Paul King as managing director and Adrian Mitchell as production director. Early in 1997, however, the receivers were called in as a result of difficult pork prices and an experimental marketing drive. The factory finally closed in February that year.

PART FOUR - THE VILLAGES
CHAPTER THIRTY-ONE
LAND OWNERSHIP

Until the nineteenth century the river Plym and all its side creeks flowed through open country. Even at its mouth the developing town of Plymouth was back from the river. The borough created in 1439 had within its boundaries all the land out to Prince Rock. There were small settlements along the foreshore associated with quarrying and shipbuilding, but Cattedown remained free from development until the early 1800s. It was originally part of the manor of Sutton Pill. The manor title, and the land, had passed from the great Elizabethan family of Hawkins to the Sparkes in 1549, and thence in 1714 to the Molesworth family of Pencarrow in Cornwall, all by marriages.

In 1785 Sir William Molesworth sold the Sutton Pill manor, which included various odd parcels of land such as the Hoe fields, the Friary, Prince Rock and Cattedown, to William Clark. He died in 1786 and his son, another William, died soon after in 1793. This left the land in the hands of three children, who finally sold up in 1820. The Hoe fields (between the Hoe and Millbay Road) went to Col James Elliot of the Barley House, hence the present names of Elliot Terrace and Elliot Street, built on these fields.

Two houses on the south side of the present Exeter Street (one of which might be the First and Last Inn) and the field which stretched up to the present Cattedown roundabout were bought by Lockyer (remembered in Lockyer Street), who had made his money buying and selling the prize goods and ships captured in the Napoleonic wars. The south side of Embankment Road from Tothill Corner and the fields running down between the present Cattedown Road and Elliot Road went to a family called Julian, who were great buyers and sellers of land.

The four Prince Rock fields, on the south side of Embankment Road. on either side of the present Laira Bridge Road, were bought by Soltau. Cattedown Quarry and with this land the fields behind, called Cattedown, were leased by Symonds & Sparrow, the quarry owners, and probably bought by them.

The land north of Embankment Road seems to have been owned by the Culme family of Tothill House, who were said to own land from Cattedown to Compton. By the end of the century various pockets of Cattedown and Prince Rock were owned by Lord Graves, of Thankes at Torpoint, and Bewes of Beaumont House. Like

Efford Manor, photographed during a garden fete and sale of work in September 1909.

1833 and Soltaus were still there in 1918; the Soltaus were Plymouth business men, remembered through another marriage as Soltau-Symons.

Efford, occupying the land between Prince Rock and Marsh Mills, was in Egg Buckland parish, all very rural with little development until the end of the nineteenth century, and the real flow of houses over this land did not come until after World War II. The shores of the Plympton branch of the estuary were in the manor of Plympton, which included all Saltram.

SALTRAM

James Bagge, a Weymouth man who came to Plymouth in the 1590s to operate his Caribbean privateers, bought Saltram farm when he retired from Plymouth life, leaving his interests there to his son, another James. The old man began to build Saltram into a great house in 1624. James senior was not a popular man; his son became even more unpopular and much Government money for various contracts was suspected of drifting into his pocket. He was brought down in 1634 and Saltram forfeit to the state. During the Civil War the Royalist army was billeted in the grounds and did tremendous damage to the house and everything else. In the Commonwealth Captain Henry Hatsell, Parliament's man of business in Plymouth, lived in the house and was still there in 1662. The Carteret family subsequently held it until 1712.

Then it was bought by George Parker of Boringdon and Woodford. The house was on a long lease and Parker continued living at Boringdon. His son John moved into Saltram in 1743 on his father's death and by 1749 had built the present house around the core of the original Tudor buildings. He married Lady Catherine Poulett whose father had been Secretary of State and Lord Steward to Queen Anne. She seems to

the Soltaus, all these families were linked by marriage with Culmes.

The year before William Clark bought Sutton Pill he had bought Efford manor for £20,000 from Sir William Trelawny of Ham (who could trace his ownership back to the Domesday owners of Efford). If Clark was a local man he had obviously come into a lot of money, on the other hand he may be a rich incomer. On his death in 1786 the estates passed to his son William Clark, who in 1793 added the manor of Buckland Tout Saints near Kingsbridge to the collection. William died in 1795 and the estates had to be divided between three children. One son, Erving Clark kept Efford, and lived there. He and his widow (Ann Letitia, a Treby of Plympton) who outlived him, were at Efford until 1881; their son and grandson followed and the last Clark of Efford was Henry Clark QC. Efford manor with its 200 acres was finally sold in 1918, described as 'an old fashioned manor house with lodge, and Deer Park Farm'.

Little Efford was in the hands of Peter Culme in 1768. A Culme daughter married George Soltau in have been the driving force; when she died John lived on quietly for ten years until his death, hoarding away his money.

John, his son, was entirely different; he was a member of Parliament and a great gambler who built up a string of racehorses. He was an enthusiastic buyer of pictures and a boon companion of Sir Joshua Reynolds from Plympton, for whom the Parkers were very early patrons. He knew all the best people, many of whom were entertained at Saltram and it is said that the first waltz ever in the West of England was danced in the saloon there.

King George III and Queen Charlotte spent a fortnight's holiday at Saltram. As a result of this visit Parker was raised to the peerage as Lord Boringdon. He still spoke with a Devon accent and was a countryman at heart. He was also an agent for progress in the whole area, altering the shape of the Laira with his Plymouth and Chelston Meadow embankments, building Laira Bridge and the new turnpike to Elburton. Deservedly he was made Earl of Morley in 1815, but when he died in 1840 he left the estate saddled with enormous debts.

His son, the second earl, sought to reduce the debts by launching the Lee Moor China clay company but this only increased his liabilities. He could not even afford to live at Saltram, which was let out. His son Albert, the third earl, was like his grandfather an active politician and became an early chairman of the new Devon County Council. But he was able to reduce the debt by selling some properties and pictures from the house, and after 23 years was able to take up residence at Saltram again in 1884.

Edmund, the fourth earl, maintained the improvements to Saltram at the cost of selling more properties. He died a bachelor in 1951 to be followed by his brother Montagu, aged 73. Faced with an imminent second set of death duties the

The east front of Saltram House in 1790, from a drawing by Lord Duncannon. With Chelston still an arm of the sea the house stands on a peninsula and the south front looks down on a stretch of water.

fifth earl made Saltram over to the National Trust, and the sixth earl, his nephew, lives at Pounds House, Yelverton.

THE EARLS OF BEDFORD

The Parkers owned all the south shore of the Laira down to Laira Bridge. The other side of the Elburton road, the manor of Plymstock, had been owned by Tavistock Abbey as a result, according to Dartmoor legend, of its monks having given christian burial to Childe the Hunter, who died in a storm on Dartmoor. They are said to have raced the monks of Plympton to the body and the historian H.P.R.Finberg set out to prove in 1952 that there is good historic grounds to accept Childe as a Saxon landowner, and that in substance the tale is true. The Russells, later Dukes of Bedford, bought Tavistock Abbey and its lands on the Dissolution of the Monasteries, and so acquired the manor of Plymstock.

William Payne's picture of Radford House, made c. 1790.

HARRIS OF RADFORD

The manor of Plymstock was not the entire parish. On the south side Plymstock manor was bounded by the manor of Goosewell, on the west by Hooe. The first Harris married the heiress of Radford and was established there by the beginning of the fifteenth century. By the end of that century more marriages to heiresses had built up the family fortunes and they owned Higher Hooe as well. They also produced successful lawyers, and by Elizabethan times ranked among the leading West Devon families. Christopher Harris was a friend of Francis Drake; he held in safe custody at Radford the admiral's share of the treasure he brought back from his voyage around the world. He was Drake's lawyer, buying Buckland Abbey for him and becoming an executor of his will.

In those days before Radford ponds had been cut off from Hooe Lake the tide came right up to the foot of the hill below Radford House; Plymouth hired a boat to take Sir Walter Ralegh there in 1601, and in later years when Ralegh was in disgrace he was under house arrest at Radford. Knowing that King James wanted him dead, he and his wife took boat at night across Hooe Lake. A ship was waiting in the Cattewater to take them to France and safety. But Ralegh had too scrupulous a sense of honour; before the ship was reached he ordered the boat to turn back; it led to his death.

By the time Christopher died he owned the manors of Goosewell and Staddiscombe as well. The family's loyalty to the King in the Civil War cost them dear. During the war they even buried their silver dinner service at Brixton for safety; it was found again in 1827 and is now the possession of the British Museum and known as the Armada Service. In the Commonwealth John Harris took part in the Penruddock rising and was sent into exile. Not until the Restoration did the family recover their sequestered lands and start rebuilding their fortunes.

They seem to have recovered very thoroughly. Harrises were partners in 1773 in the second bank founded in Plymouth, the Naval Bank. (the first was started by a Baring). Radford House was rebuilt, The Retreat and Belle Vue were established to house members of the growing family. Various marriages were made with the Bulteels of Flete and more land was acquired. In the early years of the nineteenth century John Harris of Radford exchanged some land with the Duke of Bedford which gave him land on the east side of the head of the lake. He built a dam across the lake which created the duckponds and a new lodge and carriage drive to approach Radford House. On the dam was built a mock castle which adds a picturesque touch to the area.

THE BULTEELS

In the Napoleonic Wars two young Harris sons of Belle Vue were killed in the assault on Bergen in the Netherlands. Harry Harris of Radford, on the other hand, had a distinguished army career, with Moore at Corunna and Wellington at Waterloo. By 1881 Thomas Bulteel, who had married a Harris daughter, had inherited both Radford and the Naval Bank. A Bulteel girl had married one of the rich Barings who had settled locally and became Lord Revelstoke; another married a Mildmay who inherited Flete. It seems as if Thomas Bulteel tried to live up to their considerable style. When Thomas died in 1908 his son took over, but the Naval Bank was already in trouble and in 1914 closed its doors.

The examination in bankruptcy of Captain Frederick Bulteel and his partner, Matthew Praed Parker, revealed that the bank had been in financial trouble since 1858; after the examination was closed both men were sent for trial for fraud. This was removed from Exeter to the Old Bailey in 1916 and after a ten days hearing the two of them were each sent to prison for six months.

Radford House stood at the original head of Hooe Lake, but turned its back on the water to look south to the heights of Staddon. It actually stood at the top of the hill, just where the road to Hooe swings sharp right). It is difficult now to imagine the site of the house, because of road widening, but its back was to the road. The Elizabethan house was rebuilt in the eighteenth century.

HOOE and TURNCHAPEL

The manor of West Hooe was bought in 1718 by Sir John Rogers. The first Rogers in the local scene came to Plymouth as a Custom officer, turned merchant and built up a sufficient fortune to buy Blachford at Cornwood. He and his son extended their land holding right down to Ivybridge and some areas beyond; it was the second baronet who bought Hooe. In 1861 the family sold 512 acres of this land to the War Department for £17,582.10s. This included all the present site of Fort Stamford.

In England it is very common for manors to own odd pockets of land entirely enclosed in other manors. Turnchapel and Mount Batten were part of the manor of Plympton, even though in Plymstock parish and entirely surrounded on the landward side by the manor of West Hooe. It was owned by the Crown before the Norman Conquest. It remained Crown property until the manors began to break up, and was bought by the Parkers of Saltram in the eighteenth century.

THE BREAK-UP

Oreston, Hooe and Turnchapel developed slowly, while the land was still in the hands of large landowners. But the Morleys in the nineteenth century had to sell off outlying tracts of land, such as Woodford. The Bedfords sold off their Plymstock manor in 1911. Radford House was sold in 1917 as bankruptcy stock and bought by Billy Mitchell for £11,000. It was pulled down in in 1937 and the land was rapidly built over.

The floodgates were open to housing development. Percy Loosemore, the clerk to Plympton Rural District Council, was a great believer in increasing the rateable value in his area and encouraged development; farmers and other landowners saw the money to be made and so in the 1920s houses spread across the hills around Plymstock right down to the back of the old waterside villages. The idea spread to the owner farmers of Plympton, notably at Woodford, and the process accelerated after World War II.

As a result the only areas around the Plym clear of houses now are the valley of the Plym above Marsh Mills, the Saltram estate and the Mount Batten peninsula because of its Ministry of Defence ownership.

CHAPTER THIRTY-TWO

CRABTREE AND LAIRA

On the north side of the Laira, between Prince Rock and Marsh Mills, there were originally only two waterside settlements, each at the base of a river crossing. The Ebb Ford approach on the Plymouth side was marked by the Crabtree Inn, probably nearly as old as the ford itself. At the Efford base of the Long Bridge was Crabtree proper, once dominated by the Rising Sun Inn and now on the north-western side of the Plymouth approach to the Marsh Mills roundabout.

LOWER CRABTREE

The base of the Ebb Ford crossing, the original Crabtree and for long centred in the Crabtree Inn, was called Lower Crabtree. Its site is now marked by the turning off the main road of the Military road, just east of the petrol filling station. By 1856 the pub had gathered around it a group of cottages and even a post office. They stood where the old road dipped down and ran for a short distance beside the lines of the horsedrawn china clay trucks. On the river side of the clay line was the main line railway, hidden from the road by a wooden barrier built to prevent the steam trains frightening the horses! The post office had vanished before 1939, and pub and cottages all

Crabtree Inn, once a lonely tavern on the Efford side of the Ebb ford, seen in its latter life with the old Plymouth and Dartmoor railway passing its door as well as the main road from Plymouth to London. It was demolished to make way for the present six-lane highway to Marsh Mills.

disappeared when the road was made a dual carriageway in 1985.

CRABTREE

The little community facing east over the Longbridge was better known by Plymothians as the Rising Sun, after the prominent public house there. Probably the pub was built when the turnpike was constructed in 1758 and traffic used this route, rather than the Ebb Ford.

After the construction of the Parkway and the building of the roundabout the pub was renamed the Roundabout in 1973, but further road

The roundabout at Marsh Mills before the flyover carrying traffic from the A38 to the Parkway was constructed. The Rising Sun was still there.

improvements led in 1986 to its demolition. In 1995 a 'travel hotel' and a combined pub and Beefeater restaurant were opened on the sites of the pub and Marsh House, called the Marsh Mill.

The Rev John Swete on one of his tours of Devon wrote in 1793 that he 'rode towards Saltram and saw limekilns, slate rock and the houses of Crabtree on the opposite shore'. The pub was certainly there in the 1830s. Close by were two lodges. One guarded the drive to Marsh House, where David Derry (whose family built Derry's Clock), lived when he was Mayor of Plymouth in 1850. Marsh House was north of the Rising Sun, and finally disappeared with the building of the Parkway. The other lodge guarded the drive to Efford Manor, home of the Clark family since 1784. When Efford Fort and Laira Battery were built on the hilltops above Crabtree in the 1860s a tunnel had to be built to take the drive under the link between the forts, and is still there. Between these two lodges a number of houses grew up, some of which survive and are now encompassed by modern houses. There was even a shop.

In 1923 Efford Ex-Servicemen's Colony, for men suffering from tuberculosis, was created here and on either side of the drive to Efford Manor. It was opened by Prince George (later Duke of Kent) in 1924. Seventeen families lived in pleasant wooden bungalows set in little gardens, with their fifty-odd children. Another twenty-five men living in Plymouth had their daily fares paid by the committee, and they were taught carpentry and joinery, and shoe-repairing. They made all kinds of furniture, garden sheds and hen houses, and took in boot and shoe repairs, to augment the income generated by the charitable donations. But it seems not to have paid its way, and in 1930 was up for sale by auction. Some of the families with their children stayed on, and one or two of their houses still survive.

THE MAYOR OF CRABTREE

Crabtree had twenty years of notoriety in the early 1800s. Plymouth has just ended fifty years of acrimony between freemen and freeholders about who should elect its mayor, aldermen, and councillors. In 1834 the last mayor was elected under the old charter and the patrons of the Pack Horse Inn in Treville Street ('sundry sons of Crispin', which presumably means a group of cobblers) decided to elect their own. (Treville Street disappeared when Bretonside bus station was built, and the Pack Horse was gone long before that.)

This 'mayor choosing' became an annual event, when children would line Treville Street, Exeter Street (now Bretonside) and Jubilee Street (now Exeter Street) to watch a coach containing the jokers, led by a band, travel in procession all the

No. 3 Arnold's Point, the central and oldest house in the terrace, dating back to c 1810.

way out to Crabtree. A large crowd would escort them, and the Embankment tollhouse was often so overwhelmed that no tolls were paid at all. At the Crabtree Inn the mayor-elect was presented with a large bowl of cockles by Granny Tipper, who was duly rewarded with a piece of silver.

Another crowd met the cortege at the Rising Sun where the dignitaries paraded into Crabtree Town Hall (a back room of the pub). They were preceded by the Bearer of the Great Cockle, carrying a giant cockle borne on a crimson velvet cushion. The mayor was then robed and adorned with his chain of office, and took an oath that, having been elected by the burgesses of the ancient cockle borough of Crabtree, he would preserve their rights to the catching and selling of cockles from Laira sands.

The date was fixed as Good Friday in 1845, and on Whit Sunday the Mayor and Corporation of Crabtree would (soberly) attend the the morning church service at Egg Buckland. Sadly, it all came to an end in 1854.

ARNOLD'S POINT

The Embankment was finally closed in 1802, and in 1808 one of the promoters of the Act of Parliament which permitted the enclosure of the land, John Pridham, bought from the Embankment company six acres of the new land at Arnold's Point (the name was already in use for the Mount Gould promontory which touches the Embankment between Tothill Bay and Laira Lake. A kinsman of John Pridham, Joseph Pridham, was solicitor to the Shoulder of Mutton Club which had fought for the right of the freeholders of Plymouth to elect the town council, and finally won in 1802. Joseph was elected Mayor in 1808 and another Pridham, a captain RN, became mayor in 1827. It was a prominent family.

Pridham's plot, which he carved into three

fields, was described as in Tothill Bay. In the northern field he built a house, the present centre block of Arnold's Point Cottages, Nos 2, 3 and 3a. In 1811 he leased the house, described as 'newly erected', to Lieut Richard Dechamp RN, aged 52, and his wife. On John Pridham's death in 1835 his son sold the house and large garden outright to Dechamp, a commander by this time.

Dechamp died in 1840 and his wife died in the same year. She left the house to her 'old and faithful servant', Thomasin Colwill. Four years later Thomasin married Henry Bone, a labourer in the Dockyard. Henry was no fool; by 1850 he had built two houses in the garden of the house his wife had inherited, one on each side. In that year he sold the original house for five shillings to Thomas Pearse, a pawnbroker of Pembroke Street, and to Lewis Pode, a clerk in the Custom House longroom at Plymouth. who lived in the new house on the eastern side.

It looks like a kind of mortgage, which would explain how a Dockyard labourer was able to raise the money to build two houses, because the deed of sale also guarantees that Thomasin and he shall live in their house for as long as either one of them lives, and their children after them.

In 1901 Caroline Bone, widow of Henry Bone, a retired beer house keeper, took over Nos 2, 3 and 3a Arnold's Point. This Henry was probably the son of the Dockyard labourer and Thomasin. He had carved the original house into the three separate dwellings that they are today, still with the same numbers. Caroline married again and sold off 3a in 1906 and her executors sold No 2 in 1910, after her death. She had lived in the centre property, No 3, still distinguished by being slate hung and with a pointed arch recess over its elegant glass porch.

The Ordnance Survey six-inch map of 1856 names the three houses, from the south-west, as Adelaide Cottage, Rose Cottage (the original

bigger one) and Arnold's Point Cottages, being a whole row on the north-east. All but the south-west cottages of this row (one had been converted to a shop) were knocked down after World War I to make way for a garage, now a petrol station. The 1856 map shows the square quay on which today stands the clubhouse of Plymouth Rowing Club, and just to the southwest, 'Round House' and Arnold's Point is marked on the map. In 1820 Arnold owned odd fields in the area and probably the quay as well. The round house is a puzzle because drawings of this time show a square building on the site with a pointed roof.

In the 1920s the Corporation built, just west of the quay, changing rooms for men and women swimmers, with steps leading down to the water. It was still in use until the late 1930s, when the medical officer of health for the city closed it down. At that time the main sewer for Laira and Efford took all its untreated waste into what was called the Mullet Pond, in the middle of Laira railway yard. There was a pump house alongside which, just after high water every day, pumped the raw sewage into the river. It has long been closed, but at least one distinguished Plymothian of the present day swam there regularly as a boy without any ill effects! The building housing the changing rooms is still there.

LAIRA GREEN

As late as 1880 the traveller on the old main road to Exeter, once past Lipson Vale, would have found few houses before Laira Green. After passing through the narrows today the road dips to the junction with Pike Road, but an older road on the right, passing the Old Road Inn, dips even lower. Behind the inn was Laira Green, originally a group of quite elegant houses. The most distinguished, Cleve Villa in Laira Avenue, is said to be on a site bought from the Saltram Estate. It

Cleve Villa in Laira Avenue, a Regency house built when Laira Green was extra-parochial and so not charged rates.

A train made up in the style of the Plymouth suburban services took railway enthusiasts on a tour of the local network; it is passing the 'mullet pond' in Laira railway yard with the houses of Laira and Efford behind.

claims a date of 1749 but it is generally accepted that these houses came into existence after the construction of the Embankment in 1811. This would be in keeping with the Strawberry Hill neo-gothic appearance of Cleve Villa, the best preserved, and in keeping with its grade two listing by the Department of the Environment as an 'early/mid C19 stuccoed house'. It is also in keeping with the story that a friend of Keats (1795-1821), named Brown, lived in one of these villas.

Before the Embankment this area was part of Laira Lake, under water at high tide. All this new 'dry' land (it would have taken a time to recover from its daily flooding) was outside the boundaries of the neighbouring parishes and so was 'extra-parochial', and thus not liable to any

kind of rates or taxes. This may have encouraged the building of the first houses. But the authorities soon acquired a private Act of Parliament which in 1856 turned all the one-time Laira Lake into the civil parish of Laira Green. The South Devon Railway had arrived in 1848, passing in front of the Laira Green villas and making this a little enclave between road and railway.

The railway changed the whole area. Behind the Embankment, on the recovered land, it laid out a large marshalling yard where goods trains were made up. This led to much employment, and a need for housing. The land north of the railway was in Egg Buckland parish, its rates very low compared with the Borough of Plymouth. So, between 1881 and 1896, fields on both sides of Old Laira Road, outside Plymouth, were sold for housing. Wycliffe Road was the western boundary, Bramley Road the eastern, and Beverley Road served four little streets running up to the field boundary. Federation Road was added later. This group of streets is still very distinctive, the houses with their newly-fashionable bay windows, little front gardens, and larger back yards. With the post-1948 spread of council housing over Efford its northern edges have become blurred.

It was estimated in 1890 that the population of Laira had increased in twenty years from 46 ratepayers to nearly 600. When Plymouth extended its boundaries in 1896 to take in Compton Giffard its new boundary was drawn very neatly along the northern edge of this group of streets, taking them into the borough, but leaving the fields outside still in the rural parish. The extension also took all the civil parish of Laira Green into the borough. So rates moved from 3s1d in 1893 to 7s in 1898!

Laira had another fillip in 1901 when the Round House was built at Laira Junction; not a round house at all but so called because its central feature was a turntable from which engines could be stabled on radiating lines. Gradually Laira took over the maintenance of locomotives in the region until in 1934 the official Plymouth Motive Power Depot at Millbay was closed down. Most of the goods marshalling has long since moved to Tavistock Junction at Marsh Mills, but Laira now services the InterCity trains.

In 1904 the Great Western was building up its suburban railway services and Laira Halt was opened at the bottom of Brandon Road that year. The opening in 1921 of the No 3 Corporation bus service between the town centre and Laira hit the railway passenger traffic, and Laira Halt closed in 1930.

The Laira 'narrows', the part of the main road built up at the end of the nineteenth century and still unchanged in the motor car age.

Laira Green when the clay wagons still came through and the modern links with the Embankment road system had not been built, showing how horse-drawn trucks were mixed up with cars, pedestrians and houses.

Railway building at the southern end of the Embankment also had its effect on Laira. Two railway bridges were built across the road, which had been the main road into Plymouth from the east, and one, which carried the GWR's Yealmpton branch trains over the road, imposed a height limitation on road traffic using the Embankment. So it ceased to be the main road from Plymouth to the east, and traffic, including buses, had to use North Hill, Alexandra Road and Old Laira Road.

The bridge was erected in 1897, by which time the houses on either side of Old Laira Road had been built, leaving a road between them unsuited for heavy traffic. There is still just room for two vehicles to pass in these 'Laira narrows'. But the weight of traffic was removed with the rebuilding of the bridge in the 1960s and the restoration of the Embankment as the main road east of the city.

The now-vanished Laira Inn, opposite the china clay line tunnel, with its steps up to the Embankment and its sign on the roadside.

From the late nineteenth century a railway village was created at Laira, with the majority of its inhabitants working for the Great Western; the grades of employees ranking from greasers to firemen to drivers reflected in the social structure; link one engine drivers who handled the crack expresses were the aristocrats.

Where the Embankment meets Laira Road was the Laira Inn, in a row of cottages. It was probably built soon after the Embankment was completed; it was certainly there in 1856 and seems to have survived until the present road system was developed; it would be almost under the roundabout at the end of Laira Road. On the other side of the road was the lodge guarding the main drive to Efford Manor. The Old Road Inn was built to stand out from its neighbours; locals claim that it is 200 years old. The road improvement which left it on one side was made in 1912, part of the new borough's improvements. The area also acquired a police and fire station on the main road with the borough coat of arms; later it became a branch library.

SCHOOLS and CHURCHES

The growing population had other needs. By 1870 a British School had been established in Laira Green, which also served Crabtree. But the new school inspectors found its premises unsuitable and a long debate opened on where a new school should be. Crabtree had recently had a large influx of population through the building of the two forts, used as barracks for soldiers and their families.

Crabtree already had an independent chapel, and the Vicar of Egg Buckland, whose ecclesiastical parish included both Laira Green and Crabtree. proposed building a combined school and chapel at Crabtree. G.W.Soltau of Little Efford, twice Mayor of Plymouth and a member of the Plymouth Brethren, who paid most of the expenses of Laira Green School, was at first enthusiastic about the new scheme but then withdrew his support: perhaps he did not like the Church of England's involvement. Anyway, the chapel was built at Crabtree but never used as a school, and the Laira Green building stayed in use. There were always problems from the position of this school. It was close to the river which sometimes flooded the building, and there are reports of children being caned for playing in the tide. The china clay tramway was also close by, and children would play on the line, jumping on wagons for a ride. This culminated in the death of one boy.

By 1890 the need for a new school at Laira was pressing. An Egg Buckland and Laira Green School Board was set up, in the teeth of opposition from people who wanted to keep the voluntary system. A site was found in a field at the end of Bramley Road, right next to the new housing development, and in 1892 what is now the single storey buildings of Laira Green School were opened. Four years later Plymouth extended its boundaries and the school was taken over by the Plymouth School Board. This in turn was replaced by Plymouth Education Authority, which took over from the Board in 1903. It set about new building schemes at once, and erected the present two-storey block alongside the 1892 building. Laira Green still flourishes as a primary school, and still outside the headmaster's room is a fish tank inscribed 'Presented to the Egg Buckland and Laira Green School Board by H.O.Serpell 1895'.

The first church in Laira proper was built in 1886 by the Congregationalists in Laira Road, opposite the bottom of Bramley Road. This chapel was demolished in 1935 and new premises were built across the road, at the foot of Bramley Road. These were extended in 1956.

The Wesleyans were not far behind in starting, building their chapel in 1892 at the other end of the new houses, on the corner of Old Laira Road and Wycliffe Road. It was rebuilt in 1906. In the years after World War II, with the Efford council estate growing at great speed and with all the extra housing at Lipson, it was felt to be too small. The circuit had the war damage compensation in hand for the destroyed Zion Church, built on the edge of the Barbican by the Bible Christians in 1842. It was decided to enlarge the Laira church with this money, and cash raised locally. Isaac Foot laid the foundation stone, on the same site, in 1956. When opened it sat 550 people with a schoolroom which could take 300.

By the early 1990s the new church was in trouble. Road widening had weakened the foundations of the Sunday School building and begun to make it unsafe. The Wesleyans had long become Methodists and the Congregationalists the United Reform Church; now the two Laira churches amalgamated. The Methodist premises were put up for sale, and the United Reform building became the United Church in 1993.

This sudden start in church building, free churches starting up in 1886 and 1892, shows the population growth. The Anglican chapel at Crabtree in 1874 initially had a curate-in-charge who lived in Plymouth, but in 1902 a resident curate arrived and it was clear that the church was in the wrong place if it was to serve Laira as well. In 1906 Mrs Clark of Efford Manor (always known locally as Lady Clark; in my boyhood my father would take me through 'Lady Clark's pathfields') gave a site in Laira for a new church. A foundation stone was laid for St Mary's in 1911 and it was consecrated in 1914.

Today its style of worship is described as 'open catholic' but St Mary's always seems to have been High Church. At the consecration a noisy crowd gathered outside which included a Kensit Preacher and representatives of the Protestant Truth Society, and Bishop Robertson of Exeter had to be whisked off by car at the end to the Crabtree mission hall for lunch. Part of the protest, however, was because the Vicar of Egg Buckland was 'dispensing with the services' of the resident curate. It was one of the last churches built in Plymouth under the 1897 Three Towns church extension plans. It is now part of the North Sutton team ministry.

The Roman Catholics have had a presence in the area since 1919. Then Bishop Kelly invited a small enclosed group of Carmelite nuns to move into Efford Manor. When they went in 1957 the diocese made the church and convent buildings into a centre of a new parish of Our Lady of Mount Carmel.

In 1964 the Redemptionist Fathers took up residence. In the grounds a housing trust has built sheltered accommodation, named Stott Close after Fred Stott, a leading Laira resident of the post-war years and Lord Mayor in 1960-1.

Little Efford was for some years between the wars an open-air school for delicate children. Pike Road, a main road from Laira into Efford, runs across Pike's Field, and Manor Farm is still there. The vast postwar housing estate of Efford flows down the hill to engulf Laira, and private housing fills the fields above Lower Crabtree, which is just a petrol-filling station.

A vast community college dominates what was Laira Lake. Crabtree proper is balanced on the edge of the biggest traffic intersection in Devon. Its residents have a footbridge to enable them to cross the six-lane highway in front of their houses.

The area has seen enormous changes in the past fifty years. Teclamit, a major supplier of lubrication equipment to the motor industry, built a vast factory in what had been nursery gardens, one of the first new industries opening after the war. It gradually faded away, with its site now under the roundabout. The traffic complex is now enclosed by out-of-town shopping centres (of which Sainsbury's with its flying sail facade is the most prominent), hotels, office blocks, garages, and a fast-food drive-in eatery. Even the Royal Marines had their logistics base beside the Plym (now looking for a new use). Warehouses and factories fill the land recovered from Plympton Marshes right up to Plympton St Mary, and a new industrial park stretches from Colebrook right up the valley to Newnham and Chaddlewood.

CHAPTER THIRTY-THREE

CATTEDOWN AND PRINCE ROCK

For centuries Cattedown was a wild and windy plateau. In one attack of plague a temporary hospital was built there: in another, to avoid infection, the Town Council held their meeting there. In the Civil War a fort was built there, with another bigger defensive work at Prince Rock, to ward off possible attacks across the river. Probably the most grisly event was the execution of two women in 1675 for murder; they were dragged there on hurdles from PLymouth and one then burned at the stake, the other hanged from a gallows alongside the fire.

Plymouth developed very slowly eastwards. In 1809 the Corporation built its New Eastern Road out from the junction of North Street and Exeter Street to link up with the new Embankment. From the Coxside turning onwards it was called Jubilee Street, to mark the fiftieth anniversary of the coronation of George III. In 1811 a fine row of redbrick houses, Brunswick Terrace, was built on the southern side (pulled down, alas, in 1957 to permit road widening). An 1820 map shows fields beyond the terrace, right out to Cattedown Corner which then had a turnpike where a charge was made to travel on the toll road. Not long after the First and Last pub was built - when it was built it was the first, or the last, for the traveller entering or leaving Plymouth. By 1830 there were just a few houses around Cattedown Corner, and a few more where Embankment Road met Laira Bridge Road; nothing else.

ON THE WATERFRONT

The oldest known building on the waterfront was the old Passage House Inn, but it is likely that there were a few cottages alongside. The little community threw up one infamous son, Captain John Avery, the pirate chief who was known as 'the King of Madagascar'. He set up a base on that island and plundered East India Company vessels in the Indian Ocean. He also established a base at the entrance to the Red Sea, from which he took such toll of the ships from India that the Mogul stopped the trade of the East Indies Company. Avery decided that discretion was called for, sailed back to the West Indies, sold his ship and dispersed his crew. A number were caught and hanged but Avery died in his bed at Bideford, claiming that he had been ruined by some Bristol merchants.

There were cottages on the Cattedown waterfront by 1820, where quarrying was in full swing. At the back of Martin's Wharf, on the edge

John Avery, the eighteenth-century pirate said to have been born in Cattedown.

A vessel freshly launched from Hill's shipyard, with the houses of the old waterside settlement of Cattedown clear in the background.

of Prince Rock quarry, was one row of cottages housing quarrymen and dockers on the wharf. Behind Hill's shipyard at Cattedown there was another row of cottages. Richard Hill, the shipbuilder, and Benjamin Sparrow, the quarrymaster, both had houses in this little settlement.

By 1850 both places had acquired pubs; that at Prince Rock being called the Robin Hood & Little John, and that at Cattedown the Freemason's Arms. This pub survived, as the Mason's Arms, until the 1950s but another Cattedown pub, the Three Crowns, disappeared under the wharfs. The Prince Rock cottages never grew, but at Cattedown quite a little community developed. In 1882 there was a shopkeeper, some railway employees, four shipwrights, three quarrymen and two master mariners among the seventeen residents and their families. A Wesleyan chapel looked after their spiritual welfare. By the turn of the century they had their own post office, and a baker called Adams who also advertised ship's biscuits. Some of these cottages, and the Freemason's Arms, survived until after World War II - indeed during that war the pub was said to be a centre of black market activity, probably supplied both by merchant ships at the wharfs and the large number of American servicemen in the area.

CATTEDOWN

John Nash, an Oreston man whose memories went back to the 1870s, wrote that after crossing to Cattedown one walked up the hill between low stone walls, and on either side it could be seen how deep the quarries were (That is still true). Then the road ran through fields with only a few desolate dairy farms before reaching South Devon Place. This imposing terrace of houses was built along Embankment Road in mid-century, but on the south side, where the shops now are, a rope walk and fields stretched away southwards to the edge of the quarries. Fernley Wallis, the Plymouth pharmacist whose memories stretched back to the 1890s, remarked in his little book that the rope walk stretched from the corner of Embankment Road, where the church is now, and when the walk was not long enough for the rope being made, the men finished off in the fields. The shops do not begin to appear opposite South Devon Place until 1885. By 1901 the row was largely finished.

Beyond these fields in the 1870s was only Laira House, which was converted in 1882 by Plymouth School Board into a Truant's Industrial School. Here persistent truants were incarcerated for up to 72 days. They were boarded there, set to work gardening, chopping wood and so forth, as well as having drill and instruction in the three Rs. Prince

Rock School was built on the site in 1909 by the new municipal Education Authority; the building dominated the local skyline with its three dome-topped turrets (actually built as ventilators). It still flourishes as a school, but Cattedown Road, another elementary school of the same period, was closed and for some years housed the Theatre Royal's wardrobe department.

An article in the *Western Morning News* of 17 May 1900 said of Cattedown that it probably contained the bulk of Plymouth's manufacturing concerns, but many thousands of residents had never seen the place. If one took the high road from South Devon Place, a little forest of chimneys soon became apparent. At the foot of the hill was a really old-fashioned hostelry (one of the bits of ancient Plymouth) at the passage across the Cattewater.

'There are a few still-pleasant houses, whose gardens no doubt once sloped to the sea, but are now shut in by heavy warehouses or wharfs. Proceeding along the too, too dusty road, the explorer is struck by the ambitious sign of the modest little public house, the Freemason's Arms.'

THE CHURCHES

The town slowly spread outwards. In 1844 a new parish was carved out of Charles Church, reaching from North Quay in Sutton Harbour right out to Prince Rock. The then Bishop of Exeter was the renowned Henry Philpott, a strong high churchman who had just appointed the first Puseyite vicar in the West of England to St Peter's on the other side of Plymouth. He appointed as priest to this new parish another strong high churchman. The architect employed to build the church of St John Sutton-on-Plym was Benjamin Ferrey, a pupil of Pugin, celebrated as an architect of Roman Catholic churches. St John, with its slender broach-spire, dedicated in 1855, became with St Peter's a centre of high churchmanship in

Laira House at Prince Rock, the home of the Julian family before conversion into a truant school. Prince Rock School now stands on the site.

Cattedown photographed from Turnchapel, showing the forest of chimneys and the waterfront houses.

The church of St John Sutton-on-Plym, the parish church of Cattedown. A drawing by Chris Robinson.

Plymouth, as both of them still are. The appointment of St John vicars for the past century has been in the hands of Keble College, Oxford, a stronghold of high churchmen.

In its early days its parishioners would have been drawn from the mixture of fine houses and slums west of the church. The field beyond the First and Last pub (called Dunghill Park) which reached out to Cattedown Corner and filled the area between Jubilee Terrace and what was the line of the Great Western Railway branch to Coxside Station, was built up with Alma Street appearing in 1862. St John Street is not mentioned until 1882, Holborn Street and the shops on the main road up to Cattedown Corner in 1888 and Clare Place in 1890.

In the 1880s the Culme-Seymours sold off the land they owned around Tothill House. Grenville Road was being built in 1885, Desborough Road and Cromwell Road were started in 1888. The three must have been named by a Civil War enthusiast, for Grenville was a royalist commander in the Siege of Plymouth, Desborough the major general appointed by Cromwell to command the area in the Commonwealth. These streets filled the area between the LSWR line and Embankment Road.

On the other side of the road the land now bounded by Cattedown Road on the west, Elliot Road to Gdynia Way and then to Oakfield Terrace Road on the east and South Milton Street on the south, had been bought by the Julian family in the 1820 sale for £1,575. Their name is remembered in Julian Street, their South Hams links in Alvington Street and South Milton Street. Later it was bought by John Elliot, a colonel in the Bengal Army of the East India company. Colonel Elliot had retired to the Barley House where his estate stretched from King Street to North Road West. His son, another Colonel J.J.Elliot of Leigham House, inherited on his father's death in 1859 and

when he died a bachelor in 1892 it passed to his cousin Tracey Elliot. He in turn sold the land to the Cattedown Road Building Estate, in which he kept a share with his partners, A.G.Clifton, a Devonport architect, and J.S.Hannaford, a Plymouth builder.

Smart's Meadow has remained open as the Astor Playing Field. The rest of the fields are now covered with the succession of long. east-west running streets on either side of Gdynia Way. A typical new house in Oakfield Terrace Road was sold to George Dalley, a beerhouse keeper of Millbay, at £54 for the site and £260 for the house. This is quite an expensive house for the time, for at the other end of Devonport the houses of Keyham manor, running up the hill north of St Levan's Road, were going for £200. But if the 580-odd houses built on these fields were sold at this rate, about £300 each, then these fields which cost £1,575 in 1820 had realised something like £175,000 at the end of the century.

Not all the houses were built by Hannaford. John Pethick was probably the major builder. His father had been superintendent of work on Laira Bridge. Young John became the biggest builder in Plymouth, leader of the Conservative Party on the Council and Mayor for two terms, 1898-1900. He built Plymouth Guildhall in 1873, and later on rebuilt Smeaton's Tower on the Hoe without cost to the Council. He was also a major developer in the Lipson area, where the terraces from Lipson Road and Mount Gould Road down to Tothill were being built at the same time. Another builder was A.N. Coles, who had just started up his little firm at Queen Anne's Battery; a daughter married Alderman Billy Priest of Davey, Sleep at Prince Rock. The firm of A.N.Coles became one of the biggest building contractors in the region.

Cattedown developed with amazing speed. In 1888 the directories mention Mainstone Terrace, the first of the long streets running east from

Cattedown Road. Within five years the other four long streets were built, Julian Street, Tresilian Avenue, Alvington Street and the north side of South Milton Street. Oakfield Terrace Road (which the Ordnance Survey maps regard as the boundary between Prince Rock and Cattedown) closes the eastern end of these streets. By 1888 it only had houses from 1 to 14, with 5 to 8 still being built. By 1896 it had extended to No 53. Cotehele Avenue was half built by 1899, and Home Sweet Home Terrace, with its wonderful name contradicting the gasholders which tower over its back doors, was built in the same year. Elliot Road first appears in 1901. The houses seem to have been occupied as quickly as they were built. They are all typical products of the new Housing Acts, with streets of reasonable width and each house having a back door into a back lane.

MORE CHURCHES

The churches moved quickly into the area. The parishioners of St John's built a redbrick mission church, St Mary the Virgin and St Mary Magdalene, in 1899 on the corner of Alvington Street and Oakfield Terrace. In 1910 a larger church had been added, designed by Sir Charles Nicholson, the leading builder of parish churches of the day (he also built Yelverton Church). St Mary's became a separate parish in 1911, in an area which had virtually no houses twenty years before. The church was closed and the parish restored to St John's in 1956. St Mary's Church was closed down that year, but reopened in 1972 and eventually turned into a church hall in 1990.

A Methodist mission hall is shown in Cattedown waterside in a map of 1856. With the growth of the new community back from the river a new Cattedown Methodist Mission was opened in 1897 in Tresilian Street. It was at first in a cottage, later replaced by a terraced house. At the diamond jubilee in 1957 was John Mewton, who had been at the original opening. His grandson is a dentist in Plymouth.

In 1895 the Bible Christians moved into the area, building at Cattedown Corner. They first built the large school block, but not until 1904 was the church building completed. It is typical of the nonconformist churches of the time, with the school as big as the church. After the Bible Christians amalgamated with the other Methodist Churches it was known as Embankment Road Methodist Church, and not until 1983, when the Methodists were consolidating their dwindling congregations, were the buildings sold. It was bought by a charismatic evangelical body, the Group of Foursquare Gospel Alliance whose congregation was outgrowing their Elim Pentecostal Church in Notte Street. Now renamed Plymouth Christian Centre, the church flourishes.

East of the Methodist Church, Smart's Meadow had become a cricket ground by 1895. According to Eyre's 1900 directory Plymouth Cricket Club was there in 1900. The Astors later bought it to preserve it as an open space and playing field for the community, and it became known as the Astor Playing Field. Eventually it was taken over by the local Education Authority, but still remains an open space.

Brunswick Terrace, the elegant early nineteenth-century redbrick houses built for merchants fleeing the growing slums around the Barbican. By the time it was knocked down in the postwar years for the widening of Exeter Street, it too was swarming with tenants.

COUNCIL HOUSES

After the Housing Act of 1890 the Borough Council embarked on a slum clearance programme and needed housing for the people displaced by the demolition of Looe St and Hooe Street. So the Mayor, Aldermen and Burgesses bought the Prince Rock Estate, the fields bounded by Embankment Road on the north, Elliot Road on the west, and the present Gdynia Way on the east and south. These fields had already been crossed by Laira Bridge Road, linking Laira Bridge with Embankment Road. On the north of Laira Bridge Road the Council built Prince Rock School, on the site of its former Truant's School (it was said that there were no more candidates for this school, which suggests that it was an efficient remedy for the problem). South of Laira Bridge Road in 1895 they started building for the first time what the foundation stone calls 'working men's houses'. The little streets which serve this early housing estate. Goad, Harvey, Williams, and Risdon, are all named after members of the Housing Committee!

The houses are of a quality to merit a notice in the second edition of the Devon volume in the 'Buildings of England' series started by Nikolaus Pevsner. Bridget Cherry writes 'the two-storeyed flats and houses of 1893-6 by Hine & Odgers...red brick with timbered gables, a conscious adaptation of the English vernacular idiom...a little further out, two further blocks of two-storey flats of 1897 by Wibling and De Boinville for the Plymouth Charitable Trusts, fancy wooden balconies to the first floor entrances'.

The Prince Rock row of cottages at the back of Martin's Wharf gradually dropped out of use and became sheds as the new terraces offered better accommodation. The building and later expansion of Cattedown Wharfs bit by bit destroyed the cottages there, until only the Freemasons Arms and a couple cottages just west of the level crossing survived. They finally disappeared in the 1950s.

Cattedown waterfront as a little community is now only a memory. The Cattedown between Embankment Road and the quarries is still a community a little apart from Plymouth. Its terraces are distinctive; they were erected at a time when builders could buy ornaments ready-made from their merchants and a number of the long Cattedown roads have their house fronts smartened up with these quite elegant bas-reliefs.

CHAPTER THIRTY-FOUR

ORESTON

Plymstock, the biggest and oldest parish on the south side of the Cattewater, is back from the river but has over the years developed four waterside communities,, Pomphlett, Oreston, Hooe and Turnchapel. Of these Oreston is the oldest and the most important, because it was on the direct route from Plymstock to Plymouth and for centuries was the base of the ferry crossing to Cattedown. Its main street was the road from Plymstock village, leading down to the waterside and the ferry beach, later the Town Quay, still called the Turnquay.

The village grew up around this point, with most early development mainly to the west, where the Anglican church was planted in the middle of a densely built-up area. The age of some of the houses can be gauged from Lang's House, now the headquarters of the Plym Yacht Club. When members were converting it from its original bakery in 1970-71 they removed an oven which was dated back to the seventeenth century, Stuart times.

Marine Villas was built in 1790 by the Duke of Bedford to house his agent and the doctor. Richard Hill the shipbuilder leased the house now called Oyster Cottage (so named from the shells still found on the foreshore). Lydia Palmer lived in the next door house. She is believed to have been Hill's mistress; certainly there is a communicating door between the houses on the bedroom floor!

Richard Hill built his Oreston ships on the shore on both sides of the houses. In more recent times Lucas had his boatyard next door. It is now overbuilt by Al Brotherton's yacht storage quay. At the back of the quay an old house used to carry the royal coat of arms; the local belief is that it was a Custom House. Next door was the Forester's Arms and an area known as Captain's Court.

ROBINSON CRUSOE

Ferries breed pubs; sailors resort to pubs, and Oreston has been a run ashore for ships anchored in the sheltered estuary for as long as ships have used the port. The earliest example, almost a lesson about Jack Ashore, is provided by Alexander Selkirk. He had been marooned on an island in the Pacific in 1704 and was not rescued until 1709. He went home to Largs in Fife and made money out of writing his story. Daniel Defoe read it, and turned it into *Robinson Crusoe* in 1719. Twelve months before the book was published Selkirk married a London woman.

Oreston before the green was created, with the tide coming right up to the quay.

Then he went back to sea, and in 1720 had a spell in Plymouth. He was a master's mate, a petty officer aboard HMS *Weymouth*, which was dismasted in a blow in the Sound. While the ship was under repair Selkirk found his way into the Cattewater and to Oreston, where he got to know Frances Candish. She was the spinster daughter of a publican and ran the pub herself after his death. In spite of having a wife in London, Selkirk began to court the landlady even though she was 63 years old (he was only 44). The *Weymouth* had been damaged on November 20, and they were married on December 12: a fast worker, our Alexander. But the ship sailed on December 20. After eight days of married life Frances was left behind; a year later her husband died of yellow fever off the west coast of Africa. Both widows produced wills entitling them to all that Alexander had left, but the Oreston woman finally won the lawsuits. A house on the corner of Plymstock Road and Marine Road now bears a plaque commemorating that 'Robinson Crusoe' lived there - for eight days!

THE VILLAGE GROWS

Oreston was still a small village in those days, but it would have grown quietly for the rest of the eighteenth century as quarrying developed and shipping increased. The growth was accelerated

The back of Oreston Methodist Church with the graveyard hiding behind the high wall.

in the nineteenth century. The opening of Breakwater Quarry, the crewing of 25 barges going out to the Breakwater for 25 years, the even more rapid expansion of shipping and the growth of Plymouth, which would have needed more and more stone from the other quarries, all attracted people to Oreston. In the 1880s its men either worked in the quarries or Bayly's timber yard, while the rest went to sea.

Men even worked in the Dockyard. Uncle Ned Harper would take them over to Cattedown in the ferryboat at 5.30 am, and they then walked to Devonport for a day's work, and back in the evenings, in the days before the trams (when horse trams started they only had to walk to Derry's Clock). Uncle Ned was a popular character, he even flew flags on the ferry when his friends got married. The little community at Cattedown had a Methodist chapel but no burial ground; Uncle Ned would carry the coffins over the river for burial in the Oreston Methodist graveyard.

THE CHURCHES

The growth of the village can be measured through the growth of the Methodist church membership. An Oreston society was first mentioned in 1789, the date of Wesley's last visit to Plymouth. It had 14 members, and by 1813 it was still under 22. Then came the spurt; the Breakwater Quarry started work that year and by 1816 Methodist membership was up to 74. Two years later the society had bought land from the Duke of Bedford, and built a church to seat 306 people, at a cost of £700. In 1815 a Sunday School was started by 18-year-old William Swale, and a special building for the school erected in 1835. A Methodist graveyard was opened in 1854 on land given by the Duke, and the first person to be buried there was Martha Swiggs, whose coffin was brought over from Cattedown in the ferry boat. Methodism was so strong in the village, and its associated teetotalism, that a member, William Coombs, bought out what had been Mrs Selkirk's pub, closed it down and renamed it Minard House.

The Anglican Church, as in so many places, was remote from the new developing communities and the free churches moved in first. At Oreston the Anglicans were not far behind; the mission church of the Good Shepherd was there in 1823 (John's Guide). When in 1858 the Vicar of Plymstock petitioned for a licence for the Church of the Good Shepherd, he stated that there were 1,200 people living with a mile of the church. At the turn of the century there had only been 1,600 people in the whole parish of Plymstock. Close by the church is the church hall, carrying a quiet little shield on which appears a date, 1893, above an initial B surmounted by a ducal coronet - for the Duke of Bedford.

A new Wesleyan Methodist Church was built in 1888 on the edge of the village, next to the burial ground. The duke gave the land and £250 to the society, in exchange for the old church building. The new church cost £1,500, and the foundation stone was laid by Mr F.B.Mildmay, the MP for the area. The caretaker's cottage alongside cost £500. Methodist churches with their own burial grounds are very rare; the last interment at Oreston was in 1990. Since then family graves can be opened up for the burial of relatives, or cremation urns; but it is still alongside the church.

The old Methodist Church was rechristened the Chievely Hall, and became the village hall, standing in the main street running back from the water. It flourished for years. In 1929 for example, the Plymstock Amateur Operatic Society staged *HMS Pinafore* there for six nights; in 1997 they are still going strong and take the Athenaeum Theatre in Plymouth for a week! When the old church fell into disuse as a public hall it was sold on to various people who used it as a shop; in 1995 it was standing empty.

Apart from dame schools, the first school in the district was the National School (which taught Anglican principles), founded in 1827 at Dean Cross. After the Education Act of 1870 a board school was built at Oreston in 1873. It is still in use as an infant's school, but with considerable additions over the years.

Not just the churches flourished with this growth in population. At one time there were five public houses, including the Old, the Ferryboat, the Forester's Arms and the King's Arms. Now only the King's Arms survives. The Forester's Arms, probably also the base of the friendly society of the same name, was a three-storey building off Marine Road and is remembered as having a large tree in its yard.

EMPLOYMENT

The seamen of Oreston were working mainly in the little coasters between Start Point and Falmouth, many in craft of 50-60 tons carrying Sparrow's limestone for the farmers. The smacks would also carry stone for road repairs to Bigbury Bay, Hallsands and Beesands. The ketches were coasting further afield, some to Newcastle for coal, others to Corunna for cattle. The schooners went to France and the Mediterranean for fruit, and Newfoundland for salt cod.

Sailing ships only faded from the picture during World War I. As late as 1930 there were still many captains living in the village; and an old man writing his memories in that year was able to name 24 of them, and their ships.

Fifty years earlier, said another veteran in his 1928 memories, 'Oreston was distinctly nautical in appearance, with many retired captains and pilots living there. There were flagstaffs in many gardens'.

The P&O steamer Dart *approaching Oreston. The ships moored at the Gut in the background are reminders of where many Oreston men found employment.*

With so many Oreston men coasting in and out of Plymouth, it is no wonder that it was Oreston men who in 1911 built the beacon on the Shagstone, a dangerous rock between the eastern end of the Breakwater and the Mewstone. Shipbuilding was another major employer. There were three or four yards at work for much of the century. Even after the biggest, Richard Hill, opened his yard at Cattedown he still built some ships in Oreston.

All this was very much the picture until the world changed in the Great War. The quarries dwindled, the small sailing ships had had their day, and even the timber yard closed in the end. But Oreston's population grew rather than otherwise; housing estates spread down from Plymstock as, in the 1920s and 30s, Plympton Rural Council pushed the growth of houses for all it was worth. The ferries and the train services gave way to buses, and buses were overtaken by private cars.

ORESTON ROVERS

One of the few links with the great days of the working village was the football team. Oreston Rovers, who always played a leading part in the Plymouth and District League. Their pitch was on top of the hill on the Plymstock road, now lost under Birch Pond Road. One set of goalposts was on the edge of Radford Quarry, and there were high nets behind the goal to stop wide kicks going into the quarry. Every now and again one would sail over the top, and the match then had to wait until it was retrieved - unless a second ball was available. It was the expansion of the quarry that eventually swallowed up half the pitch in the 1930s and brought an end to the club. The great rivals of the Rovers was the Sutton Harbour team, Green Waves - impolitely known outside fishing circles as the Barbican Ballbusters. There have been various efforts started since in Oreston to revive the old name, but none came to anything.

The first housing develoment came with the Thorneyville estate, built on former farmland, and Rollis Park Road still shows the dignified fronts of the Edwardian development. The well-to-do of the village were early residents, but commuters from Plymouth were soon buying the houses. Between the wars the green fields between Oreston and Plymstock were steadily built over and by the 1990s the houses flow without a break north to the main road and east as far as Elburton.

THE WAR YEARS

Oreston had a bad time in World War II. It shared in the alerts and the raids on Plymouth all through. Early on the Methodist minister, the Rev W.G.Spencer, was killed while visiting people in a shelter. There was a barrage balloon operated from fields opposite the Methodist Church, and in 1944 the men's billet was struck by a bomb, killing two. The survivors were then housed in the Methodist Sunday School.

Then, at about 3.30 on the morning of 29 April 1944, there was a fierce raid concentrated on the Cattewater. The bus depot at Laira Bridge was struck, and there was more damage near the Rising Sun, but Oreston suffered worst of all. Nine people were killed in a public shelter, and another six, nearly all from one family.

The biggest change to the appearance of the village came in the 1960s, when thousands of tons of Quarry waste was cleaned out of Breakwater Quarry to make way for the new gas plant. Masses of this material was used to fill in the little bay in front of the Quay. Now it is a pleasant grassed area, with a waterside promenade looking across the Plym. Where the black-hulled coal hulks and lime carriers once lay in trots offshore, now elegant white-hulled yachts ride at their moorings. It is all very attractive, but it is not the old working front that Oreston once presented to the world.

CHAPTER THIRTY-FIVE

HOOE AND HOOE LAKE

Hooe is a modest enough place now, but it is the only one of the original Cattewater settlements to have been a Saxon manor, with its own place in Domesday. The demesne, or manor house and land in hand, needed just one slave to run it, and had one plough. The rest of the manor also occupied one plough land but was cut into six farms and two smallholdings. It was sufficiently prosperous to be broken up, over the years into three manors, Radford, East Hooe (which is now called Higher Hooe) and West Hooe (Lower Hooe, or Hooe village).

WEST HOOE

Until 1964 Hooe Lake came right up to the edge of the road from Radford to Jennycliff. In that year masses of unwanted infill from other sites were dumped behind a new sea wall, from just above the Royal Oak across to the western shore. There was the stone cleared from Breakwater Quarry for the gas plant as well as material from Plymouth demolitions; even the remains of the celebrated Harvest Home pub at Drake Circus were used. Now it is a pleasant grassed area, used by children at play and for local events.

On the southern side of the road, behind a one-storey filling station and enclosed by an undistinguished shopping centre, is a big barn. It is all that survives of West Hooe Farm, which was

A 1694 drawing of Hooe Manor on the lake waterfront, with the village to the left.

pulled down in 1969. (The author remembers standing in the roadway on a black Sunday in the 1920s watching the smoke going up from half a dozen funeral pyres; foot and mouth had struck and all the cattle were being destroyed.)

Next to the barn is an ancient arch, now in peril of being destroyed by rampant ivy. According to the late James Barber, sometime curator of Plymouth City Museum and a considerable archaeologist, the barn and arch are all that is left of the manor house and the chapel of St Lawrence, licensed in 1417. The barn is Elizabethan, the arch fourteenth-fifteenth century. The farmhouse stood south of the barn, a sixteenth-century building on the site of the older manor house. G.W.Copeland, the pre-war archaeological adviser to the Old Plymouth Society, considered that the arch was in its original position and led to a courtyard in front of the farmhouse.

For some years now the Radford Park and Hooe Lake Preservation Association has been trying to get the City Council to put a plaque on the side of the barn. There are long-standing plans to convert the barn into a community centre, and it was restored by a voluntary body for that purpose in the 1970s.

Stamford Fort, built in 1865 as part of the ring of forts guarding Plymouth, became a nightclub in 1970 and has since changed into a sports club.

The original Hooe village hides away at the end of Lake Road, tucked in behind the Royal Oak pub. The oldest part of the village is here, grouped around the quay on the corner of the lake. The area has been cleaned up by the City Council with some houses demolished, and an attractive square created from which to view the lake. Hexton Hill climbs steeply up to the east, now lined by modern houses. The old cottages had deteriorated into slums and were cleared away in the 1950s and 60s. Yonder Street runs out to the east from the Square, and this still retains some pleasant cottages which give a hint of how attractive the village was. They were built in 1736 by Lady Rogers, whose husband owned the manor. The row is built on the floor of a shallow quarry; the quarry face is tight up against the back of the houses. The old houses on Hexton Hill were built at about the same time, adding to the older cottages which stood around the square. The row of cottages which line the north side of what is now the main road, up to the Baptist Chapel, is older than the outside appearance suggests.

The members of this waterside community have over the centuries earned their keep from the sea, fishermen, longshoremen, 'lumpers' unloading the ships that came into the Cattewater. Some were quarrymen. Powderham Cottage has been occupied by a blacksmith and a boatbuilder, the little slip beside his garden was where he built his boats. Another boatbuilder was located beside the Royal Oak. John's 1823 Guide describes Hooe as a group of neatly whitewashed dwellings surrounded by fruit trees which attracted numerous visitors in the summer. There were also a number of tea gardens, renowned for their strawberry teas and used by many Plymouth churches for their Sunday School outings. But quarrying, the development of the timber yard across the lake, and the growing volume of shipping from the middle of the eighteenth-century all would have provided new employment and increased population.

Just as the Methodists moved into Oreston in 1798, so the Baptists were in Hooe soon after. Members of George Street Baptist Church in Plymouth started a Sunday School in the village in 1820, using a room in a Yonder Street house. Soon they were running Sunday evening services and converting a barn or outhouse behind Hooe House (now the Fanshawe Nursing Home) into a chapel. In 1876 work began on a proper church,

A postcard of Lower Hooe before the green was created, with the tide reaching up to the road in front of the shops. The Royal Oak is in the background.

which was opened in 1877 and has flourished ever since, with its own minister. It 1958 it became independent of George Street, its mother church.

The Baptist Church appears to sit uncomfortably next door to the Victoria Inn, which looks like a conversion from a couple of the older cottages. The pub predates the church, however; its landlord in 1850 was Abraham Ryder and another Ryder, Thomas, had the Royal Oak. The Royal Oak was only converted from a farm in 1847. The Mount Batten Social Club was built, on a smaller scale than it is now, in 1936. It was originally the Hooe Social Club, and is on the site of Harris's farm and tea gardens.

The village suffered a number of air raids during the war. On 27 November 1940 ten people were killed in the village, in two houses, and the next night the oil tanks across the water in Turnchapel Quarry were set on fire. During the raids the tunnel from Hexton Quay back to the quarry was used as an air raid shelter. Tickets were issued by the rural district council to limit the numbers, but the night the oil tanks were set on fire, everybody (so it is said) took shelter in the tunnel. The air was so thick that even the candles went out! The whole village was evacuated to Plympton for several nights.

HIGHER HOOE

At the top of the hill between Radford and Hooe village, approached by turning from the main road into Belle Vue Road and Hooe Lane, are two eighteenth-century houses enclosed by modern housing. The three-storeyed Retreat of 1775 has a rendered front and slate-hung sides. Hooe Manor, formerly Belle Vue and built in 1777, is a more imposing-looking house with a pillared portico.

The Retreat is now a nursing home. Hooe Manor still stands in a walled garden, but has been rented out as council flats since 1948. The first council houses in the area were built in 1932, on the north side of the road to Radford. Building resumed in 1947, and more were built on the other side of the road in 1956.

PARISH CHURCH

The Anglicans were served by the parish church at Plymstock, a mile and a half away from Hooe. until 1855. Sir Frederic Rogers, who became the eighth baronet and lord of the manor of West Hooe in 1851 on the death of his father, was an earnest forty-year-old who had made a lifelong friend at Eton of Gladstone. At Oxford he had come under the influence of J.H.Newman, the high church don who later became a cardinal of the Roman Catholic church. At Sir Frederic's initiative a new church, dedicated to St John, school and schoolmaster's house was built in 1854 between Hooe and Turnchapel. It was not very convenient for either village but meant to serve both, because the third Earl of Morley (another Gladstone supporter), who owned most of Turnchapel, also helped finance the building.

Sir Frederic (who later became Lord Blachford) engaged the young William White of Truro, a first-class church architect, who produced the present group of buildings. Modest as they appear in their external grey limestone ashlar, the church interior has the wealth of coloured marble and rich ornaments that mark out the Victorian Tractarian. It was one of the earliest high church buildings in the Plymouth neighbourhood. Hooe became an ecclesiastical parish in 1856, including Turnchapel and Mount Batten and reaching out to Bovisand. The vicarage, also designed by White, is now St Anne's House and has been the residence of the officer commanding HMS *Cambridge*, the gunnery school at Wembury. Hooe still has its own vicar but he lives in a much more modest house.

The school inevitably became a National School, teaching Anglican principles. It was only replaced in 1931 by a new school at Hooe which also amalgamated Turnchapel junior and higher schools. In 1955-6 a new infants' school was built opposite the Baptist Church.

HOOE LAKE

Entered from the Cattewater by a narrow break in the limestone ridge, Hooe Lake is today a rectangular basin so choked with mud that it dries out at low tide. Actually the depth through the mud to the underlying rock is nearly as deep as in the main channel of Plym outside. Before the war its south and west beaches were lined with old hulks used as houseboats. Just one or two are left now and the old collection of derelict hulks and rotting skeletons of once-proud craft are slowly being cleared away. With its mud, its graveyard of half-submerged and mouldering hulks, its fringe of worn-out industrial sites, the lake has hardly been a beauty spot. The quarries are owned by English Clays and they have tried several times to

William Paynes' 1790 drawing of Belle Vue from the entrance to Hooe Lake, showing how it stood alone on its hillside with a splendid outlook to justify its name.

Hooe Lake after the infill, an aerial view of the village c.1985.

The ornamental 'castle' on the dam cutting off the duckponds from Hooe Lake, an old photograph with stone barges at the quay behind.

the preservation association. In 1974 an arboretum was created in the park by the Radford Heritage Group.

On the south side of the lake is what was the quay serving the old house and a cottage. When Radford House was rebuilt in the eighteenth century bits of the Elizabethan house were incorporated in the cottage and boathouse on the quay. The group of ruins is known as St Keverne's. The remains of Pond Farm, at the head of the lake, was taken over in 1978 by an enthusiastic body and turned into an adventure centre, very much used .

polish up the area with housing schemes and marinas. Locals, however, are devoted to their lake as it is and so far have resisted all developers.

HARRIS and BULTEEL

Radford was sold up in 1922. It was bought by Billy Mitchell who demolished the house and sold off much of the estate as housing estates. The park of the great house had been laid out around the duck ponds and lake, and escaped the rash of modern housing. In 1956 Mr Mitchell's son Gordon transferred Radford Lodge, the lake and associated grounds to Plympton Rural District Council as an open space. After a great struggle the eighteenth-century Radford Lodge was restored and put to use. With the boundary extension of Plymouth in 1967 the park passed to city ownership and is zealously watched over by

CHAPTER THIRTY-SIX

TURNCHAPEL

Turnchapel, nestling below cliffs on the south bank of the Cattewater, looks to be a village of real antiquity, but not even the name is known until three centuries ago. There is no trace of a place called Turnchapel until Captain Greenville Collins's collection of charts, *Great Britain's Coasting Pilot*, published in 1693, marks 'Turn Chaple'. The authoritative Devon Place Names gives Donn's map of Devon, published in 1765, as the earliest use of the name, which was 'Tan Chapel olim St Anne's'. *The Place-Names of Devon* uses this as an explanation of the name, saying: 'There was formerly a chapel dedicated to St Anne here'. But there is no other knowledge of an early chapel of St Anne. It has been suggested that the chapel of West Hooe manor is the chapel in question, but modern scholarship suggests that this was dedicated to St Leonard, and it is hardly likely that a chapel beside Hooe Lake would give its name to a place over half a mile away. So whatever the derivation of Turnchapel, St Anne's Chapel seems to be unlikely.

Not until the end of the eighteenth century do maps begin to show any houses at Turnchapel. Over the years several of these old houses have been pulled down and rebuilt; others have been so changed that it is hard to attribute any antiquity to

Turnchapel as it was for so many years after 1920, with the cable ships at their moorings, a flurry of P&O ferries hovering around their pier, and the RAF oil tanks in the quarry overlooking Hooe Lake.

them. The only exception is the row of Harbour View Cottages. This area, at the foot of the road into the village, seems to be the kernel of the village, and probably started about the end of the seventeenth century. It may well have housed men working in the quarries at Mount Batten or at the back of Turnchapel itself, or fishermen and longshoremen picking up odd jobs connected with the shipping of the increasingly busy estuary. Smuggling too was a profitable enterprise in those years.

The Manor House at the end of Boringdon Terrace in Turnchapel.

Certainly we have industrial activity at this time. Lord Boringdon (who owned the area as part of his manor of Plympton) built his shipbuilding yard at what is now Turnchapel Wharf. He was taking over the site used for earlier government shipbuilding and repairs. In 1809 a dry dock was added and his tenant Blackburn was building ships for the Royal Navy. About this time Lord Boringdon also built Boringdon Terrace, which is still the backbone of the village. Like the older houses further west, these properties back on the cliff face of a quarry,

Chris Robinson's drawing of Boringdon Terrace, Turnchapel.

which makes it clear that quarrying here had finished before this time.

Boringdon Terrace consists of the Manor House at the eastern end, a building intended to be impressive and probably designed as the house and office of the manor agent. West of that are eleven single-fronted houses with pedimented entrances and then the double-fronted Boringdon Arms, a storey higher and believed to have been built originally about 1760 as the quarry master's house. Four houses west of this completes the row, of a different pattern. The end property, Hydes House, has an interesting double-storeyed entrance porch.

At the eastern end of the terrace, the third house from the corner was until the interwar years the Shipwright's Arms. This was perfectly positioned to serve the workers in the shipyard, which continued under various ownerships until the end of the century. In fact when ships were being built in the dock closest to the village the bowsprit would overhang the road opposite the Shipwright's. At other end of the village and at the bottom of the hill is the New Inn which was set up by John Parker in 1770.

There was plenty of work in the nineteenth century. The quarries from Mount Batten around to Hooe Lake, the shipyards at both Batten and in the villages, the Oreston timber yard just a short ferry journey over the entrance to Hooe Lake, all were near at hand and needed labour. The enterprising could take a ferry from Oreston to Cattedown and have all Plymouth, and the Dockyard, within reach. After the steam Oreston & Turnchapel Ferry Co opened up in 1869 it was much easier to reach Plymouth for work, and a new alternative came with the arrival of the railway in 1897. There was also work as longshoremen, stevedores and lumpers on the coal hulks, and general dock labour across the river.

The village grew quickly enough after the start of the nineteenth century, for the Methodists established a church at the bottom of the hill in 1817, about the same time as at Oreston. The church was restored in 1879, according to a rondel on the northern gable, about ten years before Oreston built its new church. But while Oreston's Methodist Church still flourishes, that at Turnchapel closed about 1960.

The village itself, perched on the narrow floor between the quarry face and the sea, cannot expand. The houses on the eastern side of St John's Road were added in the late nineteenth century. In the post-war years more houses have been built on top of the quarry cliffs, and fourteen more added at the western end. Government land on both sides of the village has stopped further expansion There were rows of married quarters west of St John's road inside the R.A.F. station, but with the arrival of Plymouth Development Corporation these have been demolished. It is now likely that new houses will be built in this area (the old Well Field, one-time playground of Turnchapel), and along the waterfront.

The village was created a conservation area in 1977, with Boringdon Terrace from the Manor House to the Boringdon Arms declared grade II listed buildings. The study recognised that the major problem of the village was the appalling wirescape (the tangle of overhead electricity and telephone cables), car parking, and the narrow hill down. The wirescape has been cleared up. The new marina of 1990 created some parking for the yacht owners, and another small car park was added at the eastern end of Boringdon Terrace. There is a good road to the east past the Royal Marines establishment and along the shores of Hooe Lake, but the road is government property and is closed by a locked gate for most of the time. Common sense dictates that this should be opened to create a one-way traffic system through the village.

CHAPTER THIRTY-SEVEN

POMPHLETT,
AND MOUNT BATTEN BEFORE 1917

Pomphlett appears on the 1809 Ordnance Survey map as just the mill at the head of Pomphlett Creek and two or three houses close around. *White's Directory* of 1850 lists one resident, John Eva, stone agent. In 1856 there is a row of cottages running up the hill to the south.

At the top of the hill where the road turns sharp right to Oreston, a smaller turning to the left indicates 'Honcray'. This road crosses a bridge over the former railway cutting and in front is a house with the name on the fanlight, 'Wesley Cottage'. Running back down the hill, facing west, is a row of cottages. The second block carries a rondel on the central pediment inscribed 'John Coombs 1868' and the third block of cottages has a similar rondel, 'Barn Park Cottages, 1877'. On the other side of the road the row of houses has a tablet on the side of the top house, 'W.A.M. Millway Cottages 1905'. W.A.M was the mill owner in 1905, William Mitchell, who built the cottages when he was extending the mill.

The story behind Wesley Cottage is that a new miller arrived at Pomphlett in the nineteenth century and was saddened that there was no Methodist place of worship there. So he set aside for the purpose a room in the mill. The congregation grew, and in the 1860s built a chapel at the top of the hill, at the entrance to Honcray.

By the end of the century the congregation was outgrowing this chapel, and with a great effort they raised the £2,000 to build a new chapel, opened in 1909, on the main road to Plymstock, on land given by the Duke of Bedford. Wesley Cottage is the former chapel.

The growth of population indicated by the need for chapels would have been mainly quarry workers, for the area is surrounded by limestone workings. The present Pomphlett Road, where the Methodist Church still flourishes, has a terrace of 1890-1900 bay window houses on the north side, indicating the surge in population at the time. The other side of the road has even newer houses, but in the area behind the church and at the foot of Millview Place are houses that may be of about the same age as the dated cottages. This area, and the cottages up the hill, form the original nineteenth-century settlement.

MOUNT BATTEN BEFORE THE AIR STATION

Mount Batten ...before the Great War...was a playground for young folk...a bit of unspoiled rough land...apart from the old castle - we never called it a tower as folks appear to do now - and the public house facing across to Queen Anne's Battery, there was nothing to detract from its wild nature.

Mount Batten beach, a favourite resort for Plymothians before the airmen took over in 1916. Once the P&O ferry service began to include Batten in their calls it became easily accessible and the crowds justified the tent selling teas.

So wrote R.V.Walling in the *Western Morning News* of 27 February 1967. For Boy Scouts, bathers, ramblers, fishermen, courting couples or just plain idlers, he went on, it was a paradise. There was a wonderful profusion of valerian growing from the limestone rocks. Near the public house was a pontoon landing stage at which the ferryboats from Phoenix Wharf to Turnchapel called, fare one penny. For the same price a waterman on the Barbican would 'put you over' if he could get a minimum of six passengers.

Sea anglers used to congregate in strength on the inshore side of the breakwater (The largest octopus ever taken in British waters was caught there). Bathers delighted in the little sandy beaches on the seaward side of the peninsula. Men would extemporise a bathing costume from a handkerchief and a piece of string; boys did not

bother but bathed 'in the raw'. 'Of course no female of any age would dream of bathing other than in the ladies' pool under Plymouth Hoe.' In those days the United Services Golf Club was between Batten and Jennycliff (today it is the Staddon Heights Golf Club and has moved to the top of Staddon).

Mr Walling is not quite right in his memory of the number of houses. There was the Breakwater Inn, built in 1884, facing the base of Batten Breakwater, which still survives. It ceased to be a pub when the RAF arrived in 1916, but the Development Corporation hopes to see it enlarged and revived again as a pub. There was also the the Castle Inn which faced across to Plymouth. It is believed that this was originally built as a bothy for quarry workers. On the seaward side of the mass of rock on which stands the tower was a row

Another pre-1914 view of Mount Batten, from the river, with the Castle Inn in the foreground and the sail trawler fleet well in evidence.

of cottages originally built for the Coastguards. The Coastguards had gone in those pre-war days, and the cottages sold.

Hedley Foot, the elder brother of the Liberal leader Isaac Foot, had one which he and his family used in the summer months. Each day he and his son, another Hedley, would row across to the Barbican to the family building business founded by father Isaac in Notte Street. Next door in the summer months lived R.B.Wigfull, the jeweller of Windsor Lane. After the war his son Bertie revived the business in a City Centre shop.

The one blemish to this paradise, the fish manure factory, with a tall red chimney, started in 1906 'just in the lee of the castle', with its dreadful stench. This building, of limestone with brick quoins bears a date 1834; it may have been built as a fish manure factory at that date away from the town because of the smell, and later closed down. After 1900 the new steam trawlers had been landing big catches of dogfish in Sutton Harbour, which produced large quantities of waste. So

much so that the Corporation stopped removing waste from the fish market in 1906. A new company which called itself Plymouth Fish Guano and Oil Co took over the old Batten building and began making fertiliser from the waste. Complaints about the smell arose almost at once. In 1911 the Corporation and Sutton Harbour Improvement Company sorted out (in theory) the offal problem. A new company was formed from the old Mount Batten firm, apparently called Climo Works, but by 1913 the old cry about the stink was back again; 'it could be smelt as far away as Mutley'. The Mutley nose seemed always the one offended.

All this came to an end when the Royal Naval Air Service took over Mount Batten in 1916. The peninsula was closed to the public, the holiday-makers in the coastguard cottages were turned out, and the fish manure factory went as well. It can only be hoped that with the completion of Plymouth Development Corporation's plans that the public will be able to enjoy this paradise again.

EPILOGUE

THE BRIGHT FUTURE

In 1987 Plymouth City Council set afoot a major study of the future of the city, and a large part of this was devoted to the regeneration of the waterfront, reaching from the south yard of the Dockyard to Laira Bridge. In 1988 a Waterfront Development Strategy was commissioned, which focused on tourism and leisure, all with an eye to creating employment opportunities. One of the major schemes for the whole of Cattedown was the formation of a company which embraced both private and public capital: New Cattedown Ltd. It was formed of a partnership between a national development company, Bellway Urban Renewals, Carkeek Developments (a subsidiary of a big Plymouth builder) and the City Council. Bellway dropped out quite early on, and the scheme became a joint venture between the City Council and Carkeek.

The first need was for improved roads. By the end of 1994 two new roads had been made into the area, opening up approaches to the Prince Rock end from the Plymouth side of Laira Bridge, and to Cattedown from the western end of Gdynia Way. Gdynia Way was also connected with a direct road to the new fish market at Coxside. About £7 million was spent on the road infrastructure, partly funded by the Government's Urban Partnership Fund. The new company had over a hundred acres of land planned for varied development, including 'affordable' housing, industrial units, a high tech business park and leisure facilities.

THE NEW CATTEDOWN

The small housing development at the end of South Milton Street was finished by 1994. The next step was to demolish the 'Shapter's Field mountain', a mass of inferior limestone left by the quarrymen. This is turn was te be deposited on the Cockle Bank to create a new area of land ready for development. The scheme, which was launched in May 1995 with a £3.9m grant from the government's English Partnership Agency,, was to dredge a trench outside the bank, fill this with large stones and then build up on top of it with rather smaller stone to make a dam all around the site. Then the soft top mud would be dug out of the enclosed dry area until a firmer surface was reached, and the whole area filled with still smaller stones. The road entry to this area would be at the end of the newly-created Shapter's Road. This would circle the recovered land with access to the new industrial sites as they developed.

Following this the area cleared by the removal of Shapter's Field would also become available for industrial development. The two schemes would create an additional twelve acres.

SEWAGE TREATMENT

Of the existing available areas, South West Water acquired from the Central Electricity Generating Board the old power station site for a new sewage treatment plant to serve the 95,000 people in the central area of Plymouth. In this scheme all the sewage at present discharged directly into the sea, notably at West Hoe and Fisher's Nose, would be piped to the new plant at Cattedown. Here modern treatment was planned which would leave treated waste water to be returned to the present exit at West Hoe. The extracted solid sludge will be disposed of in accordance with European and United Kingdom regulations. The waste water would immensely improve the quality of water in the Sound, and the sludge would be available for use in agriculture as a soil improver.

Two similar sewage plants were already in operation in the Plym Valley, at Marsh Mills (serving Plympton) and at Radford (serving Plymstock and Hooe). Both have been extensively modernised to conform with modern requirements.

MOUNT BATTEN DEVELOPMENT

In March 1994 the RAF finally left Mount Batten and Plymouth Development Corporation took over. The organisation was set up by the Government with a funding of £45 million to find new uses for sites being given up by the Ministry of Defence. The basic plan was to landscape most of the 77 acres as a public open space. Within a year a great deal had been achieved. Batten Breakwater had been strengthened by dropping masses of large boulders outside the breakwater. Cavities in the internal structure created by heavy seas were filled in, and a new road laid along the length of the breakwater. This had been estimated to cost over £4 million; it was achieved for under a million, and a tablet commemorating the completion was unveiled in March 1955.

Many buildings regarded as surplus to need were demolished - 168 by March 1995. These included the married quarters inside the gate, as well as many of the buildings that always grow on Service establishments. The rubble was used to fill in the bomb bays higher up the hill, a labyrinth of tunnels cut into the hillside which first had to be made safe. More buildings went, such as No 1 hangar (built in 1921) under the lee of the tower massif. It stood in the way of a new buttress needed to support the cliff face below the tower. If no use is found for the barrack blocks on the Sound side of the tower rocks, then they too will go.

St John's Road, which leads both to Turnchapel village and the station entrance, has been widened, and a new road has been driven into Mount Batten, running along the top edge of the Clovelly Bay quarry.

A car park to serve Turnchapel has been created at the entrance, and a two-acre playing field will be made for local people in front of St Luke's Hospice. The 'plateau' area in between will be given over to residential housing, and the developers, Westbury Homes, signed an agreement in June 1996 to build 57 three- and four-bedroomed houses on the site. Work on the £4.9 million scheme, to be called Admiral's Reach, started right away.

An Astral Space College, an idea new to this country which has been very successful in the United States, was planned for the area of the officers' mess, but the developers then decided that the site was too small.

The giant Nos 2 and 3 hangars, only matched in the world by similar hangars at Calshot and Pembroke Dock, were each built to house several large flying boats. In front are large concrete aprons, built very thick to carry great weights, and a slipway down to the water. The idea is that the hangars will be used for marine-related industries The old fish factory, which became he first station headquarters in 1916, may become a visitor information centre.

In all the work going on over the site, a close archaeological watch is being kept. Sites in sensitive areas previously covered by buildings, as well as sites likely to be built on, are all being investigated by a team of experts. But all the development is being kept to a minimum, enough to make the site viable. The bulk of the 77 acres will be kept as a public open space. The coastal footpath will come down from Jennycliff and follow the water's edge right around to

Mount Batten cleared for the future by Plymouth Development Corporation, with the spine road running from the new car park at the bottom of a widened St John's Road down to the base of the breakwater. The two hangars are destined for maritime activities and the former sergeants' mess nearer the camera will become the West Country Sailing and Watersports Centre.

Turnchapel. Contracts were signed by a Torquay company in July 1996 to build an esplanade from the base of Batten Breakwater around to the planned marina, concrete paved, and with street lighting and seats. It was completed early in 1997.

NEW MARINA

After Plymouth Development Corporation took over Mount Batten the Clovelly Bay company, still led by Jim Gill, put up a scheme to extend the marina westwards. A new entrance was proposed at the foot of St John's Hill, thus avoiding the narrow approach down Turnchapel Hill. All the present shore-based activities linked to the marina would move from the centre of the village to the new site. The waterfront car park there would be made into a sitting area for the villagers, and there were ideas of importing sand to restore the beach.

In spring 1995 Clovelly Bay Company sold its management company to Yacht Havens Ltd of Lymington, which would relieve the local shareholders of the burden of raising the cash for so ambitious a development. They still retained the holding company, which would continue to allow them their berthing privileges.

Yacht Havens Ltd is one of the biggest marina operators in the country, and in July 1996 they applied for planning permission to build a 500-berth marina complete with ancillary office buildings, workshops, chandlery, car park, and boat storage area. Land would be recovered from the sea to allow the operation of a 60-ton boat hoist to handle craft up to 80 feet in length. The eastern, No 2 hangar, was included in the plans, to house yacht-related industry, with a restaurant built as an extension of the eastern end. The company also intend extending the esplanade to reach to Turnchapel village. The little dock, which is dated 1936, will be the base of a water-taxi service linking the marina with Queen Anne's Battery and the Barbican.

The largest area of Mount Batten will be kept as open country with full public access.

In the summer of 1996 the Mount Batten Sailing Association announced its plans for a sailing and watersports centre. A long lease was taken on the sergeant's mess, just west of the hangars, and with private and public funds, supported by an application to the National Lottery sports fund, it was intended to convert the building into a regional centre with a well-equipped clubhouse with residential and full catering facilities, bars, changing rooms, lecture and meeting rooms. The idea was developed by the Port of Plymouth Sailing Association and founder members included Devon County and Plymouth City, together with most Cattewater-linked members of the port sailing association. The non-profit making body, which aims to open its £3 million centre in spring 1998, will have ample parking for cars and dinghies, wide launching slipways, a landing pontoon and full facilities for all forms of watersports.

AQUARIUM

In Deadman's Bay, between Queen Anne's Battery and the entrance to Sutton Harbour, a National Marine Aquarium is being planned, on a two-acre site. It is the dream child of Dr Geoffrey Potts of the Marine Biological Association's Laboratory on Citadel Hill. He began developing the idea in 1988, and first publicised it in an exhibition in what was then the Polytechnic South-West but is now the University of Plymouth, when the British Association held it annual meeting there in 1991.

It has received a £5 million backing from the European Regional Development Fund as well as promises from national and local funds. Visitors will walk through reproductions of various aquatic environments, from a mountain stream with waterfalls and whirlpools to a mature river containing salmon and trout, an estuary and a

A drawing by Gordon Fricker from the brochure advertising the future Mount Batten watersports centre.

shallow sea area. Finally visitors will walk through a six metre high tank with a living coral reef, reproducing tropical seas with sharks and giant rays swimming all around and overhead.

It will share a road approach and a car park, already built, with the new Sutton Harbour fish market, but will also be reached by way of the footbridge across the lock gates of Sutton Harbour.

The Cattewater Commissioners plan to transfer their offices, and the pilots' base, to a new building near the foot of Batten Breakwater. From this point they will be able to see much of the activity both in the Cattewater and the Sound. The Commissioners were also chosen by PDC to take over the freehold and management of the north shore of Mount Batten, and resume responsibility for the maintenance of Batten Breakwater. This will enable them to exercise better control over the expanding commercial and leisure uses of the busy harbour.

For some years the Commisioners have been very active in the affairs of the Atlantic Arc, a project fostered and financed by the European Union to encourage trade along the western

An architect's drawing of the new National Marine Aquarium on which building started in November 1996. It clearly shows its relationship to the new fish market and lock gates of Sutton Harbour.

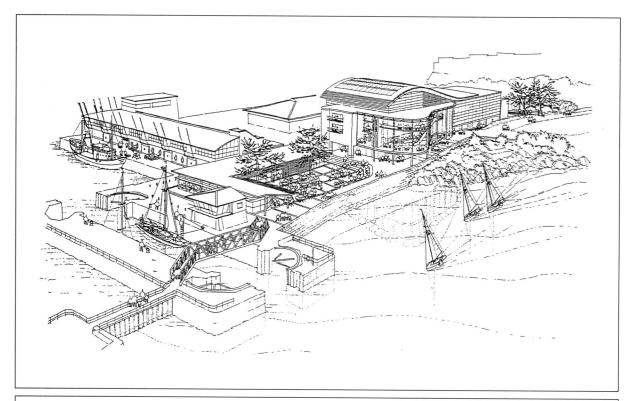

A drawing of the proposed offices and lookout for the Cattewater Commissioners at the end of the Mount Batten peninsula.

seaboard of Europe. As far back as man can go, to prehistoric days, there was a constant movement of men, ideas and trade between Spain and Portugal, western France and Britanny, the West of England, Wales, Ireland and Scotland. It is this area that the Atlantic Arc hopes to see developed and expanded. Plymouth already has a share in this traffic through Brittany Ferries's routes between Plymouth, Santander, Roscoff and Cork. It is argued that the Plymouth base would be better in the Cattewater, with easy road access to A38 and dual carriageway links with the motorway system, rather than in Millbay Docks which necessitates all the traffic moving through the centre of Plymouth. But without stealing from Millbay, the Commissioners would like to see a roll-on-roll-off facility developed in the Cattewater and greater commercial development of the harbour. Under its new and local ownership Victoria Wharfs is already building new dockside facilities and expanding its wharf space.

The whole area at the time of producing this book is in a state of flux; a time of dramatic change in many directions.

ACKNOWLEDGEMENTS

Roy Edison of Plymstock, for many years managing director of Victoria Wharf and with a prodigous memory of many things connected with the Cattewater, lent me his collection of newspaper cuttings and other memorabilia and really set me off on these researches.

My old friend Martin Langley, who with Edwina Small has written a history of the Port of Plymouth but only had two chapters published, nobly allowed me access not only to his published but his unpublished work, and to his collection of photographs.

Other people such as Alan Kittridge (on ferries), Doreen Mole (on Laira and Efford) and Arthur Clamp have made me free of their unpublished notes and photographs. This is indeed generosity.I have made great use of Chris Robinson's three books, *Plymouth, As Time Draws On*, vols one (1985) and two (1988), and *Victorian Plymouth* (1991). They are invaluable for anyone working on nineteenth-century Plymouth, and to acknowledge every little fact that I have taken from him would take pages. I also am most grateful to Chris for allowing me to use his drawings and raid his library.

Plymouth Local Studies Library's collection of directories, and the map collection both there and in West Devon Record Office yielded much material. I have had generous assistance, as ever, from John Elliott, the West Devon Area Librarian, Ann Landers, until recently Plymouth Local Studies Librarian, and Paul Brough, senior archivist, West Devon Record Office. The curator of Plymouth City Museum, Stephen Price (now moved on), and the keeper of pictures, Maureen Attrill, have again helped considerably in finding old pictures.

On the Plymstock side of the river I have relied heavily on my cousin June Whyte and the late Mary Anthony of the Radford and Hooe Lake Preservation Association. Mary's unpublished typescript on the Cattewater's history has provided odd facts for many chapters, June has directed me to the right contacts, and provided masses of photocopies from their extensive records. *The Plymstock Connection* by Ivy M Langdon (Devon Books, 1995) was published too late for me to have used to any great extent, but I have taken some information from its pages.

Many people in fact have been generous with their time, Lionel Stribley and Tony Dyer, chairman and harbourmaster of the Cattewater Commissioners at the time of writing, Robin Love, managing director of Cattedown Wharfs, and innumerable owners, directors, officers and managers of firms and bodies like yacht clubs concerned with this study. I can only hope that this book is an adequate reward for the time they have given me.

Finally, Mrs Doreen Mole joined me as picture researcher and turned out to be an indefatigible worker of infinite resource. And as ever my wife Betty, who had so often had to explain either why I was not at home or just plain absent-minded, by saying that I 'was up the Cattewater', has been a constant source of strength and encouragement.

SOURCES AND REFERENCES

ABBREVIATIONS.

TransDA. Transactions of the Devonshire Association.
TransPI. Transactions of the Plymouth Institution.
WDRO. West Devon Record Office.
LSL. Plymouth Local Studies Library.
WEH. *Western Evening Herald.*
WMN. *Western Morning News.*
WDM. *Western Daily Mercury.*
SDT. *South Devon Times.*
NMM. National Maritime Museum.
PDC. Plymouth Development Corporation.

INTRODUCTION
PART ONE - THE EARLY DAYS

1. CATTEWATER: ORIGINS AND NAME
Glover, JEB et al, *Place Names of Devon*, Part One, Cambridge 1931.
South Devon Monthly Museum, December 1835.
Pitts, Thomas, Memoirs, typescript in possession of author.
Perkins, John W., *Geology Explained in South and East Devon*, Newton Abbot 1971.

2. THE LAIRA, NAME AND ORIGINS
Gill, Crispin, *Plymouth: a New History*, Tiverton 1993.
Rowe, J.Brooking, *History of Plympton Erle*, Exeter, 1906.

3. FORDS,BRIDGES AND EARLY ROADS
Beckerlegge, J.J., 'Eastern Plymouth, Yesterday and Today', TPI, vol 17, 1944.
South Devon Monthly Magazine, May & June 1835.

4. FERRIES
Anthony,Mary, *The Red Funnel Line*, Plymouth 1981.
Kittridge,Alan, *Passenger Steamers of the River Tamar*, Truro 1984;
Langley, Martin and Small, Edwina, *Estuary and River Ferries of South West England*, Wayne Research, Wolverhampton, 1984.

5. EMBANKMENTS
Embankment Act, 1802, WDRO P346.
Woolcombe, Henry, Diary, 10 Oct 1802, unpublished MSS, copy held in LSL
Saltram, National Trust guide.

6. LAIRA BRIDGE
Rendell, JM,'The Iron Bridge', Trans PI, 1830.
Welch, Edwin, '.Laira Bridge', Trans DA, 1968.
Biography of John Pethick, *Comet*, 11 Feb 1893

PART TWO - MAN ON THE RIVER

7. EARLY COMMERCIAL SHIPPING
Burnard, Robert, Notes on Cattewater, Plymouth 1887, reprinted from the *Western Antiquary*.
Cunliffe, Bary, *Mount Batten, a Prehistoric Port*, Oxford, 1988.
Gill, Crispin, Commercial Port of Plymouth, unpublished lecture to Dartington Maritime History Seminar, 1977.
Carpenter, AC, Ellis, KH, McKee, JEG, *The Cattewater Wreck*, Greenwich, 1974.
Gill, *Plymouth*.
Lord Boringdon's mooring chains and other related material, WDRO 69/M/6/487-499. 468, 472, 475, 481, 482,

8. THE ARMED FORCES
Cramp, Arthur L. *United States Advanced Amphibious Base, Plymouth 1943-5*, Plymouth,1994.
Gill, *Plymouth*.
Hunt, Leslie, 'RAF Mount Batten - home of the Flying Boats', WMN, 26 Aug 1966.
Robinson, C., 'Queen Anne's Battery', *Plymouth: as Time Draws On*, 1988.
Stuart, Elizabeth, *Lost Landscapes of Plymouth*, 1991, Map No 22, p.87.
Twyford, HP, *It Came to our Door*, Plymouth 1945.
Wasley, Gerald, *Blitz*, Tiverton 1991.
Woodward, FW, *Plymouth Defences*, 1990.
'American Naval Base at Plymouth', WMN Mayflower Supplement, 1920.

Oil tanks, WEH 14 July 95

Talk with SC Stephens (driver of crane on Batten Breakwater, World War I), and John Lyle Carter (PDC).

9. SHIPBUILDING AND SHIP BREAKING

Burns KV, *Plymouth's Ships of War 1694-1860,* NMM 1960; Devonport-built Warships since 1860, Maritime Books, Liskeard, 1981.

Colledge, JJ, *Ships of the Royal Navy,* vol one, Newton Abbot 1969.

Davies, Orlando, 'Plymouth and Commerce, Cattewater Harbour', *The Book of Plymouth,* ed. Bracken,CW, NUT Conference 1910.

Fice, RHC, SDT, 22 April 1960.

Gill, Shipbuilding in Plymouth, Unpublished lecture 1972.

Godfrey, Judith,, extensive researches on Hill's shipyards.

Greenhill, Basil & Giffard, Ann, Westcountrymen in Prince Edward's Isle, Newton Abbot 1967.

Kittridge, Alan, notes on Cattewater shipbuilding.

Merry, Ian D., *Shipping & Trade of the River Tamar,* Parts One & Two, NMM monographs, 1980; *Westcotts and their Times,* NMM Monograph, 1977; letters from Mr Merry.

Pearce, Richard, 'Batten Castle,the account book of a home-trade sailing vessel 1852-66', *Westcountry Maritime and Social History* (ed. Stephen Fisher), Exeter University 1980.

Pitt, Dorothy Warley, newspaper cuttings in LSL 'Turnchapel' envelope.

Sargent, Julia, research notes, Castle's Ship-breaking Yard, 1994

Starkey, David,' Devon's Shipbuilding Industry, 1786-1970', p.88, *New Maritime History of Devon,* Vol II, 1994.

Stoggall, Emma, Plymouth Hookers, unpublished thesis, University of Plymouth, 1995.

Whitfeld, Henry, *Plymouth and Devonport in times of War and Peace,* p534. 1900.

Worth, RN, *History of Plymouth,* 1890

Davies & Cann ship-breaking, talk with Michael Smith and Kenneth Isaac.

10. CATTEWATER COMMISSIONERS AND BATTEN BREAKWATER

Early Cattewater Acts, WDRO.

Dyer, Lieut Com A., Notes on Plymouth Breakwaters, lecture to RWYC 1995.

Farr, Grahame, *Wreck and Rescue on the Coast of Devon,* Truro 1968.

11. LAIRA and CATTEDOWN WHARFS

Kendall, HG, *Plymouth & Dartmoor Railway,* Oakwood Press, Lingfield, 1968.

Worth, RN, 'Cattedown Caves' Trans PI, vol 10, 1887.

Cattedown Wharfs Ltd 1920-1980. Old cuttings books and diary, company typescript.

Obituary, WH Alger, WDM 22 Feb 1912,

Talks with Lionel Stribley and Robin Love, directors Cattedown Wharfs.

12. VICTORIA and CORPORATION WHARFS

Letter from Bolt, AJ, Plymouth, great-nephew of Cornelius Duke.

Various scrapbooks.

Victoria Wharf, talks with Roy Eddison and Michael East, managers, and Mark Gatehouse. Eddison papers.

Coast Lines 1995 brochures. Papers deposited with WDRO.

Sale, WEH 8 June 93.

13. TURNCHAPEL and POMPHLETT WHARFS

Turnchapel Wharfs Act, Vic 61, 1897.

Various cuttings books.

Pomphlett quays, letter from G.Hicks, manager Moorcroft Quarry, Camas Aggregates, 1994; talks with Brian Skelton and Jack Skelly.

14. OYSTERS, CABLE SHIPS and COAL HULKS

Oysters, Saltram papers, WDRO 69/M/6/450-472, 480-3, 1321-2.

Cable ships: Talks with Captain Cecil Hunt, Tavistock: and with Frank Attwood of Lanhydrock Road, who has a large collection of memorabilia.

Letters from Captain WD Harper (Lincoln), PR Dart, Plymouth, Mrs JA Whitfield, Plymouth.

The Cable Ship John W. Mackay Trust, 1978 appeal leaflet.

Cattewater Wharfs scrap books.

Cattewater Commissioners.

Blood,Arthur, 'Oldest Cable Ship', WMN, 31 Aug 72.

Langley, Martin; Cattewater Harbour, unpublished Mss.

15. DEAD HAND OF THE ADMIRALTY

Scrapbooks of Cattedown Wharfs, Roy Eddison and the late Ald. WHJ Priest, borrowed from his daughter, Mrs Joan Lister.,

Selleck, Douglas. 'What Might Have Been at Wembury', WEH, 11 May 91,

Ford Motor Co, Ernie Male, Horrabridge;

Nevins, A & Hill, FE, *Ford, Expansion and Challenge, 1915-33..* New York, 1933.

Collins, P and Stratton, M, *British Car Factories,* Godmanstone, 1993.

16. MODERN SHIPPING

Langley, Martin, Cattewater Harbour, unpublished Mss

Gill, *Plymouth* and *Sutton Harbour* (revised 1976)

Cattewater Commissioner records.

RP Rowe, 'The Port of Plymouth', TPI, 1890.
Review of Shipping 1900, WMN Jan 1901.
Notes from Sutton Harbour Co Ltd scrap book,

17. TURNCHAPEL PILOTS
Langley, Martin,and Small, Edwina, The Plymouth Pilots, unpublished Mss
Milford, Herbert, notes on forebears, and Carne, Tony, The Cawsand Pilots, unpublished Mss; both descendants of pilots.

18. COASTGUARDS and ROCKETS .
Farr Grahame, *Wreck and Rescue on the Coast of Devon*, Truro 1968.
Talks with Ronald Demellweek, Pomphlett (newspaper cuttings book), Eric Burridge, and Ian Baker, coastguard sector officer, Tamar Section.
Letter from Robert Perkins, Bath.

19. YACHTING and WATERSPORTS
Plymouth Rowing Club, talk with David MacLeod, old programmes.
Plym Yacht Club, SDT. 26 Feb 81.
Talks with Don Thompson (Plym Yacht Club), Brian Collinson (Cattewater Cruising Club), Sam Rogers (Hooe Point Sailing Club), Alston Kennerly (University of Plymouth Sailing Centre), Walter Hobson and Stanley Vincent (Mayflower Sailing Club),
Plymouth Classic Boat Rally 1994 and 1995 programmes

20. MARINAS AND BOATYARDS
Queen Anne's Battery brochure, 1994. LSL file, cuttings, WMN and WEH between July 1985 and Feb 1989.
Talks with Mark Gatehouse (QAB), Jim Gill (Clovelly Bay), Andrew Sleep (Ship Store), Arthur Blagdon and Ken Morgan (Blagdon's), M.B.Pindar, John Skentelbery (Skentelbery fire, WEH 21 Sept 95), Ron Greet (Boat Services), Capt Nigel Boston.
Rico Powerboats, WEH 19 Sept 95, 2 Oct 95

PART THREE - MAN ON SHORE

21. WATER MILLS
Directories and maps.
Gaskell-Brown, Cynthia, 'Plympton', *Industrial Archaeology of Plymouth*, 2nd edn, Plymouth WEA 1980.
SDT (from neg of page lent by Arthur Clamp)
Finberg, HRO, *Tavistock Abbey*, Newton Abbot, 1969.
Minchinton, Walter, and Perkins, J.,'Pomphlett or Abbot's Mill, Plymstock', *Tide Mills of Devon and Cornwall*, Exeter 1979.
Particulars of sale of Pomphlett Mills, 1922. WDRO.

22. QUARRIES
Prideaux, John, 'Geology of Plymouth Area', Trans PI, 1830.
Vancouver, *Agriculture*, 1808.
Talk with Andrew Moore, USA
Unpublished MSS by DL Evea, written in 1896, held by AL Clamp, details of quarries worked by FJ Moore,
Robinson, 'History that was Carved in Marble', WEH, 6 Feb 94

23. RAILWAYS
Anthony GH, *Tavistock, Launceston & Princetown Railways*, Lingfield, Surrey, 1971.
Gibson, Bryan, *Lee Moor Tramway*, Plymouth Railway Circle, 1993
Kendall, H.G., *Plymouth & Dartmoor Railway*, Lingfield, 1968
Kingdom AR, *Turnchapel Branch*. Oxford Publishing Co, Poole, 1982
Thomas D StJ, Regional History of the Railways of Great Britain vol One, the West Country, Newton Abbot 1960

24. FERTILISERS AND CHEMICALS
Burnard & Alger, old cuttings books in Cattedown Wharfs archives.
Fisons, WMN, 10 apl 57
Talk with Neil Files (Independent Fertilisers).

25. CEMENT, SAND AND TIMBER
Caldwell & Almond, directories, talk with David Hussell.
Talk with Scott Norman,(Regional Manager Devon & Cornwall, Blue Circle Co Ltd); *Cement in the Making*, Blue Circle leaflet; WEH, 22 Dec 1993, 28 Oct 1995.
Talks with Alan Purchase and members of staff (Heywoods).
Bayly records, WDRO ACC242, Plymouth & Oreston Timber Co, WDRO 1195/2; Gill files on Bayly family; development plans, WEH 7 Sept 1995.
Coles timber company, letters from George Burr, Solihull.

26. GAS, ELECTRICITY AND OIL
SW Gas Historical Society, via Michael Parriss, Plymouth.
'Plymouth Tar Distilleries' *Gas Journal*, 12 Oct 1927.
Breakwater, brochure from *South-West Gas*, 1966; cuttings from *Sou'wester*, South West Gas magazine c/o Mr Parriss
Elford, PWT, cuttings book on Turnchapel Petrol Depot fire.
Petrol. companies, talks with local managers, Barry Price (Shell), David Williams (BP), Colin Jeffs (Esso), Michael George (Conoco).
Esso, WMN, 9 Feb 87,29 Aug 87, 3 Sept 1988
Shell & BP, 24 Sept 69, 4 Sept 70, 18 Aug 72, 27 Dec 91

27. IRON MINING AND FARM MACHINERY
Baker,Owen, 'Wheal Morley Iron Mine', *Industrial Archaeology of Plymouth* (ed. Gaskell Brown, Plymouth WEA, 1973.

Hamilton Jenkins, A.K. *Mines of Devon*, Vol One The Southern Area.

Davey Sleep, Chris Robinson, *Victorian Plymouth* p 184. *Commercial Guide to Plymouth*, 1894

Talk with Mrs Joan Lister, daughter of WHJ Priest.

28. CHELSTON MEADOW AND PLYMOUTH RACES
Whitfeld, Henry, *Plymouth and Devonport in Times of War and Peace*, Plymouth 1900.

Advertisements in contemporary journals, old maps.

Airfield, Gill, *Plymouth*, p178.

Tip, visit to Reclamation Visitor Centre.

29. THE OPENING OF PRINCE ROCK
Papers held in City Solicitor's archives, Plymouth.

Acheson Colloids: Szymanpwitz, R, Raymond *Gordon Acheson* (New York 1971); company brochure, 1993; Talk with Anthony V.Parry, General Manager Plymouth;

Various Directories

Talks with Ken Newton (factory manager Croda Colloids) and Alan Blencoe (BOC).

Cattedown smells, Mrs M Hassall of Peverell and her mother, 'Seen & Heard', WEH, 5 Jul 93.

30. INDUSTRY SINCE 1945
Search of directories, LSL.

Blight & White: Talk with C.J.Woodrow, various company leaflets and brochures.

Power, WJ, Business Houses of Plymouth, 1982,, typescript LSL

English, Ernest T., *The Browns of Plymouth,* privately published, 1971_

Eagle Eye, various copies of magazine of Eagle Signs Ltd.

Corporation Depot: WW Jackson,retired city engineer's staff. Mrs Valerie Wells, Senior Adminiaration Officer, Manufacturing and Highways, Contract Services Group;

Members of City Engineer's Dept, Plymouth, 'Post-war Municipal and Reconstruction Works in Plymouth', *Journal of the Institution of Municipal Engineers*, 1953.

Ken Newton, Factory Manager Croda Colloids 1985 Croda Colloids, Croda staff magazine,booklet *Edible Protein*, International Protein Products Ltd, 1968.

Talks with Jan Colan (Interfish), Julian Anthony (manager, Severnside), Mike Hocking (Faraday Mill), Keith Fleming (Plymouth Quality Meats Ltd),Roy Herbert (Counter Spares),David Luke (W.Luke & Sons).

Wallsend Industrial Estate, WEH 13 Jul 1982, WMN 5 Dec 1984.

PART FOUR - THE VILLAGES

31. LAND OWNERSHIP
Deeds held by City Solicitor.

Particulars of sale of Sutton Pill, 1785 and 1820, WDRO

Culme papers, WDRO. Talks with Sir Michael Culme-Seymour.

Efford and Laira researches by Doreen Mole.

Finberg, HRP, 'Childe's Tomb', *Devonshire Studies*, 1952.

Gill, *Plymouth*.

Saltram, National Trust guide, 1988

32. CRABTREE AND LAIRA
Anon, Efford Ex-Service Colony, booklet published 1929.

Webb, John , 'History of the Mayor and Corporation of Crabtree', *Doidge's Annual* 1882.

Boundary extension 1896, WDM, 15 Oct 96.

Talks with Len Hill, RW Butler (headmaster Laira Green School), Rev Stuart Dobson (vicar St Mary's Laira), Percy Luscombe,

Deeds in posession of Barry Evans, 3 Arnold Point Cottages.

Sawle, AC,*The History of Laira Primary School 1870-1970,,* Privately published.

Brown, J. ' The Life of a Teacher', WEH, 10 June 1992.

Perkins, J.W., 'The Crabtree Limeworks', *Devon & Cornwall Notes & Queries*, 1968.

Camp, Rev Peter, *The First Fifty Years*, St Mary the Virgin Church, Laira, 1964.

Mss notes by Doreen Mole

33. CATTEDOWN AND PRINCE ROCK
Old maps and directories.

'Plymouth, Cattedown Reclamation Scheme,' *Wessex Archaeology Annual Report*, 1992-3

Cherry, Bridget and Pevsner, Nicholas, *The Buildings of England, Devon*, 2nd edn 1989.

Talks with Father Brian Lay (vicar, St John-Sutton-on-Plym) and Gordon and Ron Nichols (Plymouth Christian Centre).

34. ORESTON
Miss Susan Cattley, Oreston

Crooks, Will D.,' Oreston Memories', WEH, 4,11 and 16 April 1930.

Glover, JEB et al, *The Place-Names of Devon*, Part One page 256, CUP 1931.

Hammerton, Brenda, 'Oreston etc', *Industrial Archaeology of Devon* 1980.

Nash, John, 'Childhood memories of fifty years ago', 1928, quoted by Robinson.

Pitt, Dorothy Warley, 'Old Oreston', SDT.

Robinson, Chris, 'Boringdon Arms', *Plymouth; As Time Draws On*, vol 2, p186.

Tope, Arthur T., *Oreston Methodist Church*, Plymouth,1988.

Wallis, Fernley, *Gone are the Days*: Reminiscences, Plymouth 1965.

Village of Oreston, typescript compiled by Social Studies Group, Plymstock TWG, 1966.

35. HOOE
Reports by James Barber, Keeper of Human History, City Museum, 1988,and by GW Copeland on West Hooe Farm, held by the Plymouth Archaeological Officer, Dr Keith Ray.

Clamp, Arthur L, *Hooe & Turnchapel Remembered*, Plymouth 1981

Gray, Todd, *Garden History of Devon*, Exeter University 1995.

Reichel,Rev OJ, *Domesday Book Manors*, Vol VI, Hundreds of Plympton and Ermington, Devonshire Assocn, 1933.

Selleck, Douglas, 'The Alexander Selkirk Story', WEH, 25 Aprl 1984.

Steele, Brian DR, *A History of Radford*, Radford Centre, 1990

Circular walks from Jennicliff. Radford Park Preservation Association, 1990.

Turnchapel & Hooe Trail, Hooe Junior School, July 1981.

Talks with Miss Sheila Coleman,Yonder Street (general), Rev AB Robinson (vicar, St John's Church) and Ronald Cooke (Baptist Church), Charles Hankin, Ivybridge (Rogers family).

Newspaper cuttings scrapbook held by Ralph Daubeny of Burford, a Bulteel descendant.

36. TURNCHAPEL
Dorothy Warley Pitt, various articles (In LSL 'Turnchapel' envelope.

Turnchapel Conservation Study, City Planning Officer, Plymouth, 1977.

37. POMPHLETT, AND MOUNT BATTEN before the RAF
Pomphlett, talks with Roger Dodd and Michael Grundy.

Walling, RV, 'The Old Mount Batten', WMN,27 Feb 67.

EPILOGUE

38. IN THE FUTURE
West Coast Watershed, 1989;

Plymouth Waterfront Strategy, 1989

Cattedown Area Plan,consultation draft 1989.

Tomorrow's Waterfront, a Strategy, City of Plymouth, 1990

Plymouth Waterfront, 1994,

Waterfront News, spring 1995, Plymouth Development Corporation.

Cattedown proposals, Plymouth 1994, New Cattewater Ltd, WEH, 13 Mar 95

Clean Sweep for Plymouth Sound, South-West Water, 1995

Atlantic Arc, WEH, p9, 28 Sept 95

Talks and visits with John Warren (New Cattedown Ltd), John Lyle-Carter (PDC)

Mount Batten marina, WEH 22 Nov 95

Aquarium, WEH 4 Nov 95

Bayly's timber yard, WEH 7 Sept

INDEX

PICTURE CREDITS

The author and publisher are grateful for the following individuals and organisations who kindly provided illustrations for use in this book. Where a photograph is not directly acknowledged and indicated by page number, it comes from the author's collection or has been loaned to the author for specific use in this book.

Page 6 Cattewater Harbour Commissioners (T. Dyer); p. 8 Devon Books; p. 16 (top) Devon County Library Service; p. 19 (top) *Western Morning News*; p. 22 Devon County Library Service; p.24 Devon County Library Service; p. 25 Plymouth City Museum and Art Gallery (Robert Chapman Photography); p. 26 (lower) Devon County Library Services; p.31 Devon County Library Service; p. 38 A. Kittridge Collection ; p. 39 *Western Morning News*; p. 40 and 42 Arthur Clamp; p. 43 A. Kittridge Collection; p. 51 and 53 Cattewater Harbour Commissioners; p. 55 Devon County Library Service; p.60 Cattewater Harbour Commissioners; p. 66 *Evening Herald* Newspaper; p. 67 Devon County Library Service; p. 78 Martin Langley; p. 79 D. McLindon; p. 83 Devon County Library Service; p. 85 (top) Chris Hockaday; p. 85 (lower) D. McLindon; p. 88 (top and lower) E. Burridge; p. 90 E. Burridge; p. 92 *Western Morning News*; p. 93 and 94 D. Baker; p. 101 (lower) Cattewater Harbour Commissioners (T. Dyer); p. 102 Plymouth City Museum and Art Gallery; p. 108 Devon Record Office; p. 109 Plymouth City Museum and Art Gallery; p. 112 (top) Devon County Library Service; p. 116 The National Trust; p. 122 and 123 Alan Lathey; p. 132 *Evening Herald* Newspaper; p. 138 *Western Morning News*; p. 149 *Western Morning News*; p. 160 and 161 Devon County Library Service; p. 162 Devon Record Office; p. 165 *Western Morning News*; p. 168 Peter W. Gray; p. 174 The National Maritime Museum; p. 175 A. Kittridge Collection; p. 176 Chris Robinson; p. 177 Moseley Museum; p. 180 and 187 Devon County Library Service; p. 188 Western Morning News; p. 190 Chris Robinson; p. 193 Mole Postcard Collection; p. 197 Trevor Burrows Photography.

All the aerial photographs in the colour plate section were taken in June 1996 by Peter Holdgate, Picture Editor of the *Western Morning News*, and are reproduced as are all the photographs from the *Western Morning News* and *Evening Herald* files, by courtesy of Westcountry Publications Ltd. The credits for the colour plate section, running in sequence, are as follows: plates 1-5 *Western Morning News*; plate 6 Jacques Vapillon (Mark Gatehouse); plate 7-8 *Western Morning News*; plate 9 the author; plate 10 *Western Morning News*; plate 11 the author; plate 12 *Western Morning News*; plate 13 (inset) D. McLindon; plate 14 the author; plate 15 Judith Godfrey; plate 16 Plymouth City Museum and Art Gallery; plate 17-20 *Western Morning News*; plate 21 Conoco; plate 22 D. McLindon; plate 23 Conoco; plate 24 the author.